Taxcafe.co.uk Tax Guides

# Putting It Through the Company

**Tax Planning for Companies & Their Owners**

By Carl Bayley BSc FCA

and

Nick Braun PhD

# Important Legal Notices:

Taxcafe®
Tax Guide - "Putting It Through the Company - Tax Planning for Companies & Their Owners"

**Published by**:
Taxcafe UK Limited
67 Milton Road
Kirkcaldy KY1 1TL
Tel: (0044) 01592 560081
Email: team@taxcafe.co.uk

Third Edition, August 2024

ISBN 978-1-911020-95-0

**Trademarks**
Taxcafe® is a registered trademark of Taxcafe UK Limited. All other trademarks, names and logos in this tax guide may be trademarks of their respective owners.

**Disclaimer**
Before reading or relying on the content of this tax guide please read the disclaimer.

# Disclaimer

This guide is intended as **general guidance** only and does NOT constitute accountancy, tax, investment or other professional advice.

1. The authors and Taxcafe UK Limited make no representations or warranties with respect to the accuracy or completeness of this publication and cannot accept any responsibility or liability for any loss or risk, personal or otherwise, which may arise, directly or indirectly, from reliance on information contained in this publication.

2. Please note that tax legislation, the law and practices of Government and regulatory authorities (e.g. HM Revenue & Customs) are constantly changing. We therefore recommend that for accountancy, tax, investment or other professional advice, you consult a suitably qualified accountant, tax adviser, financial adviser, or other professional adviser.

3. Please also note that your personal circumstances may vary from the general examples provided in this guide and your professional adviser will be able to provide specific advice based on your personal circumstances.

4. This guide covers UK taxation only and any references to 'tax' or 'taxation', unless the contrary is expressly stated, refer to UK taxation only. Please note that references to the 'UK' do not include the Channel Islands or the Isle of Man. Foreign tax implications are beyond the scope of this guide.

5. All persons described in the examples in this guide are entirely fictional. Any similarities to actual persons, living or dead, or to fictional characters created by any other author, are entirely coincidental. Likewise, the companies described in the examples in this guide are similarly fictional corporations created specifically for the purposes of this guide and any similarities to actual companies, past or present, are again entirely coincidental.

6. The views expressed in this publication are the authors' own personal views and do not necessarily reflect the views of any organisation they may represent.

## About the Authors & Taxcafe

Carl Bayley is the author of a series of Taxcafe guides designed specifically for the layperson and the non-specialist. Carl's particular speciality is his ability to take the weird, complex and inexplicable world of taxation and set it out in the kind of clear, straightforward language taxpayers themselves can understand. As he often says himself, "My job is to translate 'tax' into English."

In addition to being a recognised author, Carl has often spoken on taxation on radio and television, including the BBC's It's Your Money programme and the Jeremy Vine Show on Radio 2.

A chartered accountant by training, Carl is a former chairman of the Tax Faculty of the Institute of Chartered Accountants in England and Wales. In June 2023, he stepped down after almost twenty years on the institute's governing council.

Nick Braun founded Taxcafe.co.uk in 1999, along with his partner, Aileen Smith. As the driving force behind the company, their aim is to provide affordable plain-English tax information for private individuals and investors, business owners, accountants and other advisers.

Since then Taxcafe has become one of the best-known tax publishers in the UK and has won several business awards.

Nick has been involved in the tax publishing world since 1989 as a writer, editor and publisher. He holds a doctorate in economics from the University of Glasgow, where he was awarded the prestigious William Glen Scholarship and later became a Research Fellow. Prior to that, he graduated with distinction from the University of South Africa, the country's oldest university, earning the highest results in economics in the university's history.

# Contents

# Introduction

When we sat down to plan a new guide aimed at company owners, we discussed what it was people running a company most wanted to know. "Well," I said, "what people usually ask me is what they can put through the company."

That simple observation gave us the title for our new guide, and the broad scope of what we wanted to cover. 'Putting It Through' is about the question of what you can get the company to pay for. But it's not a simple 'yes you can' or 'no you can't', because within this one overarching question lie a number of others.

Yes, there is the basic question of whether the company can pay for it, but then we also need to look at whether the company will get Corporation Tax relief, and how much; whether it can recover VAT on its purchases; and whether the payment will have Income Tax or National Insurance consequences for the company owner themselves, or a National Insurance cost to the company.

When it comes to buying property, other long-term assets, or investments, we also need to think about the capital gains consequences when those assets, or the company's shares, are sold, and the impact on the company owner's Inheritance Tax burden.

We will look at all these issues and, while the original question, 'Can I put it through the company?' can nearly always be answered with, 'Yes, you can if you want,' that answer will often be followed by 'but...' and the question company owners really ought to be asking is, '*Should* I put it through the company?' That can sometimes be a much more difficult and complicated question: but it is the question we will be answering in this guide.

This guide isn't generally about the simple, obvious stuff, like paying regular employee's wages, or the electricity bill for the company's premises. Yes, the company can pay those things, put them through its accounts and get Corporation Tax relief for the expense; and there will not usually be any tax consequences for the company owner. But most people know that already.

What we are more concerned with in this guide is the less obvious stuff, like paying wages to the company owner's children, putting part of a director's household costs through the company accounts, or dozens of other things where it is not immediately clear whether you should put it though the company, or what the tax consequences will be if you do.

In Chapter 1 we'll start by looking at some of the fabulous savings that may be available when you are able to put expenses through the company. We'll also look at what happens if you try to put the wrong thing through and how much it costs.

We then move onto the first major source of tax savings. In Chapter 2, we look at the general principles governing Corporation Tax relief for items you put through the company and cover a few quirky ideas like pantomime horses and Ferraris.

Chapter 3 moves onto the issue of recovering VAT on items put through the company. We look at some of the practicalities, potential savings and the detailed principles involved. 'Similar but different' probably sums up the contrast between Corporation Tax relief and VAT recovery and you need to know those all-important differences if you're going to get the best results.

In Chapter 4 we focus on director's expenses, all those costs you tend to incur when you're away from your workplace or through buying goods and services yourself personally. We look at how and when you can recover these costs from the company, what's included, and what to do if you get it wrong. We will also see the value of putting it through the company when you can: even when there's no Corporation Tax relief or VAT recovery.

Chapter 5 expands on this last idea by giving you a thorough understanding of how much Income Tax you can save by putting expenses through the company instead of having to pay them yourself out of after-tax income. In this chapter, we also look at the benefits of putting your own income through the company: salary, dividends, and interest. There are important savings to be made as sometimes these items can be paid to you at no tax cost, or even with an overall tax saving.

In Chapter 6, we start to look at some more specific areas, with a focus on the tax costs involved in employing people and how to minimise them, or even, in some cases, how to maximise the savings. We'll also see how employing your children could keep you, them, and the company accountant all happy at the same time.

As well as wages and salaries, there are a host of useful tax-efficient benefits that can help to both keep staff happy and keep your payroll costs down, and we look at these in Chapter 7. Often you can benefit too. Everything from mobile phones to buying pizzas for your staff, or sending the receptionist to the local cafe so the rest of you can have a tax-free lunch on the company, is covered.

Next, in Chapter 8, we look at tax relief for capital expenditure on machinery, equipment, computers, furniture... you name it. There is a dazzling array of allowances available to companies at present, and we navigate you through the maze to show you how to get the best tax savings for your company.

Chapter 9 looks at motoring and shows you what you can claim back on vehicles you put through the company, and what it costs in benefit in kind charges. In some cases, the overall cost of a company vehicle in tax terms can be horrendous, but in other cases the savings are astounding. Plus, there are details on exactly what you and your employees can claim back from the company and how to get the best tax relief for motoring expenses.

We move on to property in Chapter 10 with a detailed examination of some critical issues like whether to rent or buy, whether to hold the company premises personally yourself, and what you can claim if you're working from home. We also look at the property running costs you can put through the company and what tax relief is available for property expenditure like fixtures and fittings, renovations, conversions, and improvements.

In Chapter 11 we catch up with a few last, but still really important, items that you can put through the company, including arguably one of the best tax-saving strategies for small company owners: pension contributions.

Lastly, Chapter 12 covers the new Corporation Tax regime applying since April 2023 and explains why, for many small companies, putting expenses through the company now saves even more tax than before. This final chapter also includes detailed guidance on the costs and benefits of forming additional companies, deferring or accelerating tax-deductible spending, and other ways to get the best out of the Corporation Tax regime.

Once you've been through the whole guide, you should be fully armed with the information you need to know what you can put through the company and to do so with confidence. In the end, we hope you can do what we start with in our very first section: Win Win Win!

# Scope of this Guide

This guide covers UK tax issues for UK resident companies and their owners. Unless specifically stated to the contrary, it is assumed company owners are individuals and are:

i)   UK resident and domiciled for tax purposes
ii)  Not subject to the 'off payroll working' rules (sometimes known as 'IR35')
iii) Not subject to the Child Benefit Charge
iv)  Not claiming the marriage allowance
v)   Not Scottish taxpayers

Scottish taxpayers pay Income Tax at different rates. However, this will have little impact on the issues discussed in this guide as this does not affect Corporation Tax, VAT, National Insurance, or Income Tax on dividend income.

Additional reliefs available to companies operating within designated Freeports, Investment Zones, or Enterprise Zones are beyond the scope of this guide. By exception, such reliefs may occasionally be mentioned, but our coverage of these issues is by no means meant to be comprehensive.

Non-tax factors affecting the decision whether to put an expense through the company are generally beyond the scope of this guide, although we will sometimes mention them where relevant, including the important issue discussed in Section 1.5.

The reader must also bear in mind the general nature of this guide. Individual circumstances vary and the tax implications of an individual, company, or other entity's actions will vary with them. For this reason, it is always vital to get professional advice before undertaking any tax planning or other transactions that may have tax implications. The authors and Taxcafe UK Limited cannot accept any responsibility for any loss that may arise as a consequence of any action, or any decision to refrain from action, taken as a result of reading this guide.

Unless stated to the contrary, it is assumed throughout this guide that company owners extracting funds from their company have already paid themselves sufficient salary and dividends to fully utilise their personal allowance and dividend allowance for the relevant tax year.

## Tax Years, Financial Years, and Accounting Periods

Income Tax, National Insurance, and most other personal taxes operate by reference to the tax year ending on 5$^{th}$ April. In this edition, unless stated to the contrary, we will be using the tax rates and allowances for the 2024/25 tax year, ending on 5$^{th}$ April 2025. For further details, see Appendix B.

Corporation Tax rates are set for Financial Years ending on 31$^{st}$ March. For the majority of this edition, unless stated to the contrary, we will be using the Corporation Tax rates for the 2024 Financial Year, ending on 31$^{st}$ March 2025, as detailed in Section 2.1. A company's Corporation Tax liability is, however, calculated for its own accounting period, which may end on any calendar date, although this is usually the end of a calendar month. This means many company accounting periods span two Financial Years. Often this makes no practical difference, as Corporation Tax rates do not change every year. We will take a more detailed look at the Corporation Tax regime in Chapter 12.

Lastly, on the subject of years, 2024 is a leap year with 366 days; you will see this reflected in a few calculations in this guide.

## Terminology and Abbreviations

For the purposes of this guide, a spouse includes a civil partner, but only includes spouses who are legally married (or legally registered civil partners).

Receipts, invoices, etc, are often important for evidencing business spending. Electronic or paper documents are both equally valid for this purpose, even if we do not always explicitly mention it.

We generally like to avoid abbreviations at Taxcafe, as we hate jargon. We will, however, adopt a few that are in common usage or will save you having to read the same phrase over and over again, including:

- BADR     Business Asset Disposal Relief
- CGT      Capital Gains Tax
- CT       Corporation Tax
- HMRC     HM Revenue and Customs
- SBA      Structures and Buildings Allowance
- SDLT     Stamp Duty Land Tax
- VAT      Value Added Tax

Large amounts, such as £1,000,000 or more, are sometimes abbreviated by use of the letter 'm'. For example, £2,500,000 may be written as '£2.5m'.

# Chapter 1

# Why Put It Through the Company?

## 1.1    WIN WIN WIN!

If you are running any kind of business through a company, it generally makes sense to put as many expenses through the company as you can. There are several potential benefits, including:

- Corporation Tax (CT) relief
- VAT recovery
- The expense does not need to be paid out of your own after-tax income

Where all three of these benefits apply, it truly is a 'win win win', and the potential savings are phenomenal.

### Example

*Bryce is the owner and director of MacFinnan Ltd, a VAT-registered company that faces a marginal CT rate of 26.5% (see Section 2.1). He is a higher rate taxpayer, having already taken a salary of £12,570 plus dividends of £50,000 out of the company this tax year.*

*Bryce now wants to buy a new computer. He will use it at home, but he will use it exclusively for business purposes. He's giving his old computer to the kids on condition they don't touch the new one.*

*The new computer will cost £2,500 plus VAT at 20%, a total of £3,000. If Bryce wants to make this purchase personally, he will need to take a further dividend of £4,528 out of the company so that, after paying Income Tax at 33.75%, or £1,528, he will be left with the net £3,000 he needs. So, in effect, the total cost is £4,528.*

*On the other hand, if the company buys the computer, the first thing it will do is recover £500 in VAT, leaving a net cost of £2,500, on which it can claim the 100% annual investment allowance (see Chapter 8). The company will thus obtain CT relief of £663 (£2,500 x 26.5%) meaning the net, after tax, cost of the computer is now just £1,837.*

A cost of £1,837, instead of £4,528, the difference is astounding! That's a saving of £2,691, which is more than the actual net (before VAT) price of the computer, and it's made up as follows:

| | |
|---|---|
| Income Tax avoided | £1,528 |
| VAT recovered | £500 |
| Corporation Tax relief | £663 |
| Total | £2,691 |

As we can see, by far the largest part of this saving is the Income Tax Bryce has avoided by getting the company to buy the computer. This means that, while the other savings are important, it is the simple fact that the company has borne the cost that produces the greatest benefit. We will see this principle in action many times throughout this guide.

Bryce's position is fairly typical for a small company owner, but the amount of Income Tax avoided by getting the company to pay will vary from one person to another, so we will take a more detailed look at this element of the savings arising in Section 5.1.

At this stage you may be tempted to think it might be a good idea to put absolutely everything through the company, but that's not the case and, in Section 1.3 we will look at some of the potential pitfalls to be wary of, as well as the potential cost of putting the wrong thing through the company.

In Bryce's case, there was no benefit in kind charge because he fell within the exemption for home office equipment (Section 7.11).

Bryce's example also demonstrates a simple, but important principle regarding the interaction between VAT and CT. Where the company recovers the VAT on goods or services, it only claims CT relief on the net cost before VAT (£2,500 in this example, rather than the gross cost including VAT of £3,000). Hopefully this is a fairly obvious point, but we will look at it in more detail in Section 3.8.

In many cases, all the benefits enjoyed by Bryce will apply where an expense is put through the company. In other cases, it may only be one or two of them. Nonetheless, as we will see later, it is often still worth putting the expense through the company.


## 1.2 WHAT DOES 'PUTTING IT THROUGH' MEAN?

Putting something through the company ultimately means the company is bearing the cost, assuming the liability, or recognising the expenditure in its accounts.

The exact way this is done can be important for a number of issues including Income Tax and National Insurance on any potential benefit in kind, and VAT recovery. The key point in many cases is whether the company or the director incurred the liability in the first place. Generally (though not always) this in turn depends on who the bill was issued to.

However, subject to these points, an expense can be put through the company in a number of ways, including:

- The company pays the expense
- The director pays the expense and the company reimburses them in cash
- The director pays the expense and the company reimburses them via a credit posted to their director's loan account (Section 5.5)
- The company recognises the expense in its accounts and pays the director in cash
- The company recognises the expense in its accounts and pays the director via a credit posted to their director's loan account

Not all of these methods are appropriate in all cases, but we will see examples of each of them in this guide.

## 1.3    IS IT ALWAYS A GOOD IDEA?

No, not always: there are occasions when putting something through the company can backfire. This can happen for a number of reasons, including long-term issues like future capital gains on property and other assets, and the eventual impact on your Inheritance Tax burden. We will look at these issues in Chapter 10.

But the main pitfall to watch out for is the risk of creating a taxable benefit in kind. You could actually put nearly anything you like through the company, but if it creates a taxable benefit in kind, it will often end up costing you more than simply paying the expense yourself.

### Example
*Lucinda decides to go on a world cruise. The ticket costs £8,000 and she gets her company to pay for it. It's purely a holiday; there is absolutely no business purpose behind the expenditure. Hence, it must be taxed as a benefit in kind. Lucinda has already taken a salary equal to her personal allowance, plus sufficient dividends to make her a higher rate taxpayer this year, so the benefit in kind will cost £3,600 in additional Income Tax.*

*(The benefit itself is taxed at 20%, costing £1,600, but it also means a further £8,000 of Lucinda's dividends are taxed at 33.75% instead of 8.75%, increasing the tax on her existing dividend income by an additional £2,000: 25% x £8,000.)*

*The company will suffer employer's National Insurance at ~~13.8%~~ on the* benefit, costing a further £1,104, and bringing its total costs to £9,104 *(£8,000 + £1,104).*

15% from April 2025

*To pay the extra Income Tax caused by her benefit in kind, Lucinda also has to take additional dividends of £5,434. She needs this much so that after paying Income Tax at 33.75% on **these** dividends (£1,834), she is left with the £3,600 she needs to pay the tax on her benefit in kind.*

*The only bit of good news in all this is that the company will get CT relief on the cost of the cruise and the National Insurance it has suffered, generating a potential saving of up to £2,413 (£9,104 x 26.5%).*

*Nonetheless, taking everything into account, the cost of the cruise can be summarised as follows:*

| | |
|---|---|
| *Ticket price* | *£8,000* |
| *Employer's National Insurance* | *£1,104* |
| *Corporation Tax relief* | *(£2,413)* |
| *Income Tax on benefit in kind* | *£1,600* |
| *Increased tax on existing income* | *£2,000* |
| *Income Tax on additional dividends* | *£1,834* |
| *Total cost* | *£12,125* |

*Instead of facing all this grief, Lucinda could simply have taken a dividend of £12,075 out of the company, paid the Income Tax arising at 33.75% (£4,075) and been left with the £8,000 she needed to pay for the cruise. In short, the cruise would have cost £12,075 instead of £12,125.*

Admittedly, the cost is not much greater in this case, but it is more, and there is a lot of extra admin involved. And it could be worse. I made a few assumptions here that tipped the balance in Lucinda's favour, but they would not always be guaranteed in a case like this.

Firstly, I assumed the benefit in kind did not attract employee's National Insurance. If it had, this would have led to an additional National Insurance cost of £640 (£8,000 x 8%) plus a further £326 in Income Tax on the extra £966 of dividends Lucinda would have needed to take out of the company as a result.

9

For details of how and when you can avoid employee's National Insurance on benefits in kind, see Section 7.33.

Secondly, I assumed the cost of the cruise and related employer's National Insurance would attract CT relief. This was because I assumed the 'employee benefit override' discussed in Section 2.2 would apply in this case. But this is not guaranteed and this issue is discussed further in Section 2.2.

Thirdly, I applied the maximum possible rate of CT relief (26.5%). But relief may only have been obtained at 25%, or even just 19%, meaning the overall net cost of the cruise would be higher, even when CT relief is available. (See Section 2.1 for details of applicable CT rates.)

Furthermore, if you think there may have been a VAT advantage in putting the cost of the cruise through the company, think again. There are a number of reasons why that wouldn't help in a case like this. We'll look at the main one in Section 3.5.

Hence, as we can see, putting the wrong thing through the company can prove extremely costly. We will see more examples of how this can happen, and how you can mitigate the position if it does, in Section 4.3.

Generally, getting the company to pay for something that will form a taxable benefit in kind for the company owner is a bad idea. But not all benefits provided to directors will have such disastrous consequences and some benefits can be worthwhile. We will look at this area of tax planning in Chapter 7.


## 1.4    WHO ARE YOU TO DECIDE?

One really important thing you have to understand about owning a company is that you and the company are separate legal entities. The company is not simply an extension of you. In law, it is a separate legal person, albeit an artificial one. This distinction is especially critical when we begin to consider payments from the company to its owners.

You own a company by owning shares in that company, i.e. by being a shareholder. Company share structures can be extremely complex, with multiple classes of shares, some having long, complicated names like 'Class A Redeemable Preference Shares'.

However, the majority of small private companies have a single class of shares known as 'Ordinary Shares'. In these simple cases, anyone who owns more than 50% of the shares controls the company. In this guide, we will refer to such a person as the company owner.

You may also control a company if you, together with connected persons, own more than 50% of the ordinary shares. Connected persons include your spouse, children, and certain other close relatives (see Appendix C for details).

Most small private company owners are also directors of their company and manage the company's affairs on a day-to-day basis. These company owners are often referred to as 'owner/managers', 'owner/directors', or 'shareholder/directors', as if this were a single role. For most practical purposes, this is a reasonable approach. However, when it comes to deducting expenses for tax purposes, it remains important to remember, as an owner/director or shareholder/director you have two distinctly different roles:

- As a shareholder, you own the company
- As a director, you run the company on behalf of the owners and, most critically, for the purposes of this guide, you are an employee of the company

It is your role as a director that gives you the ability to put expenses you incur personally through the company: but only if you meet the relevant criteria. This ability to deduct personal expenditure will be a major focus of this guide, beginning in Chapter 4, where we will look at the basic principles governing directors' expenses.

Sometimes an individual who controls a company on a day-to-day basis is not formally appointed as a director. Such an individual is known as a 'shadow director'. The principles covered in Chapter 4 apply equally to such a person.

Directors' expenses can effectively be regarded as a sub-category of company expenses. Hence, before we look at directors' expenses, we need to look at the principles governing the deductibility of company expenses. In Chapter 2, we will look at deductions for CT purposes; in Chapter 3, we will consider VAT.

## 1.5   NON-TAX FACTORS

There are often non-tax factors to consider when deciding whether to put something through your company.

As explained previously, these are generally beyond the scope of this guide, but one thing we thought worth mentioning is consumer rights.

The Consumer Rights Act 2015 gives individuals the right to ask for a full refund within 30 days of buying a product that turns out to be faulty. This includes major items like cars (new or used) but the protection only extends to individuals, not companies.

It may be possible to change the terms of a purchase contract to include the same protection as the Consumer Rights Act, although we suspect many sellers (e.g. car dealers) may not be prepared to do this.

So, when buying through the company, it's *caveat emptor*: buyer beware!

## 1.6 CHANGES AHEAD

In all our Taxcafe guides, we keep one eye on the future and, while we always cover the current rules as they apply at present, we also strive to forewarn readers about proposed, or potential, changes in the pipeline that may affect your plans.

However, the status of proposed future changes is not always clear, especially when there is a change of Government.

### Furnished Holiday Lets

At present, furnished holiday lets meeting specific qualifying criteria (see the Taxcafe guide *Using a Property Company to Save Tax* for details) enjoy a special, beneficial tax regime.

This special regime impacts the CT treatment of furnished holiday letting businesses run by a company, although only to a limited extent. The main point being that capital allowances are available on furniture, equipment, and other qualifying assets within a furnished holiday let (see Section 10.5).

The regime has a more significant impact on the owners of companies carrying on a furnished holiday letting business, as it can affect the Capital Gains Tax (CGT) treatment of their company shares, or a property they hold personally that is used in the company's business (as discussed in Section 10.3).

However, under draft legislation published on 29th July 2024, this beneficial tax regime is expected to be abolished from 6th April 2025 for Income Tax and CGT purposes, and from 1st April 2025 for CT purposes.

Nonetheless, the furnished holiday letting tax regime is still with us until at least 31st March 2025. That means owners of companies carrying on a furnished holiday letting business still have time to carry out a number of tax planning measures, as covered in the Taxcafe guide *Furnished Holiday Lets: Big Tax Changes Ahead*.

As far as this guide is concerned, we have prepared this edition on the basis of the current rules that apply until 31st March 2025, and which still provide some significant final tax saving opportunities for owners of companies running furnished holiday letting businesses. We have also added a few pointers on the proposed transitional rules contained in the draft legislation, where these are relevant.

# Chapter 2

# Understanding Company Tax Deductions

### 2.1  HOW MUCH ARE COMPANY TAX DEDUCTIONS WORTH?

Until recently, almost all companies paid 19% CT on all their profits. On 1st April 2023, however, a new regime came into force, which creates different tax rates for companies of different sizes (and also depends on a few other factors). We will look at that new regime in detail in Chapter 12, including the total tax burden falling on companies and how it is calculated.

What matters for our purposes for the rest of this guide though is the *marginal tax rate* paid by the company.

A marginal tax rate is a measure of the extra tax suffered on each additional £1 of taxable profit. It is equally the measure of how much tax is saved by each additional £1 of deductible expenses: in other words, it tells us how much CT is saved by putting a deduction through the company.

So, marginal tax rates are vital to our understanding of how much a company tax deduction is worth.

**The New Corporation Tax Regime**
Under the new regime, for accounting periods *starting* after 31st March 2023, companies generally pay tax at the following *effective* rates:

- **Profits £50,000 or less:** Company will pay 19% tax on all its profits
- **Profits between £50,000 and £250,000:** Company will pay 19% tax on the first £50,000 and 26.5% on the rest
- **Profits £250,000 or more:** Company will pay 25% tax on all its profits

This gives us the three marginal CT rates we will be using throughout this guide to show how much a company tax deduction is worth: 19%, 26.5%, and 25%.

For example, where a company with profits of £200,000 (i.e. between £50,000 and £250,000) is able to claim a deduction of £1,000, this will save £265 in CT (£1,000 x 26.5%).

We will use the 26.5% rate often, as this is the marginal tax rate faced by most small companies. As we will see in Chapter 12, this rate does not actually appear on formal tax computations, but that does not matter: it is the marginal tax rate that determines how much a tax deduction is worth.

For the sake of illustration, we will generally assume the whole of any tax deduction provides CT relief at the same effective marginal rate. This will not always be the case in practice, however, as the deduction itself may lead to a change in the company's marginal tax rate.

For example, if a company has taxable profits of £56,000 before claiming a tax deduction of £10,000 (which thus reduces its taxable profits to £46,000), the first £6,000 of the deduction provides CT relief at 26.5% and the remaining £4,000 provides relief at just 19%. We will not get into these complexities too often in this guide, but it is important to be aware of them.

Other factors may affect your company's CT rate, including whether it has any associated companies. We will look at these issues in Chapter 12 but, until then, for the rest of this guide, we will assume they do not apply.

The effective marginal CT rates for company accounting periods that started before 1$^{st}$ April 2023 will often be slightly lower. These are set out in Appendix A, but we will not use them in the rest of this guide.

**Future Changes to Corporation Tax?**
In its election manifesto, the new Labour Government stated: *"Labour will cap corporation tax at the current level of 25 per cent, the lowest in the G7, for the entire parliament, and we will act if tax changes in other countries pose a risk to UK competitiveness."*

They made no mention of retaining the 19% small profits rate, which makes us wonder if this rate could be abolished at some point, with all companies paying 25% CT on all their profits. Time will tell!

## 2.2    DEDUCTING COMPANY EXPENSES

Like any other business entity, a company is entitled to deduct its business expenditure from its taxable income. But what is business expenditure, what can be deducted, and when?

Companies are subject to CT on their taxable income. Taxable income takes many forms, but the most common types, and the ones we will mostly focus on in this guide, are trading profits and rental profits. In both cases, the company is only subject to CT on its net profits after deducting all relevant business expenditure.

In later chapters, we will be looking at some specific types of expenditure and how and when they can be deducted for CT purposes. In this chapter, we will examine the principles that govern all tax deductions for companies.

The basic rule that governs whether any expense may be deducted for tax purposes is that it must be:

> *Wholly and exclusively incurred for the purposes of the business*

This rule lies at the heart of nearly all business deductions, but it is subject to a few quirks and interpreting this simple phrase has kept the law courts busy for more than two centuries!

Furthermore, there are a number of exclusions that must be borne in mind. These are examined in Section 2.4. There is also the question of whether an item of expenditure is capital in nature. If something is deemed to be capital expenditure, this distinction overrides the basic rule set out above. We will look at the treatment of capital expenditure in Chapter 8.

But, before we delve into these more complex areas, let's look at how the 'wholly and exclusively incurred for the purposes of the business' rule applies in practice. Perhaps the best way to do that is to break it down into its constituent parts. This, in turn, is probably best done in reverse order.

### 'The Business'

Before a company can claim any business expenditure, it must have a business. Furthermore, it is important to have a clear understanding of what the company's business is. In most cases, this is pretty obvious but it is an essential part of establishing whether expenditure is incurred for business purposes and whether it is deductible for tax.

A theatrical hire company would naturally be able to claim the cost of a pantomime horse costume, but a plumbing company probably couldn't.

There are several different types of business recognised for UK tax purposes. The most important ones, at present, are:

i)      A trading business
ii)     A 'normal' property business
iii)    A furnished holiday letting business (but see Section 1.6)
iv)    A business of managing investments

While most companies only have one business, it is possible for a company to have two or more. I once had a company client that had each of the first three types of business and, many years ago, I had a company client that ran three distinctly different trading businesses. The key point to note is that each business is eligible for its own tax deductions, even when two or more of them are in the same company.

A 'normal' property business is a property letting business that does not qualify as a furnished holiday letting business. Some of the more specialised issues faced by companies running either of these types of business, as well as property trades, are examined in the Taxcafe guide *Using a Property Company to Save Tax*, but the issues covered in this guide also apply to these companies.

Companies with a business of managing investments generally come in two varieties: holding companies of trading groups, and family investment companies. The principles examined in this guide will again apply to these companies, although the range of deductions available will be limited.

However, the vast majority of small companies are either trading companies or property companies, so that is where we will concentrate in this guide.

### 'For the Purposes of'
So, when is an expense incurred for the purposes of the business?

This part of the phrase is open to a pretty wide interpretation, as many things may be done for business purposes. For example, if a plumbing company is running a marketing event at a local fair and hires a pantomime horse costume as part of that event, then this expense would be for the purposes of the business and would therefore be deductible (which is why I only said it *'probably couldn't'* claim the expense when we discussed it above).

More importantly, anything paid to, or for the benefit of, the company's employees is generally accepted as being for the purposes of the business. One might call this the 'employee benefit override'. While this is a very useful principle, there is one major exception, and one important proviso.

The exception is where the employee is a shareholder, closely connected to a shareholder (see Appendix C), or has some other close relationship to a shareholder, outside of their employment. It applies regardless of whether the shareholder is also a director, although they often will be.

In these cases, it cannot automatically be assumed the expense is being incurred for the purposes of the business, as there may be other motives present. Hence, it remains important to fulfil the 'wholly and exclusively incurred for the purposes of the business' test on basic principles. In other words, is the payment, or the expense, justified by the work the employee does for the company.

For example, a company owner employing their seventeen-year-old daughter as a receptionist and paying her a salary slightly above the national minimum wage would be fine, but giving her a salary of £100,000 plus a company Ferrari would be totally unjustified, and it is highly probable any deduction the company claimed for this expenditure would be disallowed.

That's not to say a salary of £100,000 and a company Ferrari could never be justified, it's simply a question of how large a pay package is supported by the facts of the case. If the receptionist had a twin sister who happened to be the most talented web designer in the country, then paying **her** a salary of £100,000 plus a company Ferrari might be justified. Heaven help the poor parent trying to explain this to their other daughter!

The point is, where payments are being made to, or for the benefit of, the company owner or their family, the question of whether the expense is being 'incurred for the purposes of the business' is much more critical.

When considering what size of salary or benefits package can be justified, it is important to consider:

- The hours worked by the employee
- Their role in the business and contribution to its success
- Their competence, qualifications, and experience
- The national minimum wage and other relevant regulations

Above all, the key issue is whether you would have paid the same salary or benefits to an unconnected individual with whom you had no other relationship beyond their employment in your company.

We will return to the issue of salaries and benefits for family members in Chapters 6 and 7.

Where other employees are concerned, it will usually simply be accepted at face value that any payments to, or for the benefit of, the employee are for the purposes of the company's business. Why else would the company be making the payment after all? However, there may still be a few exceptions where the employee has some other close personal relationship with the company owner and, again, it will then be necessary to fulfil the 'wholly and exclusively incurred for the purposes of the business' test on basic principles.

Having said all that, there is nothing to stop the company being a generous employer, within reason, even if friendships develop between the company owner and some of their employees. Nonetheless, closer relationships, beyond simple friendship, will warrant the same level of scrutiny as family members.

When it comes to the company owner themselves, where they are a director, controlling and managing the company's affairs on a day to day basis, a considerable level of salary and benefits could generally be justified. Indeed, I am a strong believer in the principle that most small companies only make profits because of the efforts of their shareholder/directors and hence any salary and benefits package with a total value up to the amount of those profits must be justified. Of course, such large remuneration packages are seldom tax efficient, but this principle is important when we look at things like pension contributions for directors (see Section 11.4).

It is also the reason I assumed the cost of Lucinda's world cruise would be allowable for CT purposes in Section 1.3. While the cruise itself does not benefit the company, as a taxable benefit in kind provided to an employee (including a director) it will be allowable provided the cost, together with any salary or other benefits, is justified by the work done for the company by that employee. Of course, as we saw in Section 1.3, this does not necessarily mean putting this type of expense through the company is a good idea!

Which brings us to the important proviso about payments to, or for the benefit of, employees: namely that these payments are usually subject to Income Tax for the employee, employer's National Insurance for the company, and often also employee's National Insurance for the employee. Direct payments to the employee are, of course, subject to all three taxes.

Benefits in kind provided to employees are subject to complex rules, which we will look at in more detail in Chapter 7 for benefits generally, and Section 9.2 for company cars.

Employees, including directors, may claim exemption from tax on any reimbursement of expenses that were wholly, exclusively and necessarily incurred for the purposes of their employment. This is a much stricter test than 'wholly and exclusively incurred for the purposes of the business' and we will look at the question of what expenses may be reimbursed without giving rise to a tax liability in Chapter 4.

Apart from anything that benefits shareholders or their family, most other company expenditure will be incurred for the purposes of the company's business. The business purpose may be quite indirect and the expenditure may be totally inefficient, or even downright foolhardy. But it is not for HMRC to make these judgements. It does not matter whether, in the end, the expenditure actually did benefit the business. If the sole *purpose* of the expenditure was to benefit the business then, subject to the exclusions set out in Section 2.4, the company may claim a deduction. Remember that pantomime horse!

### 'Incurred' Part 1: When
For CT purposes, expenditure is incurred not when it is actually paid, or even when it is due; but when the relevant services are performed, the relevant supplies are made, or the relevant goods are delivered.

### *Example*
*Shebana Ltd draws up accounts to 31$^{st}$ December each year. On 10$^{th}$ March 2025, it receives an electricity bill for £3,000, covering the three months ended 28$^{th}$ February 2025. The bill is dated 4$^{th}$ March, payment is due by 18$^{th}$ March, and the company actually pays on 3$^{rd}$ April. However, the bill date, due date, and payment date are irrelevant: the expenditure was incurred over the three months ending on 28$^{th}$ February. Hence, the company may claim:*

*£1,000 in its accounts for the year ending 31ˢᵗ December 2024 and £2,000 in its accounts for the year ending 31ˢᵗ December 2025 (basing its claim on months), OR*
*£1,033 in its accounts for the year ending 31ˢᵗ December 2024 and £1,967 in its accounts for the year ending 31ˢᵗ December 2025 (basing its claim on days)*

Claims based on months or days are equally valid, as they are both reasonable methods to use. The key point is the expense may be spread over the period it was actually incurred: i.e. over the period the electricity was supplied for.

This approach to claiming expenditure is known as the 'accruals basis' and is the method all companies must use for CT purposes. A further refinement to the accruals basis is the requirement to account for trading stock and work in progress.

### 'Incurred' Part 2: How
A company may incur expenditure in a number of ways, including:

- A direct payment made by the company
- Reimbursement of expenditure incurred by directors, other employees, or another person acting on behalf of the company
- A contractual commitment, explicitly or implicitly entered into by the company
- Another type of legal commitment falling on the company

The first heading is obvious; the second is reasonably clear, although we will look at it further in Chapter 4; but what about the third and fourth?

Explicit contracts are fairly clear. A company signs a contract to purchase electricity from a power company, so it is committed to making the payments due under the contract.

Contracts may also be verbal. A company director asks a window cleaner to 'clean the office windows every week,' so the company is committed to paying the window cleaner.

So, what is an implicit contract? Let us suppose the company director just asked the window cleaner how much it would be to clean the windows. "Twenty quid," said the window cleaner. "OK, go ahead," said the director. That's an explicit verbal contract to clean the windows: but only once. This time, there was no request to clean the windows 'every week'.

However, the window cleaner then returns each week and cleans the windows again. The director sees the window cleaner doing this but says nothing. The director's silence means an implicit contractual commitment has been created, since the director already knows the window cleaner's charges and has allowed the work to be done.

The company is thus contractually committed to paying twenty pounds per week and may legitimately claim the expense (assuming it does indeed eventually pay the window cleaner).

If the director doesn't see the window cleaner returning each week, but goes ahead and pays for the work, this again creates an implicit contractual commitment and the company has incurred a legitimate business expense that it can claim.

The difficult scenario is if the director doesn't see the window cleaner returning and refuses to pay for the work: but that's one for the lawyers!

Our fourth heading, legal commitments, don't require a contract, as these are legal obligations falling on the company. As with commercial contracts, these are treated as having been incurred over the period to which they relate. The most common example is Business Rates, but there are many others, especially in any business subject to health and safety regulations.

### 'Wholly and Exclusively'
While an expense may have been incurred for the purposes of the business, the question sometimes arises as to whether it was 'wholly and exclusively' for business purposes, or whether there was also some other motive present. Where the expenditure has a 'dual purpose' and one of its purposes does not relate to the business, the strict rule is the expenditure cannot be claimed for CT purposes. However, 'dual purpose' has to be contrasted with 'mixed use', which is different. We will look at this key distinction in more detail shortly but, for now, we will focus on dual purpose expenditure: namely where both a business and non-business purpose are being served simultaneously by the same expenditure.

Remember we are talking about purpose or motive here. The fact that an incidental, non-business benefit sometimes arises from the same expenditure does not, in itself, cause any problems. For example, if a company director is travelling on business, they are allowed to enjoy the journey without it affecting the CT deduction for the expense.

Detours, sightseeing, and other deviations from the journey's business purpose are a different matter, however, and we will take a closer look at travel and subsistence for company directors in Chapter 4.

While incidental personal benefits do not generally give rise to any problems, HMRC will often take a very narrow view on what can be regarded as incidental. They will also sometimes look for a purpose or motive you may not even have considered: as we will see below, when we discuss office clothing.

Interpreting the 'wholly and exclusively' rule in practice can be difficult, and it can be something of a grey area. In many cases, the expenditure will be subject to the 'employee benefit override' discussed above. In other words, expenditure that benefits an employee is generally accepted as being wholly and exclusively for the purposes of the business and can be claimed for CT purposes. Remember, however, unless the expenditure meets the much stricter test of being wholly, exclusively, and necessarily incurred for the purposes of the individual's employment, it will usually represent a benefit in kind and give rise to Income Tax charges, and possibly also National Insurance (although there are some exceptions to this, as we shall see in Chapter 7).

Where the employee concerned is a shareholder/director, or closely connected to a shareholder, the position may be different and we will look at this situation, together with some suitable examples, in Chapter 4.

But, apart from something that benefits a shareholder/director or their family, what else might be 'dual purpose' expenditure? Such cases are rare, although they do trouble the courts from time to time.

One good example is sponsorship. Let's suppose a company sponsors the local under-seventeens girls' rugby team. There are a number of ways in which the sponsorship might automatically qualify for CT relief under the special provisions we will examine in Section 11.2, but we will assume, for the sake of illustration, that none of these apply here and we must rely on basic principles.

The company does gain some benefit from the sponsorship as this generates a lot of goodwill in the local community. However, the company's business is completely unrelated to rugby, and the cost of the sponsorship package is well in excess of the value of sales generated. It also happens the company's owner is a keen supporter of women's rugby.

Clearly there is a 'dual purpose' here and one of those purposes is not to benefit the business. Hence, strictly speaking, this expenditure should not be allowed for CT purposes at all. In practice, however, a case like this often warrants a pragmatic approach.

What I would tend to do in this type of situation is to reach a broad assessment of what level of sponsorship would have been commercially justifiable for the company's business. After all, it does get some benefit through the goodwill generated in the local community. Let's say the sponsorship costs £10,000 and the value of the benefit to the company can reasonably be assessed at about £2,000. I would therefore claim 20%, or £2,000, for CT purposes, and disallow the remaining £8,000.

This, as I say, is merely a pragmatic approach as, technically, the expenditure is not wholly and exclusively for the purposes of the business. However, this type of approach has stood me in good stead throughout my career.

In this case, there does not appear to be any direct benefit to the company owner as they are simply a 'keen supporter' of women's rugby. However, if their daughter, granddaughter, or another close relative was on the team, the position might be different, and we will explore the subject of sponsorship further in Section 11.2.

**Dual Purpose versus Mixed Use**
Expenditure has a dual purpose where it serves more than one purpose at the same time in a way that cannot be separated or sub-divided. One of the best examples of this is normal office clothing, where the business purpose of looking smart and professional cannot be separated from the personal functions of providing warmth and decency, which are provided simultaneously by the same clothing. We will look at the treatment of business or work clothing further in Section 4.2.

Expenditure has mixed use where it serves more than one purpose but in a way that can be separated or sub-divided. Where it is possible to separate out the business element of the expenditure, this can be claimed for CT purposes.

This is why directors and other employees are able to claim business mileage in respect of the business use of their car (see Section 9.4). It is also the basis behind my pragmatic approach to the girls' rugby team sponsorship discussed above.

***Example***

*Some years ago, Ben bought a detached house and adopted it as his home. Later, he divided the property into two semi-detached houses. He kept one of the semis as his home and transferred the other to his company, Bakara Ltd, which runs a property letting business.*

*In 2024, Bakara Ltd carries out some repairs on the property's roof at a cost of £8,000. Half of this (£4,000) can be claimed for CT purposes as it relates to the company's rental property; the other half cannot be claimed and must be treated as Ben's personal expense (see Section 4.3 for further details of how this should be treated for tax purposes).*

The 50/50 split used here would generally be a reasonable approach provided the two semi-detached houses were approximately equal in size. There are many other approaches that could have been used, however, including apportioning the expenditure according to:

- The roof area of each house
- The floor area of each house
- The number of rooms in each house
- The market value of each house
- A more accurate allocation provided by the roofer

Other types of expenditure might be apportioned according to the same factors, or others such as:

- Time spent
- Amount of material used (by number, volume, weight, etc)
- Cost of material or goods used
- Mileage

Many methods of apportionment are often available for mixed use expenditure, so which do you follow?

In the next section, we will look at some guidelines on how to approach the apportionment of mixed use expenditure.


### 2.3    APPORTIONING EXPENDITURE

Where expenditure needs to be apportioned for tax purposes, I have a set of guidelines, or 'laws', to help you approach this task and minimise the risk of any subsequent difficulties with HMRC. I have developed these 'laws' based on over forty years' experience in the tax profession, and they have proved themselves invaluable in practice time and again.

## Bayley's Laws for Apportioning Expenditure

### 1. Be Reasonable

Fundamentally, you are trying to reach a reasonable assessment of how much expenditure has been incurred for business purposes. While you want to maximise your tax deduction, you also want to avoid any future difficulties with HMRC, so you need to use a method that you know, in your heart of hearts, produces a reasonable result. The question is, can you look yourself in the mirror and say, "Yes, that's reasonable?"

One of the methods often used for calculating a deduction in respect of business use of your own home provides a good example. As we shall see in Section 10.7, one of the most popular methods is the 'number of rooms' method, where household costs are apportioned according to the number of rooms in the house (excluding kitchens, bathrooms and hallways). Some years ago, I had a client with a very small business, producing just £2,000 or £3,000 of income each year. However, they had a large house, with annual running costs of £24,000. Despite the size of the house, it only had four rooms for the purpose of the 'use of home' calculation, one of which (the smallest) was used as an office. Using the number of rooms method would have produced a use of home deduction of £6,000. Clearly, this was excessive in this case. It did not seem reasonable. I therefore changed the allocation method to one based on floor area, which produced a much more reasonable result, and claimed this on behalf of the client instead.

Ultimately, it comes down to this: does the amount being claimed seem reasonable? If you don't think so, you're going to have a hard time convincing HMRC or the courts.

### 2. Be as Scientific as Possible

You stand a far better chance of getting your deductions accepted by HMRC in the event of an enquiry if you use some sort of scientific basis for your calculations.

Let's say you're claiming a deduction for the annual running costs of a garden office. You know you can't claim the costs in full as there is some occasional private use of the office. You could make a rough estimate of the private use, something like 'say 10%', or you could keep a log of both your business and private use for, say, the first year. Let's say you use the garden office for work a total of 1,925 hours in the first year and you've logged the private use at 225 hours. That's a total of 2,150 hours of use, so your private use restriction works out at $225/2,150 = 10.46\%$.

Some years later, you have the misfortune to have a tax enquiry. HMRC asks you how you calculated your private use restriction for your garden office.

If you answer, "I estimated it at 10%," HMRC will probably ask, "How do you know? Are you sure it isn't more?" They may go on to say, "We estimate it at 20%," and adjust your tax calculations accordingly. Without the evidence to prove them wrong, you could end up with extra tax to pay, plus penalties and interest.

Alternatively, if you are able to answer, "I kept a log for the first year and it showed my personal use to be 10.46%," you are in a much stronger position and it is unlikely they will impose any adjustments on your tax calculations. They may still ask, "Are you happy your working patterns are still the same and your private use of the office is still at approximately the same level?" but as long as you can honestly answer, "Yes, I am happy," you should be alright.

If your working patterns and/or private use do change significantly, you should prepare a new calculation, perhaps by keeping a usage log for the office for another year.

Similar principles can be applied to most mixed use expenditure, although the apportionment methods may differ.

## 3. Be Consistent

HMRC will expect you to apply a consistent approach year on year. This does not mean the proportion of business use for an item of mixed use expenditure cannot change from one year to the next and nor does it mean you must use the same approach for every type of expenditure: but it does mean they will generally expect you to use the same approach for similar types of expenditure each year, unless there is a good reason why it has become inappropriate to do so.

Let's go back to that garden office. Let's say in the first year, you used it as described above. You also logged that the garden office was used for work on 240 days and used privately on 40 days. If you had based your calculation on days instead of hours, your private use restriction would have been 14.3%, which is quite a bit higher than the calculation based on hours. Hence, you used the 10.46% produced by the calculation based on hours. No problem with that, it was a perfectly reasonable approach.

You might have just stuck with the 10.46% in the following years since, as discussed above, such a sample or trial period is a reasonable basis to use, provided the general pattern of the office's use (business and private) does not alter significantly.

Alternatively, you might have kept a usage log again the following year. Let's say this showed 2,050 hours of business use and 220 hours of private use. That's a total of 2,270 hours of use. This would give you a private use restriction of 220/2,270 = 9.69%. It would be perfectly reasonable to use this lower percentage in the second year as you have the evidence to support it. You are not being inconsistent, as you are still using the same apportionment method.

However, once again, you also logged how many days the garden office was used for work, or used privately. This time, these amounted to 255 and 25 respectively. If you now calculated your private use restriction based on days, it would amount to 8.9%, which is less than the calculation based on hours. However, changing the basis of your calculation in this way would be inconsistent and this is very much the type of inconsistency HMRC would tend to object to. Hence, I'd suggest sticking with the calculation based on hours, which is likely to be more acceptable.

The need to be consistent means it is sensible to choose an apportionment method at the outset that is likely to be the most beneficial (but reasonable) method in the long term, over a number of years, rather than simply in the first year alone.

### 4. Keep a Record of Your Logic
It is also important to document your calculations and the reasoning behind your apportionment, so you can back up what you have done in the event of an enquiry. If you have been reasonable, as scientific as possible, consistent in your approach, **and** you can produce the evidence to prove it, you will be in a very strong position.

Keeping a record will also remind you of the reasoning you applied at the time. The older I get, the less comfortable I am relying on my memory alone, and I'm sure it's the same for most people.

### 5. Be Imaginative and Choose What Works Well for You
While I would stress the importance of following the guidelines above, provided you follow these laws, there is nothing to stop you using any reasonable basis of apportionment that suits you.

Take use of home claims again. The usual method is to base these on the number of rooms. But what if your workroom/office is larger than the other rooms in the house? In that case, a claim based on floor area would be a reasonable method to use. You might consider the height of the room as well and make your claim based on volume rather than area.

## 2.4 STATUTORY EXCLUSIONS

So far, we have considered the basic principles of whether expenditure is deductible for CT purposes and how to calculate those deductions. However, in a few cases, those basic principles are overridden by statutory exclusions.

### Business Entertaining

Business entertaining is generally accepted as a business cost for accounting purposes and will not be regarded as a personal expense of any director or other employee. However, it is specifically barred as a deduction for CT purposes.

Despite this restriction, planning, and treating your business entertaining expenditure carefully can produce massive tax savings, so we will return to this subject in Section 4.8.

### Business Gifts

Business gifts are also similarly disallowed for CT purposes. There is, however, an exception for gifts costing no more than £50 per recipient (in total per year) and which prominently bear the company's name (or its trading name, if different). Gifts of food, drink, tobacco, vouchers, or tokens exchangeable for goods are excluded from this exception.

I suspect the exception for small gifts is the reason I haven't had to buy a pen since I went self-employed over twenty years ago. However, I would say the occasional gifts of food and drink I have received over the years have generally been more welcome, even if my benefactors were unable to claim the cost for CT purposes.

The serious point here, however, is that, like business entertaining, business gifts put through the company can still yield tax savings even though they might be disallowed for CT purposes, so we will again look at this issue in Section 4.8.

Samples of the company's own goods or products are treated differently to business gifts and the cost of providing free samples will generally be allowable if it meets the general principles in Section 2.2. For example, if a sausage manufacturing company gives six packs of sausages to the owner of a small chain of convenience stores with a view to encouraging them to purchase the product for sale in their shops, this cost would be allowable. However, repeated gifts to the same person will eventually become business gifts rather than legitimate samples used to promote the business. Hence, giving the convenience store owner a pack of (the same) sausages every week would constitute a non-allowable business gift.

**Fines and Penalties**
Statutory fines and civil penalties imposed by the authorities cannot generally be claimed for CT purposes. However, there are some exceptions for parking fines and we will look at this subject in more detail in Section 9.9.

Penalties levied by HMRC themselves are, of course, disallowed for CT purposes, but interest on overdue tax is allowed for CT.

Commercial penalties, such as a payment under a penalty clause in a contract, will generally be allowable, provided they meet the general principles discussed in Section 2.2.

**Car Leasing**
If the company leases a car with $CO_2$ emissions in excess of a set statutory threshold, 15% of the lease payments must be disallowed for CT purposes.

The threshold for this disallowance is 50g/km for leases commencing after 31$^{st}$ March 2021; 110g/km for leases commencing between 1$^{st}$ April 2018 and 31$^{st}$ March 2021; and 130g/km for leases commencing between 1$^{st}$ April 2013 and 31$^{st}$ March 2018.


### 2.5    TAX RETURNS AND AMENDMENTS

A company's Corporation Tax Return (known as a CT600) is generally due within twelve months of the end of the company's accounting period and must be filed electronically. Paradoxically, this deadline falls three months after the normal due date for payment of CT, which is nine months and one day after the end of the accounting period. Larger companies (generally those with annual profits in excess of £1.5m) must pay their CT in instalments, and it is due earlier.

The CT Return can be amended at any time within twelve months of its normal filing date. Hence, for example, in the case of a twelve-month company accounting period ending on 31st December 2024:

- The normal due date for payment of CT is 1st October 2025
- The filing deadline for the company's CT Return is 31st December 2025
- The company's CT Return can be amended at any time until 31st December 2026

The ability to amend the CT Return can be useful if an item of allowable expenditure has been overlooked and the company wishes to rectify the position. For example, if a company purchased new business premises during the year ending 31st December 2024 and only realised during 2026 that it could have claimed the annual investment allowance on £250,000 worth of integral features (see Sections 8.4 and 10.5), it would be able to amend its 2024 CT Return to make the claim.

In view of this ability to amend earlier CT Returns, we will generally endeavour to cover the principles applying to company tax deductions for expenditure incurred after 31st March 2021 in this edition of the guide.

However, while amending an earlier year's tax return is a useful facility for larger claims, in practice, where smaller items have been overlooked, it will generally make sense to simply claim them the following year. For example, if a £100 restaurant bill was wrongly classed as business entertaining and disallowed in the 2023 tax return, it would make sense to simply adjust the entertaining disallowance in 2024 by deducting the £100 from the disallowed figure. Technically, it isn't the correct procedure but no-one, not even HMRC, would thank you for going to the bother of doing an amended CT Return to claim such a small amount of expenditure.

In exceptional cases, it may be possible to make a tax repayment claim in respect of errors or mistakes in earlier CT Returns for accounting periods ending between two and six years previously. The claim must have been valid under the law as it was generally understood at the time (HMRC will usually interpret this as meaning valid under *its* understanding of the law at the time) and is restricted to cases of genuine error regarding an available deduction. It cannot be used to put in place capital allowances claims that could have been made (but see Section 8.9 on this point) or many other elections or claims for relief.

Nonetheless, under the right circumstances, it could be worthwhile, so it's something worth bearing in mind as you read the rest of this guide.

## 2.6   ACCOUNTING PERIODS

Companies generally draw up accounts for a period of twelve months ending on the same calendar date each year. Unless stated to the contrary, we have assumed this is the case throughout this guide. This is important as a number of allowances, reliefs, and other limits are restricted on a pro rata basis if the company draws up accounts for a period of less than twelve months.

Companies may, however, draw up accounts for shorter or longer periods (usually up to a maximum of eighteen months, although longer periods can occur in exceptional cases).

A shorter period is treated much the same, apart from the restrictions in allowances, reliefs, and other limits discussed above.

A longer period is treated for CT purposes as if it were two accounting periods: the first twelve months and the remainder. In most cases, the remainder is then a short accounting period of less than twelve months and is treated accordingly.

### Starting Business
For CT purposes, a new accounting period starts when the company starts business. This will often be some time after the date of incorporation.

### *Example*
*Trinity Ltd is incorporated on 12th May 2024 but does not commence trading until 15th September 2024.*

*The company changes its accounting date to 30th June and prepares its first set of accounts for the period from 12th May 2024 to 30th June 2025.*

*For CT purposes, the company is regarded as having one accounting period as a dormant company, from 12th May to 14th September 2024, and then a second accounting period, as an active trading company, from 15th September 2024 to 30th June 2025.*

If Trinity Ltd prepared its first set of accounts to a date more than twelve months after it commenced trading, it would have three accounting periods for CT purposes.

**Ceasing Business**

For CT purposes, an accounting period is also deemed to come to an end when the company ceases business.

**Keeping HMRC Informed**

It is important to keep HMRC informed of any changes that affect your company's tax return periods, including changes of accounting date, setting up new companies, and commencement of business. Most important of all is to advise HMRC if the company ceases business activity and becomes dormant.

Failure to keep HMRC informed may mean they issue notices requiring the company to deliver a CT Return for the wrong period. This can lead to unnecessary complications and even penalties: do not ignore a notice to deliver a CT Return just because it has been issued for the wrong period!

## 2.7    LOSSES: CAN YOU GO TOO FAR?

An important point to note is the fact that any losses arising in a company cannot be set off against the company owner's personal income. Company losses are effectively 'ring-fenced' within the corporate regime.

Having said that, the loss relief regime within companies is pretty flexible and, provided the company returns to profit in the near future, in the vast majority of cases it will soon obtain CT relief for its loss. Trading companies can also obtain relief by setting losses against profits made in the previous year, and companies that are in a group together can set losses off against each other's profits.

Nonetheless, this effective ring-fencing of company losses is worth bearing in mind, especially when considering issues such as:

* Financing: borrowing personally may provide better tax relief; getting the company to pay you interest may create, or accelerate, an overall tax cost
* Rent payments: getting the company to pay you rent may create, or accelerate, an overall tax cost
* Salaries paid to family members: payments that attract Income Tax and/or National Insurance may not be tax efficient

But it's also worth making the point that, if the company will be getting tax relief for its payments in the near future (via loss relief) then many of these strategies will remain almost as beneficial as they are for a profitable company.

Furthermore, let's not forget what we saw in Section 1.1: CT relief is not the most important issue in most cases. Throughout this guide we will see many examples of payments and expenses where putting it through the company provides a benefit, not because of CT relief, but because the expense doesn't have to be paid out of the owner's after-tax income. The ability to recover input VAT on company expenses will also be important in many cases.

So, even when a company is making losses over a number of years, it can be worth putting expenses through the company. A frequent example of this is in the case of start-up companies, many of which take a few years to show a profit. The owner will often have to rely on taking a salary for their personal income, since the company has no distributable profits. That fact alone means it will often still be worth putting expenses through the company.

### *Example*
*Simon is the shareholder/director of Startup Ltd. The company has been trading for a couple of years and its prospects are good, but it is yet to show a profit. Simon has been taking an annual salary of £60,000 out of the company and this, together with the related employer's National Insurance is part of the company's trading losses carried forward for CT purposes.*

*In December 2024, Simon holds a Christmas party for the company's staff. The party costs a total of £2,000, which amounts to less than £150 per head. (Hence, as we will see in Section 7.31, it does not give rise to benefit in kind charges for the staff.)*

*The party would be an allowable expense for CT purposes but, as the company has trading losses carried forward, it will not actually produce a CT saving for some time to come. Simon is therefore tempted to pay for it out of his own pocket but then he realises that, to fund the cost, he would need to take a bonus of £3,448 out of the company. This would give rise to Income Tax and employee's National Insurance at a total of 42%, or £1,448, leaving him with the £2,000 he needs.*

*The company will also suffer employer's National Insurance at 13.8% on Simon's bonus, costing a further £476.*

*While both Simon's bonus and the employer's National Insurance will be added to the company's trading losses and will effectively obtain CT relief at some point in the future (one hopes), for the time being, the effective cost of the party has almost doubled and now amounts to a total of £3,924.*

Hence, as we can see, when it comes to external costs (i.e. payments to outside parties, not to the company owner or their family), it can actually be even more important to put these through the company, where appropriate, when the company is making losses.

See Section 12.7 for details of group relief; see the Taxcafe guide *Using a Property Company to Save Tax* for details of the loss relief available to property companies.

# Chapter 3

# Claiming Back VAT

## 3.1 RECOVERING VAT

There is a lot of commonality between whether an expense qualifies for CT relief and whether the company can claim back the VAT on the expense. Unfortunately, however, there still remain a number of key differences.

Firstly, of course, the company has to be VAT registered. If it is registered, this applies to all its activities. While a company may have two or more businesses for CT purposes, its VAT registration applies to the whole company.

Where the company carries on any VAT exempt activities, this will restrict its ability to recover VAT. None of the VAT on direct costs relating to the exempt activities can be claimed and only a suitable proportion of the VAT on overheads and other general costs can be claimed. This is known as partial exemption and is a complex area of VAT law.

Where all the company's activities are VAT exempt, it simply cannot register for VAT. The most common exempt activity for small companies is residential property letting. If this is the only activity your company is engaged in, you will not need to register for VAT, but nor will you be able to recover the VAT on any of your business expenses. *[handwritten: exempt as it is considered an essential service]*

However, ancillary services provided to tenants (e.g. cleaning or gardening) are standard-rated and your company will need to register for VAT if the annual value of these services exceeds £90,000 (the new threshold from 1st April 2024). The company would then need to charge VAT on a suitable proportion of its rental income and could recover some VAT under the partial exemption rules.

The letting of holiday accommodation is also standard-rated for VAT, and commercial property is subject to the option to tax. See the Taxcafe guide *Using a Property Company to Save Tax* for further VAT information for companies with property businesses.

One way in which VAT is simpler than other taxes is that, apart from companies operating the flat rate scheme, it generally makes no difference whether expenditure is revenue or capital. We will look at that important distinction in Section 8.1 but, as I said, it rarely makes any difference for VAT purposes.

Companies that are VAT registered, but which are operating the flat rate scheme, are only able to recover VAT on a limited number of expenses. We will look at this further in Section 3.7 but, in effect, for most of the costs you put through the company, this means you cannot claim the VAT.

### Have You Paid Any VAT?

The next hurdle to get over is to establish whether the company has actually paid any VAT. You can't recover it unless you've paid it... and can prove it. Proof generally takes the form of a VAT invoice, but we'll take a closer look at that subject in Section 3.4.

It's worth bearing in mind that a lot of company expenditure will not have any VAT on it, including:

- Wages and salaries
- Interest, bank charges, and other finance costs
- Insurance premiums
- Travel costs (train fares, bus fares, air fares, etc.)
- Cold, takeaway food and drink (not alcohol)
- Books and publications (including electronic publications)
- Business Rates
- MOT Certificates
- Vehicle Excise Duty (Road Tax)
- Rent (if the landlord hasn't exercised the option to tax)
- Purchases from a non-VAT registered business or individual

It's not always so easy to spot these things though. Food and drink can be particularly difficult. A cold takeaway sandwich has no VAT on it, but a packet of crisps, a biscuit, or a chocolate bar is standard-rated. And if you eat in, it's all standard-rated.

Smaller suppliers may not be registered for VAT, even when making taxable supplies, so you cannot just assume you've paid VAT without some form of evidence. Even what appears to be a large supplier may not be, it could be a franchise: so evidence is key.

And it doesn't matter whether something was subject to VAT further up the line: you need to have been charged VAT by your supplier.

**Business Purpose**
As well as being VAT registered and being able to prove you've actually paid some VAT, there also needs to be a business purpose for the expenditure.

This is a similar principle to the one we looked at for the purposes of CT relief (see Section 2.2), although the 'employee benefit override' operates differently for VAT purposes. We'll look at the recovery of VAT on employee benefits in Section 3.5. Don't forget, employees include directors!

A business benefit is not sufficient, there has to be a direct business purpose. Hence, the company will not usually be able to recover VAT on any dual purpose expenditure that benefits a company owner or their family. A good example is an individual golf club membership for a director. There may be a business benefit in that the director is able to generate work for the company's business through their contacts at the golf club, but the purpose of the membership is to enable them to play golf. Hence, any VAT paid on the membership fees cannot be recovered. (Whether there is any VAT on the fees will depend on how the club is constituted.)

However, a partial recovery of VAT will be allowed for mixed use expenditure and some other cases where the business purpose is reasonably clear, even if a non-business purpose also exists. I recently saw an example where HMRC were offering to allow a company to recover 20% of the VAT on a horse box used by the director's wife to transport her horse to various events around the country. The box bore prominent advertising for the company and was painted in the company's colours, so there was sufficient business purpose to allow a partial recovery of the VAT. (For other tax consequences of this type of expenditure, see Section 11.2.)

**Statutory Exclusions/Restrictions**
Like CT, VAT has its own statutory exclusions and restrictions. The main ones to be aware of are business entertaining and gifts, which we will look at in Section 3.6, and cars and other motor expenses, which we will look at in Chapter 9.


## 3.2    SHOULD YOU REGISTER FOR VAT?

Any business entity that makes more than £90,000 of taxable supplies in any twelve-month period must register for VAT.

(There is a potential exemption where the £90,000 threshold has been exceeded due to exceptional, 'one-off' circumstances, but this must be applied for.)

Taxable supplies are the company's total gross sales income from sales of goods or services subject to VAT at any rate (0%, 5%, 20%, or anything else the Government dreams up: we also had a 12.5% rate for a while not long ago).

The company should also register for VAT if it expects its taxable supplies to exceed £90,000 in the next month alone.

Some people have tried to avoid compulsory VAT registration by splitting a business into different parts and placing them in different entities (e.g. two or more companies). Not only does this lead to potential additional costs in both CT and National Insurance (see Sections 6.2 and 12.3), it also has to be done incredibly well in order to work: so, it generally doesn't! Take professional advice if you're considering this, although we don't really recommend it.

**Voluntary Registration**
When we are looking at the issue of recovering VAT on company expenses, it is worth considering whether voluntary registration is worthwhile. A company can register for VAT voluntarily when it is making some taxable supplies, but less than the £90,000 threshold.

Voluntary registration can be beneficial under a number of circumstances as it allows the company to recover the VAT on some or all of its expenses (depending whether partial exemption applies). It does, however, mean the company must charge VAT on its taxable sales.

**Zero-Rated Sales**
Where the company's sales are mostly zero-rated (VAT is charged, but at 0%), VAT registration will generally be beneficial. Some of the businesses this may apply to include:

- Food retailers (including those selling cold takeaway food)
- Publishers (anyone selling books or publications, including electronic publications)
- Property developers developing new residential dwellings

Note that property developers selling new residential property cannot recover the VAT on any white goods or carpets they supply as part of the dwelling (although wooden flooring is permitted).

## Business to Business

Where your company's customers are mostly VAT registered businesses themselves, you will be able to charge them VAT and they will be able to recover it. Hence there should be no impact on your sales income while, at the same time, you can recover the VAT on your costs.

## Online Registration Estimator

For those considering voluntary registration, HMRC has provided an online *VAT Registration Estimator* tool designed to provide some idea of what VAT registration could mean for your business. This can be found at: https://www.gov.uk/guidance/check-what-registering-for-vat-may-mean-for-your-business

The estimator can also be used by those facing compulsory registration to see what the impact will be, but it won't affect your obligation to register!

However, while it might be useful for some, the tool is rather 'rough and ready' and assumes a great deal of knowledge (about VAT) on the part of the company owner, so it's no substitute for professional advice.

## 3.3    EXTRA CLAIMS ON REGISTRATION

When the company first registers for VAT, it can claim the VAT on purchases of goods made within the last four years, provided the goods are still held by the company at the date of registration. This covers both stock held for sale and fixed assets such as vans, furniture, and equipment.

Subject to the further points below, VAT on services supplied to the company within the six months prior to registration can also be claimed.

This ability to make back-dated claims extends to purchases made by directors or other employees, even before the company was incorporated, provided the goods or services related directly to the business carried on, or to be carried on, by the company. However, VAT cannot be recovered on items initially purchased for private use by a director or other employee personally and then subsequently introduced into the company and used for business purposes.

VAT cannot be claimed on any goods or services that formed part of an onward supply to a customer made before the date of registration.

Hence, for example, if a company paid an invoice for accountancy fees for the preparation of its annual accounts issued three months before it registered for VAT, it can claim the VAT on those fees. However, if it also paid a sub-contractor for some work on a contract that was completed and invoiced to a customer before the company registered for VAT, it cannot claim any VAT charged by that sub-contractor (on this occasion).

There is no restriction on the recovery of VAT on fixed assets purchased within the four years prior to registration, provided those assets have been in business use, even though they will of course have been used to make supplies before the company was registered for VAT.

Hence, if the company bought a van three years ago and has used it in the business since then, it may claim the VAT on the van in full when it registers for VAT (subject to any restriction for private use: see Section 9.6).

Claims for VAT on pre-registration expenditure are, of course, subject to all the normal rules on deductibility in the same way as other goods or services purchased by the company.

## The Capital Goods Scheme
A partial VAT recovery is sometimes also possible on major items of capital expenditure (including services) falling under the Capital Goods Scheme, even when the expenditure was incurred earlier than the normal time limits set out above: up to ten years previously for expenditure of £250,000 or more (excluding VAT) on land and buildings; up to five years previously for expenditure of £50,000 or more (excluding VAT) on a single item of computer hardware, or on ships, boats, other vessels, or aircraft. In these cases, the VAT is spread over the relevant five or ten year period.

For example, let's say your company bought its business premises six years ago for £300,000 plus VAT of £60,000. The company now registers for VAT. Assuming the company is fully taxable, it can claim input VAT of £6,000 (£60,000/10) each year for the next four years. The other, unclaimed, £36,000 cannot be recovered, however, as in this case it is deemed to relate to the pre-registration period. (This claim is under different rules to the full claim for items like the van discussed above.)

## 3.4    DO YOU NEED A VAT INVOICE?

Ask most HMRC staff and they will simply say 'Yes'. And obtaining a VAT invoice is by far the best way to evidence that the company has incurred VAT and to tell you exactly how much.

However, alternative evidence will sometimes be acceptable and we will look at that later in this section. First, however, let's look at what a valid VAT invoice should contain:

- Name and address of supplier
- Supplier's VAT registration number
- Name and address of customer
- Description of goods or services
- Invoice number (unique)
- Time of supply (tax point)
- Net amount chargeable
- VAT amount

However, where the supplier is a retailer, or the total value of the invoice is less than £250 (including VAT), a less detailed invoice may be issued containing:

- Name and address of supplier
- Supplier's VAT registration number
- Description of goods or services
- Time of supply (tax point)
- VAT rate and total payable (including VAT) for each applicable VAT rate

As we can see, the less detailed invoice still includes all the information needed to make a VAT claim but, most crucially, it does not need to show the customer's name and address. We will come onto the significance of that later.

### Alternative Evidence

While HMRC staff will always want to see a VAT invoice (and that's by far the easiest way to keep them happy), they are instructed to consider whether there is satisfactory evidence of the taxable supply and should not refuse a claim without giving reasonable consideration to that evidence.

The evidence they are looking for is anything that shows:

- VAT was paid to a taxable person,
- A supplier VAT number, and
- The expense relates to the business

Suppose the company's phone bill is paid automatically by direct debit. For whatever reason the company doesn't have a VAT invoice. The supplier is a large, well known company based in the UK.

The entry on the company's bank statement proves VAT was paid, the supplier's VAT number can easily be found on the internet, and it is obvious the expense relates to the business. Hence, I would argue strongly there is sufficient evidence to claim the VAT. But a VAT invoice would still be better!

## Directors' Expenses and Other Payments by Directors

A common area of difficulty in company VAT claims is where an expense was paid by a director personally and then reclaimed from the company.

For retail purchases and other purchases under £250, there should not be a problem as a valid VAT invoice can be issued without showing the customer's name and address. Hence, the fact the purchase was initially made by the director should not affect matters. Having said that, most non-retail suppliers will show the customer's name and address even when the supply is less than £250.

So, what if the invoice shows the director's name rather than the company's?

HMRC might argue this is not a valid VAT invoice. But that's when we must point them to their own instructions (see above) to accept reasonable alternative evidence.

A VAT invoice issued to a director will show the first two pieces of evidence we need (see above), so there only remains the need to prove the expense relates to the company's business. For most smaller items this should not be too much of a problem (e.g. a hotel bill when the director stays overnight on company business), although with larger purchases it is probably sensible to make sure the invoice is issued in the company's name (even if the director initially pays it).

In fact, whenever practicable it makes sense to ensure invoices are issued in the company's name (except where they are a valid, less detailed invoice issued by a retailer or another case where a less detailed invoice is permitted and no customer name or address is given).

Where an address is given, try to ensure the company's address appears as the billing address. A different address can be given as the delivery address (e.g. the director's home address). In theory, this should not present a problem in itself: but be prepared for questions. You may need to prove the purchase was for a business purpose.

**In Summary**
A VAT invoice in the company's name is always your best option, except in the case of retail purchases and other small purchases, where the less detailed invoice with no customer name or address will be sufficient. If the invoice is in the director's name, you will need to show the expense relates to the company's business.

If there is no VAT invoice, you will need to find other ways to provide the evidence required and you cannot simply assume VAT has been paid. HMRC staff are under instructions to take a reasonable approach when considering alternative evidence, but they are notoriously pedantic when it comes to VAT claims.

### 3.5    EMPLOYEE BENEFITS

In Section 2.2, we talked about the 'employee benefit override' for CT relief purposes. A similar principle applies for VAT, although there are some important differences.

Subject to specific rules for assets like cars, vans, etc, and for fuel (see Chapter 9), VAT can be claimed on the cost of any benefits provided to employees generally. For example, the company could claim the VAT on a corporate gym membership available to all staff.

However, where any benefit is provided to a specific employee (e.g. an individual gym membership) the company must also account for output tax on the benefit. The net result is the same as if the VAT claim wasn't allowed in the first place and, in practice, this is what many companies do: i.e. simply not claim the VAT.

## Mobile Phones

Mobile phones can be provided for employees' use and the company can recover the VAT on the phone itself and the line rental. The phone must remain the company's property, however.

An apportionment will be required to cover the cost of private calls, if any, unless these are only incidental. If the company charges the employee for the cost of private calls, it can recover input tax in full but must account for output tax on the charges levied on the employee.

## Staff Entertaining

VAT may be claimed on the cost of staff entertaining. There is no limit on the amount that can be spent and generally no requirement for all staff to be present (but see below regarding directors). This is quite different to the Income Tax rules on benefits in kind (Section 7.31), so don't confuse one with the other.

The VAT claim only extends to entertaining current employees; it does not cover employees' spouses or partners, past or future employees, sub-contractors, or non-employee shareholders. Any costs relating to entertaining any such people are classed as business entertaining and no VAT claim is permitted.

Hence, in the case of a staff party where other guests are also invited, it will be necessary to apportion the VAT costs and only claim the element relating to current employees.

An alternative and more beneficial approach in such a case is to levy a small, token charge on the non-employees (e.g. £5 per head). Input VAT can then be claimed in full and output VAT only needs to be accounted for on that small token charge.

*Input Claimed as*
*Counts as providing a*
*taxable*
*service.*

Where non-employees are present at an event, it is important that the staff present at the event are not acting in a capacity as hosts to the guests. If they have hosting responsibilities, this turns the costs into business entertaining.

### *Example*

*Emeka is the director of Conquest Ltd. He hires a box at the local racetrack for the day and invites his wife, the company's six staff, and two key business contacts to join him. Emeka and his wife act as hosts and he also instructs two of his staff to help look after the business contacts for the day. However, the other staff are invited purely as a reward for their hard work and have no hosting responsibilities.*

*The event costs £6,000, including £1,000 of VAT. Conquest Ltd can claim £400 of the VAT, representing the proportion (4/10ths) relating to the staff with no hosting responsibilities. The remaining 6/10ths of the cost must be treated as business entertaining.*

### Alternative Scenarios
*If only Emeka and his wife had hosting responsibilities, 6/10ths of the VAT could be claimed.*

*If all the guests were employees apart from Emeka's wife, 9/10ths of the VAT could be claimed. If, additionally, Emeka's wife was an employee of the company (even in a very minor capacity) all the VAT could be claimed.*

You might also wonder if Conquest Ltd could claim all the VAT if Emeka's wife and the business contacts each paid a token £5 to attend the event. This depends very much on whether the main purpose of the event was staff entertaining or whether it was mainly business entertaining with some incidental benefit to a few of the staff. Any hosting from anyone, including Emeka, really turns it into business entertaining so, in practice, it seems unlikely this would work in a case like this. The token charge is really more of a solution to the problem where a few non-employees attend a staff party, rather than a business event like the one in the example.

### Directors
Subject to the issue regarding hosting non-employee guests, there is no restriction on an input VAT claim where a director attends a staff party or other staff entertaining event, provided the event is open to staff generally.

### Subsistence
The company can claim the VAT on subsistence costs (meals, etc) incurred by directors or other employees when working away from the main business base. As a general rule of thumb, this applies when working at least five miles away from the main business premises.

It is important that the cost is genuinely subsistence necessitated by a business journey and not a meal whose main purpose is to entertain customers or business contacts.

### Gifts
Gifts to an individual employee will be subject to output VAT on the cost of the gift (thus cancelling out the input VAT claim). As explained above, some companies simply choose not to claim the input VAT. Small gifts may, however, benefit from the exemption discussed in Section 3.6.

## 3.6 BUSINESS ENTERTAINING AND GIFTS

Subject to a few minor exceptions, VAT cannot be claimed on business entertaining or gifts.

This contrasts with staff entertaining, where the VAT can usually be claimed, and we saw how the two sets of rules interact with each other, and some tax planning opportunities arising, in Section 3.5.

For VAT purposes, entertaining is defined as 'hospitality of any kind', so the bar on VAT claims is very wide-ranging and would even cover the cost of buying a customer a cup of coffee.

### Overseas Customers

Input VAT can be recovered when entertaining overseas customers, but output VAT is also due (thus effectively cancelling out the claim) unless:

- The entertaining relates to a business meeting, and
- It is reasonable in scale and character

HMRC interpret this very strictly and effectively restrict it to working lunches essential to a business meeting. Their guidance is extremely miserly and refers to sandwiches and soft drinks only.

Even this small, miserly exception only applies to customers or potential customers and not to other business contacts.

### Business Gifts

VAT can be recovered on gifts made for business purposes where the cost of all gifts to the same individual within any twelve-month period does not exceed £50, excluding VAT.

There is no need for the company's name or logo to appear and no restriction in the type of gift, so even alcohol is covered (unlike for CT relief!)

The £50 limit applies on an individual basis, so you could give £50 worth of gifts to each of several people working at the same business if you wish.

Where the cost of gifts to the same individual in any twelve-month period exceeds £50, VAT can still be claimed on the cost, but output VAT must also be accounted for.

## 3.7    THE FLAT RATE SCHEME

VAT registered companies with annual sales not exceeding £150,000 (excluding VAT) may generally join the VAT flat rate scheme. Joining the scheme does not alter the amount of VAT the company must charge its customers, or the amount of VAT it pays on its purchases. What it does alter is the amount of VAT paid over to HMRC.

Under the flat rate scheme, a special reduced rate is applied to calculate the VAT payable to HMRC on sales. The rate to be applied depends on the nature of the company's business and currently varies from 4% to 14.5% (ignoring the rate for 'limited cost businesses' discussed below).

The rates used under the scheme can be found at www.gov.uk/vat-flat-rate-scheme/how-much-you-pay but are not as generous as they seem because they are applied to the company's gross, VAT-inclusive sales: remember the VAT element within the gross sales price for standard-rated goods and services is actually one sixth (20/120ths), or 16.67%.

Furthermore, the downside to the scheme is that the company is unable to recover the VAT on most of its purchases: with the exception of certain capital expenditure of £2,000 or more (including VAT). We will look at this exception in more detail later in this section.

Another drawback to the flat rate scheme is that any company, or other entity, registering for the scheme must apply the appropriate reduced VAT rate to *all* its business income, including income that would normally be exempt from VAT, or zero-rated. Among other things, this generally makes the scheme unsuitable for any company that has residential rental income, or that sells a higher than usual proportion of zero-rated goods.

The rates used for the flat rate scheme are set on an industry-wide basis and hence, as a general rule of thumb, a company will benefit by joining the scheme if the VAT it pays on its purchases is less than the industry average. This could arise for a number of reasons but the main things to watch out for are:

- Rent: if the company is not paying rent for its business premises, or is not paying VAT on it
- Labour: if the company employs more people than is usual for a company of its size, rather than contracting for services from external suppliers, sub-contractors, etc

- Goods: if the company purchases more zero-rated or VAT-exempt items than is usual in its industry
- Small suppliers: if the company purchases many of its goods and services from non-VAT registered suppliers

The purpose of the flat rate scheme is simplification, but joining it could save your company thousands of pounds every year; or cost the company thousands of pounds; or not make much difference. It's a case of doing the number-crunching to find out where you stand.

### Example Part 1

*Candy operates a small café through her company, Candy Bar Ltd. Her annual sales, including VAT, total £120,000, and these are all standard-rated for VAT purposes. The company's annual input VAT (the VAT paid on purchases) totals just £1,800: most of its purchases are zero-rated food, and it does not pay VAT on the rent for its business premises.*

*Under normal principles, the company would calculate its annual output VAT as £20,000 (£120,000 x 20/120). After deducting its input VAT, the total paid over to HMRC for the year would be £18,200 (£20,000 – £1,800). (The company would, of course, usually be preparing VAT returns, and paying its VAT, quarterly: but I am using annual figures for the sake of illustration.)*

*Instead, Candy decides it would be a good idea for the company to join the flat rate scheme. The rate applying to 'catering services including restaurants and takeaways' is 12.5%, so the company's annual VAT bill under the scheme would be £15,000 (£120,000 x 12.5%).*

Joining the flat rate scheme will save the company £3,200 a year (£18,200 – £15,000): a substantial saving for a company with a turnover of just £100,000 (excluding VAT). But Candy needs to keep the position under review, especially if she changes her business model, or sees a significant increase in the company's input VAT: increased energy costs are one example that springs to mind, or the landlord might opt to tax the property and start charging VAT on the rent.

The company is unlikely to be forced out of the scheme any time soon, though. Once in the flat rate scheme, a company can stay in the scheme until its annual sales (including VAT) exceed £230,000, or are expected to do so within the next twelve months. This test must be applied on each anniversary of joining the scheme (although the company must also leave if VAT-inclusive sales are expected to exceed £230,000 in the next 30 days alone).

## Example Part 2

*To boost sales, Candy starts offering takeaway food, including crisps and confectionary (candy bars, appropriately enough!)*

*The company's total sales, including VAT, increase to £165,000. A fifth of these are zero-rated cold takeaway food (not the crisps and confectionary, which are standard-rated). However, under the flat rate scheme, the same percentage must be applied to all the company's sales, meaning the company's annual VAT bill increases to £20,625 (£165,000 x 12.5%).*

*Meanwhile, the company's annual input VAT has increased to £4,000 and its gross, VAT-inclusive, standard-rated sales are £132,000 (£165,000 x 4/5). Under normal principles its annual output VAT would be £22,000 (£132,000 x 20/120). After deducting its input VAT, the total paid over to HMRC for the year would be £18,000 (£22,000 – £4,000).*

The flat rate scheme is now ***costing*** the company an extra £2,625 a year (£20,625 – £18,000).

Fortunately, a company can leave the flat rate scheme at the end of any VAT quarter, although, if it does, it cannot re-join within the next year. So, if it looks like the scheme is now going to cost your company more in VAT on a regular basis, it is a good idea to leave, but if the effect is only a short-term, temporary one, it may be better to stay in. More number-crunching required, I 'm afraid.

Joining the scheme within the company's first year of VAT registration has an additional advantage as there is a one per cent reduction in the applicable VAT rate during this period. For instance if, in Example Part 1 above, Candy Bar Ltd had only just registered for VAT (perhaps Candy had only recently set the company up) its VAT rate would have been 11.5% instead of 12.5% and its total VAT bill for the first year would have been £13,800 (£120,000 x 11.5%), providing an additional saving of £1,200.

However, it is important to bear in mind the ability to make extra, back-dated VAT claims when the company first registers, as detailed in Section 3.3. This may mean the flat rate scheme is not beneficial in the company's first VAT quarter.

Hence, while each company's position is going to be different, my general recommended approach is as follows:

i)      Prepare your first VAT return on the normal basis, maximising all potential claims under the principles we looked at in Section 3.3

ii)     Assess whether the flat rate scheme is likely to be beneficial for your company, bearing in mind the one per cent reduction in the applicable rate in the first year of registration

iii)    If so, join the flat rate scheme for your second to fourth VAT quarters

iv)     Assess whether the flat rate scheme is still likely to be beneficial for your company using the usual rate applying without the one per cent reduction

v)      If not, leave the flat rate scheme at the end of your fourth VAT quarter

vi)     If the flat rate scheme is still beneficial, stay in it

vii)    Whatever you've done so far, keep the position under review, but

viii)   Remember to leave the flat rate scheme when your company's annual sales (including VAT) exceed £230,000, or are expected to exceed that level in the next twelve months (doing this test on each anniversary of joining the scheme)

And yes, the annual sales test for *joining* the scheme is based on net sales, excluding VAT, and the test for compulsorily having to *leave* the scheme is based on total, VAT-inclusive sales.

The £150,000 threshold for joining the scheme is also based on VAT taxable turnover (i.e. it excludes exempt supplies like residential rental income: although, as discussed above, it may not be a good idea to join the scheme when the company is making such supplies). The company must expect to have VAT taxable turnover of no more than £150,000 in the next twelve months when it joins the scheme.

A company cannot usually join the flat rate scheme if its business is associated with another business outside the company. Your company's business will be associated with another business if:

•   One business is under the main influence of the other,
•   The businesses are closely bound by financial, economic, and organisational links (see Section 12.3 for details of how these links are defined),
•   Another company has the right to give directions to you, or
•   In practice, your company repeatedly complies with the directions of another: the test here is a test of the commercial reality rather than the legal form

## Capital Expenditure

As explained above, the only VAT a company in the flat rate scheme can recover on its purchases is the VAT on certain capital expenditure of £2,000 or more (including VAT). Oddly, this means a company in the flat rate scheme will be better off buying a computer for anything between £2,000 and £2,399 (including VAT) than for £1,999 (including VAT).

Even this exception is not as good as it seems, since it only applies to single purchases of capital expenditure *goods* for £2,000 or more, and not to services. This distinction between goods and services does not always work how you might think. For example, if you engage a builder to build an extension on your business premises, this would be capital expenditure, but you have contracted for *services*, and hence no VAT can be recovered under the flat rate scheme.

While there must be a single purchase of £2,000 or more, a package can count as a single purchase. Hence, if you buy a computer for £1,999, you cannot claim the VAT, but if you buy the computer and a printer as a package costing £2,100, the VAT is recoverable. Items must be bought together from the same supplier at the same time to constitute a package.

The expenditure must be capital expenditure under general principles (see Section 8.1) and must not be the purchase of assets you intend to lease, let, or hire out. This even extends to assets you only intend to hire out part of the time.

Expenditure falling under the Capital Goods Scheme (see Section 3.3) is also excluded. In fact, if you are expecting to make a purchase falling under Capital Goods Scheme, you must leave the flat rate scheme and advise HMRC immediately.

## Asset Disposals

Where VAT has been recovered on the purchase of capital expenditure goods, it must also be accounted for on the sale of the asset at the normal VAT rate applying, usually the standard rate of 20%. For example, if the company bought a computer for £2,400 and recovered the VAT, then sells it many years later for £120, it will need to account for £20 VAT on the sale.

Furthermore, where VAT was not, or could not be, recovered on an asset purchase, any sale proceeds must be included in the company's taxable turnover under the flat rate scheme.

It would therefore generally make sense to leave the scheme before making any major asset disposals of this nature: for example, a commercial property on which the option to tax has not been exercised.

## Limited Cost Businesses

In the early days of the flat rate scheme, some businesses with very limited spending were able to save substantial amounts of VAT under the scheme. Sadly, those days are over, and a special rate of 16.5% now applies to 'limited cost businesses'.

The rate applies for any VAT period where the company's VAT-inclusive expenditure on goods amounts to less than either:

- 2% of its VAT-inclusive sales income, or
- £1,000 annually (i.e. £250 for a normal VAT return period of three months)

It is crucial to note the test is applied to each VAT period (usually a quarter), so companies with spending that is generally only a little over these thresholds could get caught out from time to time: and thus need to plan their expenditure carefully.

Only spending on goods is counted, not spending on services. Any goods purchased to sell or hire out as part of the company's main business activity can be counted, but otherwise a number of items must be excluded, including:

- Capital expenditure (furniture, equipment, etc.)
- Food and drink
- Vehicles, parts and fuel (except transport businesses)
- Goods the company intends to sell or hire out that are not part of its main business activity

The exclusion of services from this test means very few service companies will benefit from the flat rate scheme.

Where the limited cost business rate of 16.5% applies, it effectively removes any benefit of the flat rate scheme. Let's take the most extreme example we can think of: say a company has annual sales of £230,000, including VAT, all standard-rated. Its output VAT under normal principles would be £38,333 (£230,000 x 20/120). But let's say it's in the flat rate scheme, so it pays £37,950 (£230,000 x 16.5%).

OK, the company might save £383 a year if it has absolutely no input VAT at all: but that's extremely unlikely, especially as it cannot have any associated businesses. It only takes standard-rated purchases of £2,298 (including VAT) and the company is losing out.

In short, if your company is likely to be subject to the limited cost business rate most of the time, the flat rate scheme is probably not for you.

### The Flat Rate Scheme and Putting it Through

There are many factors to consider when deciding whether your company should join (or leave) the flat rate scheme. One important factor is how much input tax the company is able to claim and, for this purpose, it's worth considering how many expenses you are able to put through the company, as discussed throughout the rest of this guide.

If your company does join the flat rate scheme, it will not benefit from any VAT recovery on most of its costs and will generally be in the same position as a non-VAT registered company: apart from on some capital expenditure of £2,000 or more (including VAT).

For the remainder of this guide, unless stated to the contrary, we will assume the company is not in the flat rate scheme. If you are in the scheme, however, it's fairly easy to understand how the rest of the guide applies to you. For most expenditure, you cannot recover any VAT; for capital expenditure qualifying for VAT recovery as described above, you are generally in the same position as any other VAT-registered business. One area of complexity we will look at, however, is the treatment of vehicles and motoring costs under the flat rate scheme (Section 9.8).

### 3.8    INTERACTION WITH CORPORATION TAX

A company that is registered for VAT can generally only claim the net (excluding VAT) amounts of its expenditure for CT purposes.

Where VAT recovery is barred or restricted, however, the additional cost arising may generally be claimed for CT purposes (as part of the underlying cost). This includes:

- Companies operating the flat rate scheme (Section 3.7)
- Companies subject to partial exemption (see Section 3.1)
- Provision of private fuel for directors or staff (see Section 9.1)
- Capital allowances on cars (see Section 9.2)

- Leasing/contract hire of motor cars (see Section 9.2)
- Capital allowances on other assets with an element of private use (see Sections 9.6 and 9.7)

Business entertaining and gifts are not generally allowed for either CT or VAT, but if any VAT is recovered on these items, only the net cost will appear in the company's accounts.

A non-VAT registered company should, of course, include the VAT in all its business expenditure for CT purposes.

For companies operating the flat rate scheme: as well as including VAT in most of their expenditure, they can deduct the VAT paid to HMRC from their sales income (although they have to account for their gross, VAT-inclusive sales income in the first place).

For instance, if we return to Candy Bar Ltd, in Example Part 1 in Section 3.7, the company would show sales income of £105,000 (its VAT-inclusive sales of £120,000 less the £15,000 VAT paid to HMRC). It would also claim VAT-inclusive amounts for all its expenses. In this way, the company will effectively obtain CT relief for all the VAT it has paid: both to HMRC and to its suppliers (assuming it has no disallowable expenses).

The downside, of course, is that Candy Bar Ltd is effectively paying CT on the £3,200 annual saving generated by joining the flat rate scheme: but you can't win them all!

Where VAT is payable on an asset disposal under the flat rate scheme, this is deducted from the asset's disposal proceeds for capital allowances purposes, etc, rather than from sales income. See Section 9.8 for a suitable example.

# Chapter 4

# Director's Expenses

## 4.1 WHAT ARE DIRECTOR'S EXPENSES?

The term 'director's expenses' can mean a lot of different things in different contexts, and to different people, so we'd better define what we mean by director's expenses in this guide.

A good definition for us to use is that director's expenses are expenditure incurred by a director on behalf of the company. Some of the most important examples include:

- Travel and subsistence costs
- Business entertaining
- Fees and subscriptions
- Office costs for business use of the director's home

We will look at each of these items (and several others) in this chapter, except business use of the director's home, which is covered in Section 10.7.

In each of the above examples, there is an element of personal involvement for the director as an individual and this is perhaps another good definition of director's expenses. In other words, there is some personal liability or personal benefit involved.

### Settling Company Costs or Liabilities
Directors might make other types of payment on behalf of a company where there is no personal element. For example, the director might pay the rent for the company's business premises one month. While it remains perfectly reasonable for the company to reimburse the director and claim the cost for CT purposes (and VAT, where applicable), this is not really what we mean by director's expenses.

### The Admin Process
Generally, the way director's expenses are dealt with is as follows:

- The director incurs the expenditure
- The director claims a reimbursement from the company, either in cash or by way of a credit to their director's loan account (we'll see more about director's loan accounts in Sections 4.3 and 5.5)

- The company puts the expenditure through its accounts as if it had incurred it directly itself

Sometimes, however, this type of expenditure may be paid directly by the company. The company might settle a hotel bill directly where a director is booked to stay at the hotel while travelling on business. This is still classed as director's expenses because it is the director personally who is receiving the hotel's services. The same can apply to travel costs, subsistence, fees, subscriptions, and many other items that involve a personal service to the director, albeit that service is being used for business purposes.

## Tax Treatment
There are two distinct elements to the tax treatment of director's expenses:

i)     Is the expenditure allowable for CT purposes: this follows the principles we looked at in Chapter 2

ii)    Has the expenditure been incurred wholly, exclusively and necessarily for the purposes of the director's employment?

While these two elements are related, they do not always work in tandem. Furthermore, in most cases, it is the second element that is harder to satisfy (and more costly when not satisfied). Let's look at some examples.

***Example 1:*** *A director catches a train to London for a business meeting. The director buys the ticket and the company reimburses the expense. The expense was incurred **both** wholly and exclusively for the purposes of the company's business **and** wholly, exclusively and necessarily for the purposes of the director's employment. The company obtains CT relief; the director is not taxed on the reimbursement.*

This is the type of expenditure we are mainly concerned with in this chapter. It is fully allowable for both the company and the director and is thus the best kind of expenditure to put through the company. When we talk about 'allowable expenditure' in this chapter, this is the type of expenditure we generally mean.

***Example 2:*** *A director takes a business contact out to lunch. The director pays the bill at the restaurant and the company reimburses the expense. Business entertaining is specifically barred from CT relief under tax legislation. However, the director has still incurred the expense wholly, exclusively and necessarily for the purposes of their employment.*

*The company does not obtain CT relief, but the director is not taxed on the reimbursement.*

Putting this type of expenditure through the company remains beneficial and we will look at it further in Section 4.8.

**Example 3:** *A director takes a two-week holiday, completely unconnected with the company's business. The company pays the director's hotel bill in recognition of all the hard work the director has done on its behalf. The expense is regarded as being wholly and exclusively incurred for the purposes of the company's business, due to the 'employee benefit override' (see Section 2.2). However, the expense has not been incurred wholly, exclusively and necessarily for the purposes of the director's employment. The company obtains CT relief; the director is taxable on the cost of the hotel bill as a benefit in kind. The company will also be liable for employer's National Insurance on the hotel bill; whether the director is liable for employee's National Insurance will depend on whether the company contracted directly with the hotel (see Section 7.33).*

This type of expenditure is generally not tax efficient where the director is also the owner of the company. Let's say the hotel bill amounts to £5,000 and the director is a higher rate taxpayer. Instead of paying the hotel bill, the company could have paid a dividend of £7,547 to the director instead. After paying Income Tax at 33.75% on the dividend, the director would have been left with a net sum of £5,000 to pay the hotel bill. Total cost £7,547.

By paying the hotel bill directly, the company will face an employer's National Insurance charge of £690 (£5,000 x 13.8%). The total cost before tax would be £5,690. After CT relief at, say, 26.5%, the net cost would be £4,182.

But later, the director will have an additional Income Tax bill of £2,250 to pay. How do we arrive at that? Many small company owners pay themselves a small salary equal to the National Insurance primary threshold and personal allowance (we'll take a closer look at this topic in Section 6.4). They then take any further sums they require in the form of dividends. This means that, while any taxable benefit in kind will most likely attract Income Tax at just 20%, an equal amount of dividend income will be taxed at 33.75% instead of 8.75%, an extra cost of 25%. That brings the total effective Income Tax rate on the benefit in kind up to 45%, or £2,250 in this case.

To fund this extra Income Tax, the director will need to take an additional dividend of £3,396 out of the company (after paying Income Tax at 33.75% this leaves them with a net sum of £2,250). Total cost £7,578 (£4,182 + £3,396).

If the director also has to pay employee's National Insurance at 8%, their total tax bill rises to £2,650 (an effective overall rate of 53%), meaning they now need to take dividends of £4,000 and the total cost is £8,182 (£4,182 + £4,000).

Either way, the company payment route costs more and leads to a lot of extra admin. And it would be worse if the company's marginal CT rate were less than 26.5% (see Section 2.1). Paying the shareholder/director a dividend to cover the cost of the holiday is easier and cheaper.

But, for a non-shareholder director, this type of perk may be quite attractive and we will look at this further in Section 7.33.

*Example 4:* *A company pays the school fees for one of the shareholder's grandchildren. The shareholder still carries the title of director but has done no work for the company for many years. The expense cannot be regarded as being wholly and exclusively incurred for the purposes of the company's business, even considering the 'employee benefit override'. It cannot be regarded as wholly, exclusively and necessarily for the purposes of the director's employment either. The company will not be eligible for CT relief on this expense; some form of tax charge will also fall on the director, with the school fees either treated as a taxable benefit in kind (taxed in the same way as the hotel bill in Example 3, but with no CT relief for the cost) or a dividend in specie (taxed at the same rates as a cash dividend).*

This type of expenditure is generally best avoided as the tax consequences can become both complex and expensive. Paying a dividend to cover the cost will be simpler and will avoid the danger of potentially greater tax charges arising. Another possible approach is considered in Section 4.3.

## In Summary

Our examples have demonstrated the impact of the two elements to the tax treatment of director's expenses. Generally speaking, the more important issue is not CT relief, as this will often be obtained under the 'employee benefit override', even if nothing else, but the issue of whether the expense gives rise to a taxable benefit in kind for the director. In the following sections, we will look at how this issue is dealt with in practice.

There is, of course, also the question of whether VAT can be recovered on the cost. This depends on a number of factors, including whether your company is registered for VAT, whether the supplier is registered for VAT, and the nature of the expense itself. As there are so many other considerations involved, we will generally leave VAT to one side for most of this chapter, but the VAT treatment of director's expenses will follow the principles we covered in Chapter 3.

## 4.2 WHAT ARE NOT DIRECTOR'S EXPENSES?

When I started training as a Chartered Accountant, I was quite surprised by some of the things I learned about UK tax, which seemed quite contrary to basic common sense or morality.

There's the fact they tax you for dying for a start, but that belongs in another book (the Taxcafe guide *How to Save Inheritance Tax*).

Another surprise was the fact that home to work travel is not an allowable cost. We will look at this further in Section 4.4, but what struck me as odd was the fact HMRC regard going to work as a personal, private journey. We go to work to work, for business, we don't do it for some private purpose; morally it's obviously a business journey. Sadly though, the law says otherwise: but we will look at this area in greater depth later.

The point is, when it comes to director's expenses, we cannot rely on common sense or what feels equitable; we (sadly) have to follow the law. But understanding the law will help you claim as much as you can and put whatever can be justified (legally, rather than morally) through the company.

Another surprising example of disallowable expenditure is business clothing. Let's say your company runs an estate agency business and it buys you a new suit to wear at work. There is a business motive here, as the suit is meant to make you look smart and the idea is this will impress potential customers and bring in more business (I'm not convinced a suit still impresses people these days, but that's the idea!)

However, tax law tells us that most normal office clothing also provides you with warmth and decency and hence is not 'wholly and exclusively' for business purposes. Furthermore, as we saw in Section 2.2, these personal functions cannot be separated out, so the whole cost will generally have to be treated as a taxable benefit in kind: unless there is another approach we can follow (see Section 4.3).

Specialised or protective clothing and uniforms are a different matter however.

## 4.3    WHAT IF YOU GET IT WRONG?

As a practising accountant for over thirty years, I was constantly dealing with the problem of director's expenses paid by the company, or reimbursed to the director, that were not allowable.

Here, I am not talking about something that is planned and expected; such as some of the more beneficial types of benefit in kind we will see in Chapter 7. Here, I am talking about simple errors or misunderstandings: like the things we talked about in Section 4.2. Perhaps the company has bought the director a new suit, for example, or paid for a private journey.

In the case of a shareholder/director, the way in which such a payment is treated depends on whether any personal benefit derived is deemed to be in their capacity as an employee or as a shareholder.

Generally speaking, where the benefit is derived in their capacity as an employee, it will be a taxable benefit in kind. It will then be allowable for CT purposes (under the 'employee benefit override'), but subject to Income Tax, employer's National Insurance and possibly also employee's National Insurance. This would generally be HMRC's preferred approach for most active, working directors and, as we saw in Section 4.1 (Example 3) is not tax efficient. Further costs in terms of penalties and admin time/accountancy fees often arise owing to failure to report the benefit on time. In short, it is not generally a desirable outcome.

Where the benefit is deemed to be derived predominantly in their capacity as a shareholder and not as an employee, there will be no CT relief. The individual will then be taxed either on a benefit in kind (as described above) or a dividend in specie (taxed at the same rates as a cash dividend). The benefit in kind route is the more expensive in tax terms and is to be avoided whenever possible (it's a harsh approach where CT relief is being denied, but is not unheard of). Either way, there are again likely to be further costs in terms of both penalties and admin time/accountancy fees.

### The Third Alternative: Posting to the Director's Loan Account

These kinds of mistakes can prove very costly, but there is an easier way to deal with them in practice than the benefits in kind or dividend in specie routes.

Posting the payment to the director's loan account effectively means the director has now paid the cost. Hence, there cannot be a dividend in specie or benefit in kind in respect of that cost.

The effect of posting the payment to the director's loan account will depend on whether the account is in credit (the company owes the director money) or is overdrawn/in debit (the director owes money to the company).

Overdrawn director's loan accounts can have tax consequences in their own right. In brief, these are:

- An additional CT charge at 33.75% on any balance still overdrawn nine months after the end of the accounting period
- Benefit in kind charges on notional interest at HMRC's official rate (see further below)

However, these problems can generally be avoided by making sure the director's loan account is never more than £10,000 overdrawn and by repaying the balance in full within nine months of the end of the accounting period. In other words, that gives you nine months to rectify mistakes totalling up to £10,000 at no tax cost.

If your director's loan account is in credit, it is simply a case of posting the non-allowable expense to the loan account (as a debit, or deduction from the amount due to you). This is one of the reasons it's worth building up a credit balance when you can and we'll look at some ways you might do this at little or no tax cost in Section 5.5.

### Official Rates

HMRC publishes two types of official rate for the purpose of calculating the benefit in kind charge on overdrawn director's loan accounts:

- An average rate for the tax year, which may be used where the loan account was overdrawn throughout the year
- An actual rate, which may be varied at any time: this must be used where the loan account was not overdrawn throughout the year, and may also be used as an alternative option in other cases

The average rate for 2024/25 is 2.25% which is very generous given that, at the time of writing, the Bank of England base rate is 5.25%. The actual rate is currently also 2.25%.

Where the average rate is used, it is applied to the average of the balance at the beginning and end of the tax year. There are anti-avoidance rules to prevent this rule from being excessively abused.

For the latest published rates, see: https://tinyurl.com/official-rates

### National Insurance Risks

Under certain, limited circumstances, there is a risk of National Insurance costs arising when a payment posted to a director's loan account is seen as an advance on the director's salary. However, this risk is only relevant where:

- The payment was made to settle the director's personal liability (i.e. the bill or invoice being settled by the company was in the director's name),
- The loan account is overdrawn, or becomes overdrawn as a result of the posting, and
- A salary payment due to the director is subsequently posted to the loan account

Even in these cases, there may be no additional National Insurance cost as the deemed advances can only alter the timing of when salary is treated as paid. This will often be in the same tax year.

There is also some doubt over the validity of regarding such payments as an advance of salary unless the director has an employment contract requiring the company to make the payments: which will be very rare for a small company.

Furthermore, where dividends or other payments due to the director are also posted to the same loan account, it will be unclear what exactly was supposedly being paid in advance.

In short, this is a risk to be aware of and to be avoided whenever possible, but there are also grounds for resisting any attempt by HMRC to collect National Insurance under these circumstances.

### 4.4    BUSINESS TRAVEL

One of the most important areas of director's expenses is travel and subsistence. This covers:

- Travel costs, including air fares, train fares, buses, taxis, etc.
- Business mileage and parking (Sections 9.2 and 9.4)
- Subsistence: Food and drink (Section 4.5)
- Accommodation: Hotels, etc.

In order to be allowable, all these costs need to be incurred in connection with a business journey. Hence, the first thing we need to do is look at what constitutes a business journey. You would think this would be a simple matter. Straight away though, we run into a problem.

**Principle 1: Home to work travel is not allowable**
Imagine a director called Serwaah, travelling to her company's business premises every day. To a reasonable layperson, this journey is clearly made for business purposes. Sadly, tax law states otherwise and this journey is classed as personal.

**Principle 2: Travel from home to a temporary workplace is allowable**
What if Serwaah needs to carry out some work at a customer's premises and travels there directly from home? Now the journey is classed as a business journey.

In general, travel to a workplace remains allowable unless that workplace is intended to be the individual's permanent base, or actually becomes their main work base for a period of two years or more. Serwaah cannot claim the cost of travel from her home to her company's premises but can claim the cost of travel from her home to any other business destination, unless it becomes her main base for two years or more.

Directors who are permanently, *and exclusively*, based at home can therefore generally claim all their business travel costs since there is no 'home to work' element to be disallowed. We'll look at the position where directors are based at home, but not exclusively, later.

**Principle 3: Where there is Triangular Travel involving home, work, and another business destination, two sides of the triangle will be allowable (but not the 'home to work' side)**
If Serwaah leaves the customer's premises and goes straight home, this journey is again allowable. Alternatively, if Serwaah travels from the customer to her company's premises, this journey is also allowable.

Let us suppose Serwaah lives in Luton and her company is based in St Albans.

A journey from her home to a customer in Stevenage would be fully allowable and the subsequent journey from Stevenage either to St Albans or back to Luton would also be fully allowable. However, if Serwaah goes to her company's business premises in St Albans after visiting the customer, her later journey back home to Luton will not be allowable.

**Principle 4: Any part of a journey that is part of, or similar to, an individual's usual home to work journey is not allowable**
HMRC views journeys that are similar to an individual's regular commute as still being home to work travel.

Where there is a clearly separate additional business element to a journey, however, that element should remain allowable.

Let's say Serwaah visits another customer based a few miles from her company's business premises. She catches the train to St Albans as usual but, instead of walking to her office nearby, she takes taxis to the customer and back to her office afterwards. Serwaah's taxi journeys are allowable since they are clearly not part of her usual journey to work. However, her train journeys to and from St Albans are part of her usual home to work travel and are thus not allowable.

**Principle 5: There is generally no restriction on the standard, or class, of travel for the purposes of tax relief (but you can push it too far)**
Serwaah visits Manchester on business and travels first class. Despite the increased cost, the journey remains fully allowable.

However, there is a limit to how far a director could push this principle. Fundamentally, the expense must be wholly, exclusively, and necessarily incurred for the purposes of their employment. A first class train fare would generally remain acceptable and would be deemed to meet this criterion. But let's say Serwaah needs to go to New York for business. She could fly, and any class of air fare would remain allowable as it was 'necessary' for her to fly. But what if she went by luxury cruise liner?

A few years ago, I would have said the cost of the journey would not then be allowable and I imagine that would still be HMRC's view today in most cases.

However, there could be an argument that this mode of transport was 'necessary' for the purposes of Serwaah's employment if her company's business is to promote sustainable development and part of her job is thus to discourage air travel.

As with many things in the tax world, the outcome would depend on the full facts of the case. Nonetheless, the key points to consider are:

- Is the journey necessary?
- Is the mode of transport used necessary in the context of the director's role with their company?

If you can answer yes to both questions then the cost of the journey will be allowable and it will not generally matter what standard, or class, of travel the director uses.

Furthermore, when we talk about 'necessary' that does not mean there aren't reasonable alternatives. If we go back to that journey from Luton to Manchester, Serwaah could drive, fly, take the train, or take the bus. These would all be reasonable ways to travel to Manchester and Serwaah is not obliged to use the cheapest method available. But hiring a hot air balloon is probably not going to meet the 'necessarily' test!

We will return to the subject of international travel in Section 4.6.

### Principle 6: Small incidental private elements to a journey will not prevent it from being allowable

In theory, a director's travel expenses are only allowable when incurred wholly, exclusively, and necessarily for the purposes of their employment. Taking this literally would mean any personal element to a journey would prevent the entire cost from being allowed for tax purposes.

Thankfully, HMRC is prepared to ignore any minor, incidental element to a journey. If Serwaah stopped at a garage to buy some milk on her way home from a customer, for example, the journey would remain fully allowable.

However, this leaves us with the problem of journeys with a more significant private element.

### Principle 7: The main reason behind a journey will usually determine whether it is allowable

Let's return to Serwaah's trip to Manchester but let's now suppose she visited two people when she was there: a customer and her brother.

Whether this will be allowed as a business journey depends on her primary purpose for making the trip.

If her main reason for going to Manchester was to visit her customer and she simply took the opportunity to visit her brother while she was there, it remains an allowable business journey.

Conversely, if she mainly wanted to visit her brother and simply took the opportunity to pop in on one of her customers, then it is a personal journey and her travel costs are not allowable.

Generally, the main reason for the journey will follow whichever appointment was booked first. Hence if Serwaah had already arranged to visit her customer before she organised her get together with her brother, this would tend to suggest it was an allowable business journey.

Here we are talking about the travel costs from Serwaah's home in Luton (or her company's premises in St Albans, as the case may be) and assuming there are no further costs involved in travelling around Manchester. Local travel at the destination is another matter.

### Principle 8: Where there is more than one purpose to the journey, it may be possible to break it down into its constituent parts and still obtain some relief

Unlike self-employed taxpayers, HMRC will not usually accept an apportionment of director's travel costs where there are both business and private elements to the same item of expenditure (and the private element is more than incidental). Hence, if Serwaah's main reason for visiting Manchester was to see her brother, none of the cost of travelling to Manchester will be allowable.

However, separate parts of a journey may attract their own individual treatment. Let's say, for example, that Serwaah caught a train to Manchester, took a taxi to her customer's premises, another taxi to meet her brother, and then caught the metro back to the train station.

We must now look at each part of Serwaah's trip separately. The question of whether the cost of her train journey to Manchester is allowable is determined under the principles we have already discussed. But, once she has arrived in Manchester, we effectively start with a 'clean slate' and look at each subsequent journey on its own merits.

Generally, in most cases, we would expect Serwaah's first taxi journey (to her customer's premises) to be classed as a business journey, and thus allowable, while her second taxi journey (to meet her brother), and her metro ride, are not allowable, as neither of these costs were wholly, exclusively, and necessarily incurred for the purposes of her employment. This is based on 'triangular travel' principles, namely on the assumption that the railway station, her customer's premises, and the place she meets her brother, are all in distinctly different locations. This would be the usual interpretation of this type of situation but sometimes things might be a bit different.

Let's say her meeting with her brother was only a short distance from her customer's premises and she only caught a taxi because she was late. She then walked back to the nearest metro station, which was also the nearest metro station to her customer's premises.

In this case, her second taxi journey (to meet her brother) will always remain disallowable, but her first taxi journey and her metro ticket may or may not be allowable: they will follow the same treatment as her train fare to Manchester.

What about another scenario? Let's say the taxi journey to meet her brother followed the same route back to the railway station but stopped a short distance away and then Serwaah merely hopped on the metro for one or two stops to complete her journey afterwards. In this scenario, both taxi journeys are allowable as they represent the cost of visiting her client while she was in Manchester.

Her metro ticket will be disallowable, however, as this cost was not wholly, exclusively, and necessarily incurred for the purposes of her employment.

Let's look at that another way. If Serwaah's main reason for going to Manchester was to visit her customer, it is only any additional costs involved in seeing her brother that must be disallowed.

On the other hand, if she went to Manchester primarily to see her brother, it is only any costs directly and exclusively related to visiting her customer that will be allowed.

**What Happens Where Home is a Workplace?**
So far, we've mostly looked at a more traditional model where a director's permanent workplace is their company's business premises; although, in Principle 2, we did consider the position where the director works exclusively from home and saw that, in this case, all business travel will usually be allowable.

Generally, of course, a director will work exclusively from home where the company does not have any business premises, and that makes the position pretty clear.

There may also be a few instances where the company has business premises, but it is not practical for the director to be based there, so they still work exclusively from home. This, for example, might include a case where the company's business premises are a noisy workshop with no office space and the director's role is purely desk-based.

This certainly helps when we are looking at Principle 4 above: there is no usual home to work journey, so no part of any business journey can be part of, or similar to it, and all business travel should generally be allowable. This would include any occasional visits to the company's business premises, perhaps for meetings with employees, or to carry out an inspection. But this all assumes there is no base (e.g. a desk or an office) available for the director at the company's business premises.

Things get more difficult when it is possible for the director to work at the company's business premises but they choose not to, including cases where the director adopts a 'hybrid' working arrangement, working partly from home and partly from their company's business premises.

HMRC sometimes allows employees with hybrid working arrangements to claim for home to work travel on the days they are normally scheduled to be working from home (e.g. to attend a meeting): but only if there is no space at the company's premises available for them to use as a base on those days (perhaps where there is a desk-sharing arrangement in place, for example).

It is, however, difficult to see this applying to many directors, and most directors adopting a hybrid working arrangement will be in the same position as we looked at under the Principles above. In other words, where the director merely chooses to work from home part of the time, but could work at the company's business premises, they are unable to claim the cost of any home to work travel. According to a rather imperious, condescending statement from HMRC, such journeys remain 'ordinary commuting', and any reimbursement of the relevant costs by the company will be treated as additional salary.

See also Section 10.7 regarding household running costs that may be claimed where a director works from home.

## 4.5    SUBSISTENCE COSTS

Almost every company director incurs subsistence expenditure, such as meals, drinks, and other refreshments, yet in practice it can often be one of the most difficult areas of tax to deal with.

Claims for director's subsistence costs must usually be based on actual expenditure and round sum allowances are not generally available. The first problem with this is evidence. Many directors neglect to obtain receipts for some of their subsistence expenditure. Here, I would make two points:

- Firstly, in an ideal world, you should really try to get a receipt for every last penny of subsistence expenditure incurred while travelling on business for your company. It doesn't necessarily have to be a printed till receipt: I have even resorted to getting a receipt written on a paper napkin!
- Secondly, don't just give up and not make a claim just because you don't have a receipt. Reasonable subsistence claims are seldom refused, especially if you make a note of the expenditure at the time: but do try to get receipts in future.

### Business Trips

The basic rule is that directors (or other employees) may claim reasonable subsistence costs incurred during a business trip. In essence, a business trip is any trip away from the director's normal business base made for business purposes and which does not form part of their normal pattern of travel (see Section 4.4). Let's look at a couple of examples to see what this means in practice.

### *Example 1*

*Mike is based in Scotland and has to spend a day in London on business. He has an early morning flight, so he has breakfast at the airport. He grabs a coffee and a Danish pastry when he arrives in London. Later, he goes out for lunch in a pub near his customer's office. He buys another coffee and some cake in the airport on the way home.*

*All of this expenditure was necessitated by Mike's business trip and can be claimed for tax purposes.*

*If, however, Mike buys himself a takeaway on the way home from the airport that evening, it would not be allowable. If he had dinner in London before catching his flight home though, this would be allowable.*

An interesting planning point emerges here. By and large, any meals, snacks or drinks you have while you're away will be allowable.

As soon as you're back on your own patch, any further expenditure is purely personal and cannot be claimed.

### Example 2
*Emma normally works from home but needs to visit one of her customers just a mile away. She buys herself a coffee on the way to her customer's office and goes for lunch in a local cafe.*

*Sadly, this expenditure is not allowable. Emma could have made herself a coffee before leaving home and could have returned home for lunch. Her subsistence expenditure cannot be claimed as a business expense because she had a reasonable alternative.*

It would have been exactly the same if Emma had her own office premises and her customer's office was only a mile away from there. Her subsistence costs would still have been a personal expense because one cannot say that her expenditure was any different to that which she might incur during a normal day at her own office.

Mike, on the other hand, flew all the way to London. It would have been ridiculous to expect him to go home to Scotland for lunch, so his subsistence costs were a reasonable business expense.

There is no set rule on how far you must travel before your subsistence costs become allowable. It is a question of whether it would have been reasonable for you to return home, or to the area in which your own business premises are located, before incurring the expense.

You must also actually incur the expenditure during the business trip. In Mike's case, it would be quite reasonable for him to have dinner in London, which would be allowable, but if he chose to go home first, he could not claim the cost of his dinner in Scotland.

While subsistence expenditure needs to be reasonable, it doesn't need to be frugal. If you're in a town with a nice Italian restaurant and a burger bar, there is no requirement for you to take the cheaper option.

### Alcohol
Some people assume that all alcohol must be a personal expense and hence not allowable. Not so! Just because something provides an element of personal enjoyment, this does not prevent it from being a business expense. You wouldn't just assume desserts weren't allowable, would you?

You have to drink, so if you choose to drink one or two glasses of beer or wine with a meal instead of water or lemonade, it's still subsistence expenditure. A single glass of beer or wine in an airport or railway station on your way home would also generally be allowable.

But any expense you claim must be reasonable. There can come a point when the expense is incurred purely for personal enjoyment and is no longer allowable. A bottle of wine is usually fine, but a magnum of vintage champagne is probably not.

Similarly, while drinks taken with a meal are usually considered reasonable, further alcoholic drinks after an evening meal would generally be regarded as a personal cost which cannot be claimed.

### Business Meetings and Entertaining
So far, we've talked about personal subsistence. Once you're with a customer or business contact, the situation changes.

For business meetings, we must again consider what is reasonable. A cup of tea or coffee while you discuss some business would usually be acceptable. Beyond that, we're into the realm of business entertaining and that's another story (Section 4.8).

In the meantime, if you're reading this in an airport or railway station on your way home from a business trip, why not have a drink on the Chancellor of the Exchequer?

### 4.6    OVERSEAS TRAVEL

In theory, there isn't any real difference between overseas travel and other business travel, so the principles we looked at in Sections 4.4 and 4.5 still apply in the same way. In practice, however, there are a few key differences:

- The trips tend to be longer
- The costs are more significant
- The likelihood of there being some personal element to the trip is greatly increased
- Home to work travel is not generally an issue
- Spouses and partners may often accompany the director

We'll cover that last bullet point in Section 4.7. For now, let's focus on the director's own costs. So, how do you get the taxman to pay for part of the cost of trips abroad?

At one end of the spectrum is the pure business trip. You may need to travel to some far-flung location to meet customers, suppliers, or business colleagues, or to view sites for some new venture abroad.

Just because your trip takes you far away doesn't prevent it from being a business trip and the travel, subsistence, and accommodation costs involved remain fully allowable for tax purposes under the general principles we have explored in previous sections.

Many business trips will have some leisure element to them. Your foreign host might take you to dinner, for example. Such minor, incidental, personal elements to the trip should not make any difference and the whole cost of the trip should still be allowable.

It would be slightly different if you paid for that dinner yourself. Your own meal would represent allowable subsistence expenditure, but the cost of anyone else's meal (other than an employee of your company) would usually represent business entertaining and hence would not be allowed for CT purposes. We'll come back to business entertaining in Section 4.8, where we will see it is still a good idea to put it through the company, even though it will not qualify for CT relief.

For longer trips abroad, the leisure element of the trip often becomes more significant. At this point, we have to start separating out the business and private elements of the trip in order to establish how much is allowable. A lot will depend on the circumstances surrounding the trip. The most important factor in many cases will be your initial rationale for taking the trip in the first place.

### Example
*James is the owner/director of an import-export company. He needs to visit Hi Fat, one of his suppliers, in Bangkok. Hi Fat organises a meeting on Monday, a factory tour on Tuesday and another meeting on Wednesday.*

*There are no available flights arriving in Bangkok on Sunday, so James has to travel on Saturday, leaving him a free day on the Sunday. James spends the day sightseeing and goes to a Thai boxing match in the evening. He spends £100 on entry fees (for museums, etc, and the boxing match) and £60 on food and drink during the day. His accommodation also costs £200 per night.*

*Although James has spent the day sightseeing, he is in Bangkok purely for business reasons, so he is able to claim the cost of his food and drink and his accommodation on Saturday and Sunday nights.*

*The cost of James's flights also remains fully allowable, as his sole purpose for taking the trip was to meet Hi Fat. The only costs James cannot claim in these circumstances are his £100 of entry fees.*

So, simply occupying your free time abroad in a pleasurable way still leaves you able to claim the vast majority of the cost.

So far, I'm assuming James flew back home as soon as possible after concluding his business with Hi Fat, but what if he extended his trip?

**Extending Your Trip**
By Wednesday night, James's business in Bangkok is finished. However, he does not fly home until Saturday and spends all of Thursday and Friday sightseeing. The position now will depend on the reason behind James's decision not to fly home until Saturday.

If Saturday was the earliest available return flight, or the cost of any earlier flight was significantly greater, then the extension to James's trip was purely business-driven. He would then be able to continue to claim all subsistence and accommodation costs in full, as well as the cost of his flights.

'Subsistence', for this purpose, would generally include all non-alcoholic drinks at any time and alcoholic drinks taken with meals. James could not claim any purely personal costs incurred, such as entry fees to museums, shows, etc.

If, however, James could have flown home on Thursday, but decided to extend his trip for personal reasons, then the situation is quite different. Here there are several potential scenarios to consider.

Firstly, let's suppose that James genuinely needed to visit Hi Fat for bona fide business reasons and then subsequently decided that, as he was going all the way to Bangkok, he might as well extend his trip to give him a chance to see the city.

The primary purpose for James's trip is therefore still business and he can continue to claim the full cost of his flights and all his subsistence and accommodation costs from his arrival on the first Saturday until Wednesday night, plus any subsistence costs during his journey home.

In other words, the only costs James cannot claim are the additional costs incurred due to extending his trip by an extra two days (as well as all purely personal costs such as entry fees for shows, etc).

James will have spent seven nights in Bangkok so a simple way to look at his accommodation costs would be to disallow (i.e. not claim) two sevenths of the total bill (his first night's accommodation remains allowable as he had no choice but to fly in a day early).

However, he only needs to disallow the additional costs of extending his trip, so it may sometimes be worth digging a little deeper. Suppose, for example, that it would have cost £1,000 to stay for five nights but the hotel only charges £1,300 for seven nights. James's disallowable accommodation cost would then be just £300.

James could also improve his position by planning his dining habits carefully. Meal costs incurred up to Wednesday night (the business part of his trip) will be allowable but his meals on Thursday and Friday are a personal expense. Hence, if there are any more expensive restaurants James would like to try out, he should do so by Wednesday night!

## Mixed Purpose for Trip

In our second scenario, let's suppose James's reasons for travelling to Bangkok were mixed. Visiting Hi Fat was useful, but not essential, and James also fancied a few days' break in Thailand. In other words, the trip wasn't **necessary**.

This poses quite a problem from a tax point of view as the trip would now appear to fail the 'wholly, exclusively, and **necessarily** incurred' test required for director's expenses. A self-employed individual could claim a proportion of the costs, but the tougher test for directors (as company employees) means that, strictly speaking, none of the costs of the trip can be claimed.

Nonetheless, it is probably still reasonable to claim any purely business elements within the costs: like taxi fares from James's hotel to Hi Fat's office or factory, and back; or subsistence costs incurred while visiting Hi Fat's offices and factory.

The bulk of the costs, however, including flights, accommodation and most of James's subsistence costs, cannot strictly be claimed. In practice, it might perhaps be possible to claim a small proportion of these costs in a case like this, but this is by no means guaranteed.

This may sound ridiculously unfair, but remember James is basically on holiday. You can't turn a holiday into a business trip just by popping in on a business acquaintance while you're there!

To avoid this fate, you need to make sure your business trip is necessary for the purposes of your employment as director of your company. Good ways to evidence this include recording the purpose and necessity of the trip in directors' board minutes and, of course, making sure the business part of your trip is arranged first, before you book your flights or accommodation.

## Internal Travel

The treatment of internal travel costs, such as taxi or train fares, incurred while abroad on business, depends on the reason for the internal trip. A purely business journey will be fully allowable, but a journey made for personal reasons, such as sightseeing or going to a show, cannot be claimed.

Travel costs incurred when going out for meals may be allowable, depending on the circumstances. In essence, the question is: was it necessary to travel to eat, or could you have just stayed in, or near to, your accommodation?

Meeting a customer or business contact for lunch or dinner would help in this regard, but could turn some or all of the cost into business entertaining: see Section 4.8.

## Business Conferences

For many directors, their main experience of foreign business travel is the business conference. In theory, the principles for claiming tax relief for the costs of attending a conference are exactly the same as for other business trips. In practice, however, conferences do seem to give rise to a few problems!

A typical business conference will involve some lectures or presentations, meals, refreshments, accommodation, and some business networking activities. It's that last category that causes the problems because 'networking' often involves some form of leisure activities.

For example, a conference in Florida might include an afternoon's golf. Is it still a business trip? If the golf is an integral part of the conference and the only people involved are conference delegates and organisers, I would argue that this is a pure business networking activity and the entire cost of attending the conference remains allowable. HMRC has been known to disagree with this view in similar situations however.

## 4.7    TAKING YOUR SPOUSE OR PARTNER

In Sections 4.4 and 4.6, we looked at travel costs and how much of them can be claimed for tax purposes. In this section, we will take a look at the tax position for trips taken together with a spouse, partner, or other family member.

For ease of illustration, I'm just going to talk about being accompanied by your spouse. As far as the tax treatment is concerned, however, being accompanied by an unmarried life partner or any other member of your family has much the same effect.

### The Nature of the Trip
The first thing to consider is: what is the main reason for taking the trip? Is your spouse accompanying you on a business trip, or are you simply fitting some business into a holiday or other private trip?

In the former case, you are likely to be able to claim a significant proportion of the cost of the trip, in the latter you will generally only be able to claim any additional costs arising as a direct result of the business element of the trip.

The mere fact your spouse accompanies you on a trip tends to suggest there is at least some private element. This can be overcome in some cases, but it is necessary to show your spouse's presence was required for business purposes.

### Working Spouses
Many small companies are owned and run by couples, so both spouses (or partners) are shareholder/directors in their own right. This makes it a business trip for each of you and a suitable proportion of the travel, accommodation and subsistence costs for both of you can be claimed following the same principles we looked at in Sections 4.4 to 4.6.

In other cases, a director's spouse might be their personal assistant, or may be employed by the company in some other capacity. This may also give rise to a genuine business reason for the spouse to accompany the director on the trip. However, this will generally only apply where the spouse has a permanent role in the company, which is consistent with the need to take them on the business trip. Hiring your spouse as a clerical assistant for a couple of weeks will not usually be enough!

The simplest solution in most cases is to make your spouse a director of the company, but they will need to play an active role to justify the business purpose behind their presence on the trip. Remember, it has to be necessary.

## That Special Person

If the spouse has some special skill that is relevant to the director's trip then the cost of taking them along might then become allowable even when they do not have a permanent role in the company. A good example might be a spouse who speaks the local language and can therefore act as an interpreter.

A director might also be able to claim the cost of taking their spouse where this was essential to their personal safety. This would be particularly relevant in the case of a female director travelling to a developing country but might also apply to a businessman whose wife has a black belt in karate!

## Social and Networking Requirements

Sometimes you might need to take your spouse on a business trip in order to meet the cultural or social expectations of a foreign host or business contact.

Let us suppose, for example, that, in order to secure a large contract in South America, the managing director (MD) of a UK company flies to Rio for some business meetings and is also invited to dinner at their opposite number's home. The South American host clearly expects the UK director to take their spouse with them and, although this is ostensibly a social occasion, the contract rides on meeting those expectations.

In this situation, the travel costs in respect of the UK director's spouse are wholly, exclusively, and necessarily incurred for business purposes and are therefore fully allowable.

However, it does not take much of a change to this situation before the spouse's travel costs cease to be allowable. If it is merely desirable, rather than essential, for the MD's spouse to accompany them to the dinner in Rio, then the spouse's travel costs become a personal expense. The company could still get CT relief for those costs, but the MD would then be personally liable for a benefit in kind charge, often giving rise to combined Income Tax and National Insurance costs of 58.8% (45% Income Tax for the MD and 13.8% National Insurance for the company), more in some cases.

As usual, we have to remember that, as an employee, the MD can only classify their spouse's travel costs as a business expense when it is essential that their spouse accompanies them on the trip.

## What to Claim and How to Support It

When a spouse's presence is essential on a trip, this will cover their travel, subsistence, and accommodation costs where these are necessarily incurred as part of the trip. It will not extend to other costs incurred in sightseeing, going to shows, visiting friends and relatives, etc.

Documentation recording the rationale for a spouse's presence on a business trip will be helpful: especially if there are other directors whose approval is required and this is recorded in the minutes of a directors' board meeting.

## Purely Private Spouses

Where a director has simply taken their spouse with them on a business trip for purely personal reasons, the director's own travel costs will be allowable on the same basis as we looked at in Sections 4.4 to 4.6, but the spouse's costs will be a personal expense.

It would, however, only be necessary to disallow any additional costs incurred as a result of the spouse's presence on the trip. For example, there may not be any additional accommodation costs to disallow, as the room charge might be the same whether the spouse is there or not. The same might apply to taxi fares or the costs of hiring a car.

## 4.8    ENTERTAINING AND GIFTS

As a company director, you may incur expenditure on:

- Business entertaining
- Staff entertaining
- Personal entertaining

The same three categories apply equally to gifts and the rules are broadly the same with only minor variations to consider.

The good news is that business entertaining and gifts can be put through the company with no adverse tax consequences for the company owner. The same is often true for staff entertaining or gifts, although it is important to be aware that any direct benefit to the owner/director themselves or their family may cause a chargeable benefit in kind. We'll look at that in more detail later.

Hence, subject to the risk of a chargeable benefit in kind on a proportion of any staff entertaining costs (see below) or gifts made directly to the owner/director themselves or their family, both business and staff entertaining (and gifts) can be put through the company as legitimate director's expenses.

Regardless of whether they attract CT relief, or give rise to a benefit in kind charge for other employees, they remain a business expense provided they are wholly and exclusively incurred for the purposes of the company's business.

However, meeting that critical 'wholly and exclusively' test remains essential and we'll look at that issue later in this section.

### Business Entertaining and Gifts

Subject to the exceptions we looked at in Sections 2.4, 3.5, and 3.6, business entertaining and gifts do not attract CT relief and VAT cannot generally be recovered.

However, where a director incurs expenditure on business entertaining or business gifts, it is still highly beneficial to put it through the company because this means the cost does not have to come out of the director's after-tax income.

#### *Example*

*Simon is the owner/director of Carpenter Ventures Ltd and is a higher rate taxpayer. He takes a group of customers out to dinner. The meal costs £750, including VAT. If the cost is put through his company, it will not be able to claim CT relief or recover any of the VAT, so the total, after tax, cost remains £750.*

*However, if Simon was to pay for the meal himself, he would need to take additional dividends of £1,132. After suffering Income Tax at 33.75% on the dividends, £382, Simon would be left with the £750 he needs to pay the restaurant bill.*

*Critically though, this means the meal has now cost £1,132, which is 51% more than if the cost were put through the company.*

Simon may not need to take those additional dividends immediately but, sooner or later, he has to fund the cost somehow, so it is right to take account of the additional cost of getting those funds into his hands.

In Section 1.1, at the start of the guide, we saw there were three potential benefits to putting expenses through the company. We also saw the fact the cost did not need to be funded out of the company owner's personal after-tax income was the greatest of those benefits.

In this example, we can clearly see this one single benefit alone is worthwhile, even in the absence of the other two: and that, in a nutshell, is why it's worth putting business entertaining and gifts through the company. Furthermore, as these costs remain business expenses, there is no benefit in kind charge for the owner/director.

But can we do better?

**Entertaining versus Subsistence**
A key area of confusion is the difference between subsistence and entertaining. If you take a customer to lunch, the cost of their meal is business entertaining and not deductible for CT purposes. If you took them to lunch locally, the cost of your own meal must be treated the same way. (As we saw above though, it's still worth putting it through the company.)

If you have travelled some distance to meet the customer, however, your own meal might represent a legitimate subsistence cost which may be claimed (see Sections 3.5 and 4.4). However, it is important for both CT relief and VAT recovery that the main purpose of your visit was for other business reasons, and not simply to entertain the customer.

Nonetheless, where other business motives are present, it will generally be a mistake to 'play host' to your visitors. A policy of 'visitor pays' could convert half your entertaining expenditure into allowable subsistence costs.

*Example*
*Every month, Crispin travels 100 miles to visit Linda, one of his suppliers. Linda pays for their lunch in a local restaurant. Linda also visits Crispin once a month and he then pays for lunch. All the costs incurred by both Crispin and Linda are disallowable business entertaining.*

*Let us suppose, however, that Crispin and Linda reverse their arrangements to a 'visitor pays' policy. Half the cost of each lunch now becomes allowable subsistence expenditure (provided there are other business reasons for their visits).*

The position changes if a visitor is actually making a direct contribution to your company's business: i.e. they are personally performing work directly for your company during their visit.

Let's suppose that Linda is an IT consultant and, during her visits, she carries out maintenance work on Crispin's computer system. If Crispin pays for Linda's lunch under these circumstances, he can claim this as part of his company's IT support costs for CT purposes. The company will probably be unable to claim the VAT on this cost though, as the test there is much stricter ('hospitality of any kind': see Section 3.6). Hence the 'visitor pays' policy probably remains more beneficial.

Where there is a contractual obligation to provide visitors with food, drink, etc, this cost is usually allowable for both CT and VAT purposes, as it is no longer business entertaining but part of the service being provided.

### Travel and Incidental Costs
Incidental costs related to business entertaining, such as travel expenses, must generally also be disallowed for CT purposes. This would apply, for example, where you invited a customer to dinner and paid their taxi fare. The travel costs for directors and other staff attending a business entertaining event are also disallowed for CT but can be reimbursed by the company without giving rise to a benefit in kind charge.

This does not affect normal travel and subsistence claims where a journey is undertaken for other business purposes and the entertaining takes place during the same visit.

### Staff Entertaining
Staff entertaining is an allowable expense for both CT and VAT purposes (see Section 3.5 for more details on the VAT position).

The drawback, of course, is that, subject to the exemptions for annual staff parties, etc, (Section 7.31) and trivial benefits (Section 7.32), the cost of the entertaining is a chargeable benefit in kind for the staff. That includes the owner/director themselves (if they are present), but only on the appropriate proportion of the cost.

For example, if a director takes five staff out to dinner, each of them has a chargeable benefit for one sixth of the overall cost. Alternatively, the director might only put five sixths of the cost through the company to avoid a chargeable benefit in kind for themselves. The position for the rest of the staff remains the same.

The miserly staff at HMRC take this to extremes, even looking to tax employees for the cost of sandwiches provided during working lunches at the company's business premises. These issues are often resolved through a PAYE settlement made by the company. We will look at the whole area of what can be provided to staff without giving rise to chargeable benefits in kind, as well as the benefits of PAYE settlements, in more detail in Chapter 7.

Food and drink provided to employees while working away from their main business base are allowable for both CT and VAT purposes, and do not give rise to benefit in kind charges, where these represent genuine subsistence expenditure. The same principles apply as for company directors (see Sections 4.4 to 4.6).

CT relief is denied where staff entertaining is merely incidental to the entertainment of customers or other non-employee guests. The test HMRC uses to assess this is to consider whether the company would still have paid for the event if the non-employee guests had not been present. If the company would not have paid without the presence of other guests, the staff entertaining is merely incidental and none of the cost is allowable for CT purposes.

Hence, if a director invites a member of staff to join them and a customer for lunch, it will not turn the cost of the meal into allowable staff entertaining: it will remain non-deductible business entertaining. The good news is there will be no benefit in kind charge for either the staff member or the director themselves.

Alternatively, a director might have already arranged to take some staff out for lunch when a visitor arrives unexpectedly. So, the director asks the visitor to join them for lunch: now the company only needs to disallow the cost of the visitor's meal.

Better still, why not invite some customers to your company's annual staff party? You would still need to disallow an appropriate proportion of the cost, but this will often be more cost effective than having to disallow the cost of separately entertaining each customer.

Look at it this way: you and two co-directors throw an annual staff party and invite your twelve staff, plus five of your customers. You will need to disallow a quarter of the cost (5 out of 20) for both CT and VAT purposes but, if you had taken each customer to lunch separately, the whole cost of all five lunches would have been disallowable.

In this case, benefit in kind charges can also be avoided if the cost per head for the party is no more than £150 (see Section 7.31).

In other cases, however, it may actually be better overall if an event were business entertaining rather than staff entertaining. While this is usually a question of fact, not choice, it's worth us contrasting the position.

**Business Entertaining versus Staff Entertaining**

### *Example*

*Marcus is the owner/director of Mamboja Ltd. He organises a day's clay pigeon shooting and invites six senior staff members and five customers. The total cost is £7,500 plus VAT, i.e. £9,000. Whether the event is classed as staff entertaining, with some customers in attendance, or as a pure business entertaining event is a question of fact: we have covered the CT principles above and we looked at VAT in Section 3.5. The event cannot qualify for the annual party exemption (Section 7.31) as only selected staff were invited (and it costs too much anyway).*

*If the event is staff entertaining, the company can claim back the VAT on 6/12ths of the cost (the proportion relating to the staff, but not Marcus himself, as this event was not open to all staff: see Section 3.5). Naturally, the VAT recovered cannot be claimed for CT purposes, and the company will also have to disallow the 5/12ths of the gross, VAT-inclusive cost of the event that related to the customers.*

*Hence, the company will recover £750 in VAT (£1,500 x 6/12) and will have to disallow a further £3,750 (£9,000 x 5/12) for CT purposes. This leaves £4,500 eligible for CT relief which, if we assume the company has a marginal CT rate of 26.5% (see Section 2.1), yields a saving of £1,193.*

*However, Marcus and his five senior staff members will all be subject to benefit in kind charges. To simplify matters, let's suppose the company enters into a PAYE settlement agreement to deal with this issue. All the attendees are higher rate taxpayers, so HMRC will gross up the VAT-inclusive cost at 40%, to reach a total of £8,750 (£9,000 x 7/12 x 100/(100 – 40)). To this, they will add employer's National Insurance at 13.8%, to give a sum of £9,958. Deducting the actual apportioned cost of £5,250 (£9,000 x 7/12), leaves £4,708 payable by the company.*

*In effect, this cost is treated like additional salary so it attracts CT relief, thus recouping £1,248 (£4,708 x 26.5%). So, this is what the event cost:*

| | |
|---|---|
| *Actual cost of event* | *£9,000* |
| *VAT recovered* | *(£750)* |
| *Corporation Tax relief* | *(£1,193)* |
| *PAYE settlement* | *£4,708* |
| *Corporation Tax relief thereon* | *(£1,248)* |
| *Total net cost* | *£10,517* |

*If the event had been classed as business entertaining, it would simply have cost £9,000.*

Like I said, it's a question of fact, not choice, but this particular event would have cost £1,517 more if it had been treated as staff entertaining with a few external guests. Generally speaking therefore, where benefit in kind charges are potentially involved, it is better if an event is treated as business entertaining.

That, of course, will happen if invited staff are there to entertain customers and other business contacts, and not just to enjoy themselves. Naturally, however, they, and you, can still enjoy themselves as well.

As for Marcus's shooting day: it looks like business entertaining to me.

### Gifts to Staff
Subject to the exceptions covered in Chapter 7, these will generally constitute a chargeable benefit in kind for the recipient. The 'employee benefit override' will generally mean CT relief is available, unless the recipient is a shareholder/director or one of their family members, in which case the cost of the gift needs to be justified under the principles examined in Section 2.2. For the VAT position on gifts to staff, see Section 3.5.

## 4.9  FEES, SUBSCRIPTIONS AND OTHER ITEMS

Fees, subscriptions and other items that are directly relevant to the company's business, or to the director's role in the company, can be put through the company and will be eligible for CT relief. There should be no benefit in kind charge provided any benefit to the director is merely incidental.

This will cover items such as:
- Professional subscriptions
- Membership of a trade body or business association
- Subscriptions to trade publications (printed or electronic)

Newspapers and other more general publications may also qualify under certain circumstances, such as:

- Newspapers and other publications provided for the use of visitors
- Where the director's role necessitates them having a thorough, up to date, knowledge of the news in general
- For a specialist publication like the Financial Times or The Economist, where a particular aspect of the news is relevant to the director's role

A club membership used purely to provide business facilities for the company (e.g. meeting rooms) will qualify for CT relief without a benefit in kind charge. If the club is also used for business entertaining, some or all of the CT relief may be lost but a benefit in kind charge may still be avoided if any personal benefit to the director is merely incidental.

However, memberships of institutions such as golf clubs, rowing clubs, etc, will not generally be covered, even if they are a good source of work for the company, as there is usually too much of a personal benefit for the director. (And hence a dual purpose, as per our basic principles in Section 2.2.) Exceptions may occasionally arise if the club is directly relevant to the company's business, or the director's role, but these are rare.

## 4.10  PRE-TRADING EXPENDITURE

As a director, you may incur some expenses on behalf of your company before it starts its business, before it has its own bank account, or even before you have formed it.

In general, deductible expenses incurred within seven years before the commencement of a business may still be allowable if they would otherwise qualify under normal principles. In such cases, the expenses, termed 'pre-trading expenditure' can be claimed as if they were incurred on the first day of the business.

In the case of a new company, a number of pre-trading expenses will often have been paid for by the company owner personally before the company has been formed or before it has its own bank account. The best thing to do in these circumstances is:

| i)   | Keep track of the relevant expenditure, retaining receipts, etc, as usual. |
|------|-----------------------------|
| ii)  | Once the company has been formed, recharge the expenses to the company. What this means in practice is that a director's loan account is set up (see Section 4.3) recording the expenditure previously incurred by the director. |
| iii) | The expenses recharged by the director may (subject to the normal principles of deductibility) be claimed in the company's first accounting period. |
| iv)  | The director may be repaid the loan account as soon as the company has available funds. |

It is generally still worth following this process where the costs recharged represent capital expenditure, as this enhances the balance on the director's loan account (which brings many benefits, as we will see in Section 5.5), and the costs may also attract capital allowances or be deductible against a later capital gain arising in the company.

However, it is not generally possible to recharge the costs of the company formation in this way, although they can be added to the director's base cost for their shares for future CGT purposes.

Some resistance can be encountered where costs recharged are not clearly for the company's benefit. It is therefore best to retain some evidence that you were acting on behalf of the company (e.g. in email instructions to a surveyor or solicitor). This can include acting on behalf of a prospective company you intend to form, although this can sometimes be hard to prove, so it is better to form the company as soon as possible.

See also Section 3.3 regarding VAT reclaims on expenses incurred by a director before the company commences business or registers for VAT.

# Chapter 5

# Saving Tax by Putting It Through

## 5.1 THE BIGGEST SAVING: INCOME TAX

In Section 1.1 we saw that, of the three potential savings you might achieve by putting expenditure through the company, the largest, most significant one was the Income Tax you save by not having to pay the cost out of your own after-tax income.

In fact, in Section 4.8 we saw this saving alone makes it worth putting the cost through the company.

All this is based on the assumption that, sooner or later, the expenditure would otherwise have to be funded by extracting funds from the company and that the director has already exhausted their opportunities for extracting funds tax free (we'll look at some of those opportunities in Sections 5.2 to 5.4).

This is a reasonable assumption in the case of most small company owners whose main source of income is their company.

**How Much Income Tax Are You Saving?**
Most small company owners needing to extract further funds from their company will do so by way of dividend and that's what we'll look at in this section. In a few cases, the extra funds may need to take the form of additional salary or a bonus payment. This will generally be a more expensive option as it will cost both Income Tax and National Insurance. For a good example, see Section 2.7.

Subject to the rather pathetic tax-free dividend allowance (see Section 5.3) dividends are currently taxed at the following rates:

| | |
|---|---|
| Basic rate | 8.75% |
| Higher rate | 33.75% |
| Additional rate | 39.35% |

However, where the director's taxable income lies in the band from £100,000 to £125,140, the effective cost of further dividends will be even greater due to the withdrawal of their personal allowance. The most common effective rate on dividends falling into this bracket for small company owners will be 56.25%.

This arises where the director is taking a salary equal to the personal allowance and the rest of their income is made up of dividends. This excessive tax rate can often be avoided with careful planning although in this section we will assume that has not been possible.

Using the above tax rates, we see for a higher rate taxpayer director to make a purchase costing £1,000 personally, they need to take £1,509 in extra dividends so that, after paying the Income Tax arising (£1,509 x 33.75% = £509) they are left with the £1,000 they need.

They may not need to take that dividend straight away but nonetheless this implicit cost needs to be taken into account.

So, using the same principle, this is what £1,000 of expenditure is actually going to cost, depending on your existing level of taxable income:

| Existing Taxable Income (Notes) | Cost |
|---|---|
| £13,070 to £50,270 (3) | £1,096 |
| £50,270 to £100,000 (4) | £1,509 |
| £100,000 to £125,140 (5) | £2,286 |
| Over £125,140 | £1,649 |

**Notes**
1. Based on 2024/25 tax rates, allowances, and thresholds (see Appendix B)
2. To simplify matters, I have assumed total taxable income remains in the same tax bracket after taking the extra dividends required
3. Assuming no other tax-free profit extraction methods remain: see Sections 5.2 to 5.4
4. Assuming the Child Benefit Charge does not apply to taxable income between £60,000 and £80,000
5. See above regarding the effective Income Tax rate used here

**Total Savings**
Using the figures in the above table, we can now see what the total savings are where purchases or costs totalling £1,000 are put through the company under three different scenarios:

**Scenario 1:** The expenditure is not eligible for CT relief or VAT recovery. A good example is business entertaining.
**Scenario 2:** The expenditure is eligible for CT relief, but VAT cannot be recovered. A good example is a train fare.
**Scenario 3:** The expenditure is eligible for CT relief, and standard rate VAT at 20% can be recovered. A good example is hot food or drinks qualifying as subsistence expenditure.

In each case, we are assuming there is no benefit in kind charge on the director. The savings under Scenario 1 remain the same regardless of the company's CT rate. For Scenarios 2 and 3, we need to consider the three potential marginal CT rates discussed in Section 2.1.

**Savings per £1,000 of Expenditure: Small Company Paying Corporation Tax at 19%**

| Existing Taxable Income | Scenario | | |
|---|---|---|---|
| | 1 | 2 | 3 |
| £13,070 to £50,270 | £96 | £286 | £421 |
| £50,270 to £100,000 | £509 | £699 | £834 |
| £100,000 to £125,140 | £1,286 | £1,476 | £1,611 |
| Over £125,140 | £649 | £839 | £974 |

**Savings per £1,000 of Expenditure: Company Paying Corporation Tax at Marginal Rate of 26.5%**

| Existing Taxable Income | Scenario | | |
|---|---|---|---|
| | 1 | 2 | 3 |
| £13,070 to £50,270 | £96 | £361 | £483 |
| £50,270 to £100,000 | £509 | £774 | £897 |
| £100,000 to £125,140 | £1,286 | £1,551 | £1,673 |
| Over £125,140 | £649 | £914 | £1,036 |

**Savings per £1,000 of Expenditure: Larger Company Paying Corporation Tax at 25%**

| Existing Taxable Income | Scenario | | |
|---|---|---|---|
| | 1 | 2 | 3 |
| £13,070 to £50,270 | £96 | £346 | £471 |
| £50,270 to £100,000 | £509 | £759 | £884 |
| £100,000 to £125,140 | £1,286 | £1,536 | £1,661 |
| Over £125,140 | £649 | £899 | £1,024 |

Some of these savings are pretty substantial. And, even if that first saving of £96 doesn't sound very impressive, if it means you can take less dividends in a future year when you have become a higher rate taxpayer, you'll actually be saving £509 or more. We'll see why in Section 5.5.

## 5.2 SAVING TAX BY PAYING YOURSELF

Basic company tax planning is to take anything you can out of the company that is tax-free, or has an overall negative cost after taking account of CT relief (better still!)

Where something satisfies these criteria, it makes sense to put it through the company, even if you don't need the cash at the moment. You can always pay it back or post it to your director's loan account (see Section 5.5).

Having said that, most small company owners will already be taking far more out of their companies than the amounts they can take tax-free or at an overall negative cost. Extracting money from your company tax efficiently is a complex area of tax planning and is covered in detail in the Taxcafe guide *Salary versus Dividends*.

Nonetheless, any amounts that can be taken tax-free, or at an overall negative cost, are a good place to start. In many cases, directors can take a salary of £12,570 this year with an overall negative cost, although a higher or lower salary is sometimes more tax efficient and we will look at this in more detail in Section 6.4.

Other options include dividends and interest, which we'll look at in this chapter; or rent (where you own the company's business premises personally), which we'll cover in Section 10.4.

Any form of payment you take out of your company needs paperwork to back it up and we'll take a brief look at some of the requirements in Section 5.5.

## 5.3    TAX-FREE DIVIDENDS

Each individual can receive up to £500 of dividends tax free this year under the dividend allowance. Hence, if you have no dividends from other sources and your company is in profit, it makes sense to take a dividend of at least £500 this year.

Note the dividend allowance applies to all dividend income for the tax year, not just dividends from your own company. If you have £100 of other dividend income, there is only £400 of dividend allowance available to cover dividends from your company.

Dividends covered by the dividend allowance remain taxable income for all other purposes: they are just free from a direct tax charge in their own right. Hence, under appropriate circumstances, they can still give rise to the Child Benefit Charge, withdrawal of your personal allowance, or result in the reduction or loss of your personal savings allowance (see Section 5.4).

## 5.4    TAX-FREE OR TAX-EFFICIENT INTEREST

Interest income is tax free if it is covered by your starting rate band (currently £5,000), or your personal savings allowance (£1,000 for basic rate taxpayers; £500 for higher rate taxpayers; not available to additional rate taxpayers).

Taking the personal allowance into account as well, it is therefore possible to receive up to £18,570 in tax-free interest where your only other taxable income is dividends not exceeding £31,700 (£50,270 – £18,570).

Where you have loaned money to your company (including where your director's loan account is in credit), you can charge interest at anything up to an arm's length commercial rate and it will be allowable for CT purposes.

What is a commercial rate depends on a number of factors, including prevailing market interest rates. It is worth remembering that most loans from shareholder/directors to their company are unsecured, have no fixed term, and no regular repayment schedule. In this sense, they are often more like overdrafts than any other form of borrowing and this, in turn, means quite high interest charges can be justified as being a commercial rate: check what the high street banks are offering on their overdraft facilities.

For the rest of this section, we'll assume any interest payments are at no more than an arm's length commercial rate, are backed up by the relevant paperwork (see Section 5.5), and are thus eligible for CT relief.

Basic rate Income Tax at 20% must be deducted from interest paid to you and then paid over to HMRC quarterly. Any excess tax deducted can be recouped through your self-assessment tax return, but this still represents a cashflow disadvantage and an admin burden. (Both can be mitigated with careful planning.)

Despite the cashflow and admin issues, it's generally worth charging as much interest as you can justify commercially, even beyond the tax-free amounts described above. If your company's marginal CT rate is 25% or 26.5% and you remain a basic rate taxpayer, there is an overall negative cost, i.e. a saving, after factoring in CT relief.

### Example

*Quads Ltd has a marginal CT rate of 26.5%. Ellie, the company's owner, has lent a substantial sum to the company, such that interest payments of up to £25,000 can be justified commercially. She needs to take a net, after tax sum of £45,000 out of the company. The National Insurance employment allowance (see Section 6.2) is available, so she takes the following sums, which are tax free:*

- *Salary £12,570*
- *Interest £6,000*
- *Dividend £500*
- *Loan repayment £25,930*

*Ellie has no Income Tax to pay and the salary and interest payments attract CT relief at 26.5%, saving the company £4,921. From the company's point of view, the net cash outflow is £40,079. However, Ellie can do better by maximising her interest payment, increasing it to £25,000. While all the interest paid is subject to the 20% basic rate Income Tax deduction, she will get a refund of £1,200 in respect of the £6,000 that is tax free and thus eventually suffer a net £3,800.*

*She then pays herself a tax-free dividend of £500 and a loan repayment of £10,730 to bring her total net receipts up to the required amount (£12,570 + £25,000 − £3,800 + £500 + £10,730 = £45,000).*

*The company has now made payments totalling £48,800. However, the salary and interest payments attract CT relief, reducing the overall net cash outflow by £9,956 (£12,570 + £25,000 = £37,570 x 26.5%) to £38,844.*

By maximising her interest payments, Ellie has reduced the overall effective cost to the company by £1,235 (£40,079 − £38,844).

Looked at another way, the company has paid out a net total of £38,844 to get a net £45,000 into the shareholder/director's hands. The extra £6,156 has come from HMRC. I would say that's well worth a little short-term cashflow disadvantage and a bit of admin.

Maximising the interest payment has also preserved an additional £15,200 of the director's loan account (£25,930 − £10,730). It's well worth preserving director's loan account balances wherever this can be done at little or no tax cost, and we will look at some of the benefits arising in Section 5.5.

In fact, in a case like Ellie's, there's a potential argument for saying it would be better to top up her income with dividends taxed at just 8.75% to preserve more of her loan account balance and allow her to maximise her tax-efficient interest payments in future years.

## Interest versus Dividends

Interest payments in excess of the tax-free amounts discussed above will have an overall tax cost if the company's CT rate is only 19%, or if you are, or become, a higher rate taxpayer.

In the case of a company paying CT at 19% and a basic rate taxpayer director, the overall net cost of paying interest is only 1%, so it's probably still worth maximising your interest payments as this is still a tax efficient way to take money out of your company and preserves more of your loan account balance for future use.

In other cases, it will only be worth paying interest beyond the tax-free amounts if you need the funds. Even then, you will usually have the option to take tax-free loan repayments instead.

But if you want to preserve your loan account balance for future use, paying interest remains cheaper than dividends in excess of the dividend allowance. For example, even if the company's CT rate is 19%, paying you interest of £10,000 will only cost £8,100 after CT relief. If you are a higher rate taxpayer suffering Income Tax at 40%, your net interest income will be £6,000.

For a higher rate taxpayer to get net income of £6,000 by way of a dividend, the company would need to pay £9,057 (this suffers Income Tax, at 33.75%, of £3,057, leaving the shareholder/director with the net £6,000 required).

Hence, the dividend costs almost £1,000 more than paying interest: even when the company has the lowest CT rate.

In short, after the dividend allowance (Section 5.3), interest eligible for CT relief is almost always better than any further dividends: although there can be occasional exceptions depending on the director's income requirements and the amount of cash available in the company.

## 5.5 MAKING THE MOST OF YOUR DIRECTOR'S LOAN ACCOUNT

A director's loan account that's in credit (the company owes you money) has many benefits. It can be regarded as money stored away for a rainy day. Not necessarily in cash, but the sum due to you from the company can be paid to you at any time (funds permitting) free from tax. Some of the benefits a credit balance on your director's loan account provides include the ability to:

- Easily rectify mistakes with director's expenses (Section 4.3)
- Pay yourself tax-free or tax-efficient interest (Section 5.4)
- Keep future dividend income at a level that enables you to:
   o Remain a basic rate taxpayer,
   o Avoid the Child Benefit Charge, or
   o Retain your personal allowance (see Section 5.1)

As discussed in Section 5.2, anything you can put through the company that is either tax-free or has a negative overall tax cost will be beneficial. So, if you don't need the cash straight away, you should still put these items through and post them to your director's loan account to create or increase that credit balance.

It's important to put the relevant paperwork in place to validate these items. For director's salaries or dividends this will typically include director's board minutes and, for dividends, minutes of shareholder meetings and dividend vouchers. Salaries have to go through the PAYE system (Section 6.1). Loan interest needs to be paid under a loan agreement between the director and company.

Subject to getting the paperwork right, beneficial director's loan account postings include:

- Salaries with an overall negative tax cost (see Section 5.2)
- Tax-free dividends (Section 5.3)
- Tax-free or tax-efficient interest (Section 5.4)
- Tax-efficient rent (Section 10.4)
- Allowable director's expenses (Chapter 4)
- Business entertaining and gifts, and any other items that don't attract CT relief but do not give rise to a benefit in kind charge
- Business mileage (Sections 9.2 and 9.4)
- The market value of any assets or goods you have transferred to the company
- Business expenses paid on behalf of the company before it was incorporated (Section 4.10)

The last heading will include set-up costs you paid on the company's behalf (but not the cost of your shares) and any director's expenses incurred before the company's incorporation (as long as they relate to the company's business and have not already been claimed for Income Tax purposes: e.g. where you were previously a sole trader).

Once these costs have been posted to your director's loan account, they may attract CT relief where they are eligible under normal principles, although many set-up costs will be regarded as capital in nature.

### Basic Rate Dividends

Where you would normally expect to be a higher rate taxpayer but there is a tax year in which you are a basic rate taxpayer, it may be worth taking further dividends that year taxed at just 8.75% and then posting them to your director's loan account. While this has an initial tax cost, it could yield significant long-term savings.

### *Example*

*Bartie is normally a higher rate taxpayer but, in 2024/25, his taxable income totals just £20,270. This already includes enough dividends to use up his dividend allowance. Bartie takes a further dividend of £30,000. He takes £2,625 of this in cash (to cover the 8.75% Income Tax) and posts the remaining £27,375 as a credit to his director's loan account.*

*In the following year, Bartie is a higher rate taxpayer but he can withdraw the sum of £27,375 from his director's loan account tax free. To obtain the same net sum after tax by way of dividend he would have to take a dividend of £41,321 and pay 33.75% Income Tax of £13,946. Taking the extra dividend in 2024/25 when he was a basic rate taxpayer has therefore saved Bartie £11,321 (£13,946 – £2,625).*

If Bartie's taxable income in the later year is in excess of £58,679, his savings will be even greater: either because he can avoid losing some or all of his personal allowance, or because he would become (or is) an additional rate taxpayer.

### A Word of Warning

HMRC has been known to challenge the treatment of salaries or dividends that are not actually paid but only posted to the director's loan account. This is usually only a problem where the company not only didn't pay the item but couldn't (i.e. it did not have the cash to do so).

The legal validity for these challenges is debatable, although there is an overriding principle that directors must act in the company's interests, so anything which, if paid, might make the company insolvent can be seen as a risk.

To be on the safe side, it may be sensible either for the company to actually pay the item and then the director pays it back, or to retain documentary evidence indicating how the company could have paid the item.

# Chapter 6

# Employing People

## 6.1 SALARIES AND WAGES

When you employ someone in your company's business, their salary or wage is a tax-deductible expense.

For example, if you pay someone a salary of £20,000 per year, your company's taxable profits will be reduced by £20,000. This in turn means your company's CT bill will be reduced by between £3,800 (£20,000 x 19%) and £5,300 (£20,000 x 26.5%).

So, you could say employing that person costs the company between £14,700 and £16,200, not £20,000. That's certainly good news but salaries are not the only expense a company incurs when it employs people. Other costs include:

- Payroll fees
- Employer's National Insurance
- Pension contributions

In the pages that follow we will attempt to calculate the true *overall cost* of employing someone in your business.

And what about the salary you pay yourself as a director of the company, or salaries paid to your spouse, partner or children: what's the position when it comes to putting these payments through the company? We'll take a closer look at these family-related payments in Section 6.5.

### Apprenticeship Levy
Another tax larger employers face is the Apprenticeship Levy. This is levied at the rate of 0.5% of the company's wage bill. However, each employer receives a £15,000 allowance, which means the levy is only paid by employers with a wage bill in excess of £3 million.

Because this guide is aimed at small company owners, we will not cover the Apprenticeship Levy in any further detail. However, it's worth pointing out that businesses in England that don't have to pay the levy can receive up to 95% support from the Government to cover staff training costs, within certain limits. This is known as 'co-investment'.

If your business has fewer than 50 employees, the Government will cover all the training costs for those aged 16-18 and certain other youngsters. Different arrangements apply to businesses in Scotland, Wales, and Northern Ireland.

For further information go to:
https://www.gov.uk/guidance/apprenticeship-funding-rules

**Payroll Fees**
It is your company's responsibility, as unofficial tax collector, to deduct Income Tax and National Insurance from your employees' salaries and pay it to HMRC. Employers must generally register for and operate PAYE where at least one employee either earns at least as much as the lower earnings limit (£6,396 in 2024/25), or has another job. Where at least one employee meets these criteria, the employer must report information about payments to all employees.

In most companies, the directors will be paying themselves a salary so the company will probably be operating PAYE already, even if it doesn't have other employees.

Employers also have to keep detailed payroll records. These have to be kept for three years from the end of the relevant tax year.

These days salary payments have to be reported to HMRC under the Real Time Information (RTI) regime. This requires submitting something called a Full Payment Submission (FPS) to HMRC at the same time or before you pay your employees.

Most small company owners should get their accountant or a bookkeeper to run the payroll. Unless you have experience in this area, it is definitely not advisable to go it alone: there's a good chance you will make mistakes which could lead to penalties.

Your company's accountant or bookkeeper will tell you exactly how much to pay each employee and how much to pay HMRC. They will also submit the Full Payment Submission to HMRC and issue you with payslips to give to each employee.

Naturally you will have to pay a fee for this service. However, if the company is already paying you and other directors a salary, employing just one or two more people should not lead to a substantial increase in payroll costs, if any.

One small firm of accountants we know charges around £500 per year for companies with 3-5 employees. Some will charge more, others will charge less. The cost can, of course, be put through the company, so the true cost in this case would be £405 net of CT relief at 19%, or £368 net of CT relief at 26.5%.

In summary, in most small companies where the directors are already paying themselves a salary, employing a few more people should not lead to a significant increase in payroll costs. As the business grows, payroll costs are likely to increase but the expense can be put through the company.

## 6.2    EMPLOYER'S NATIONAL INSURANCE

Apart from the actual salaries or wages, the biggest additional cost your company will incur when it employs people is likely to be employer's National Insurance.

Most salaried employees do not realise just how much National Insurance is paid by their employers. At present employers typically pay 13.8% on every single pound their employees earn in excess of £9,100. Unlike employee's National Insurance (see below), there is no upper limit where the rate of employer's National Insurance reduces.

It's not quite as bad as that because most businesses qualify for something called the employment allowance, which currently provides a £5,000 National Insurance saving each tax year.

Thus, a small company with just a handful of low paid employees will pay just a small amount or no employer's National Insurance. We'll take a closer look at which companies qualify for this allowance shortly. For now, we will ignore it when calculating the amount of employer's National Insurance payable.

£9,100 is known as the *secondary* threshold for National Insurance. The *primary* threshold applies to the employees themselves and is currently £12,570: it has been aligned with the Income Tax personal allowance. The Government has announced that both of these National Insurance thresholds and the personal allowance will all remain at these levels until 5th April 2028.

National Insurance is not an annual tax for most people but is levied by reference to pay periods (the position is different for directors: see below).

Pay periods are whatever the company's usual period is for paying its employees, typically weekly or monthly. Each pay period has its own primary threshold:

Weekly paid: £242
Monthly paid: £1,048

From 6th April 2024, employees pay 8% National Insurance to the extent their weekly or monthly salaries exceed these pay period thresholds, until they reach the 'upper earnings limit' when the rate falls to 2% on any further amounts.

The upper earnings limit is aligned with the higher rate threshold for Income Tax, £50,270. However, like the primary threshold, it is applied to most employees by reference to pay periods, as follows:

Weekly paid: £967
Monthly paid: £4,189

Like the primary threshold, the upper earnings limit will be the same for all pay periods until 5th April 2028.

For directors, National Insurance is calculated on an annual basis. Thus, for 2024/25, the rate of employee's National Insurance applying to director's salaries between £12,570 and £50,270 is 8%, regardless of how much salary is taken in any given month.

(Directors can opt to follow the same basis as other employees for most of the year, with a final adjustment in the last pay period of the tax year. This is not usually relevant for most small company owners, but might be useful in a case like Simon in Section 2.7.)

### Calculating Employer's National Insurance

The secondary threshold is also applied on a pay period basis for most employees but, in the vast majority of cases, we are able to calculate the total employer's National Insurance cost for the year quite simply using the annual figure of £9,100 for the threshold.

So, if you pay an employee £20,000 in 2024/25, the employer's National Insurance cost will be £1,504: (£20,000 – £9,100) x 13.8%.

And if you pay an employee £60,000, the employer's National Insurance cost will be £7,024: (£60,000 – £9,100) x 13.8%.

Just like the salary itself, employer's National Insurance is a tax-deductible business expense for CT purposes.

Thus, if you pay someone a salary of £60,000, the total CT relief could be up to £17,761: (£60,000 + £7,024) x 26.5%. So, you could say employing that person might only cost the company £49,263: £60,000 salary + £7,024 NI – £17,761 CT relief.

What this means is that a net amount of £49,263 will ultimately flow out of the company's bank account to pay someone a salary of £60,000, although the CT relief will only be enjoyed many months after the salary has been paid, when the company pays its CT bill.

Table A shows the actual net cost of lots of other salaries, taking into account the increase in the cost caused by employer's National Insurance and the decrease in the cost thanks to CT relief. To keep things simple, in the table we have assumed the company's marginal CT rate is 26.5% and this is unaltered by the payment of the salary itself.

**TABLE A**
**Actual Net Cost of Salaries 2024/25**

| Salary | Subject to NI | Employer NI | Total Cost | CT Relief | Net Cost |
|---|---|---|---|---|---|
| £10,000 | £900 | £124 | £10,124 | £2,683 | £7,441 |
| £15,000 | £5,900 | £814 | £15,814 | £4,191 | £11,623 |
| £20,000 | £10,900 | £1,504 | £21,504 | £5,699 | £15,806 |
| £25,000 | £15,900 | £2,194 | £27,194 | £7,206 | £19,988 |
| £30,000 | £20,900 | £2,884 | £32,884 | £8,714 | £24,170 |
| £35,000 | £25,900 | £3,574 | £38,574 | £10,222 | £28,352 |
| £40,000 | £30,900 | £4,264 | £44,264 | £11,730 | £32,534 |
| £45,000 | £35,900 | £4,954 | £49,954 | £13,238 | £36,716 |
| £50,000 | £40,900 | £5,644 | £55,644 | £14,746 | £40,898 |
| £55,000 | £45,900 | £6,334 | £61,334 | £16,254 | £45,081 |
| £60,000 | £50,900 | £7,024 | £67,024 | £17,761 | £49,263 |
| £65,000 | £55,900 | £7,714 | £72,714 | £19,269 | £53,445 |
| £70,000 | £60,900 | £8,404 | £78,404 | £20,777 | £57,627 |
| £75,000 | £65,900 | £9,094 | £84,094 | £22,285 | £61,809 |
| £80,000 | £70,900 | £9,784 | £89,784 | £23,793 | £65,991 |
| £90,000 | £80,900 | £11,164 | £101,164 | £26,809 | £74,356 |
| £100,000 | £90,900 | £12,544 | £112,544 | £29,824 | £82,720 |
| £110,000 | £100,900 | £13,924 | £123,924 | £32,840 | £91,084 |
| £120,000 | £110,900 | £15,304 | £135,304 | £35,856 | £99,449 |

As a general rule of thumb, for most small companies with a marginal CT rate of 26.5%, the total after-tax cost of employing someone is roughly 80% of their quoted salary: a little more for higher salaries, a little less for low paid employees.

For example, we know the total cost for most small companies of paying someone a salary of £60,000 is £49,263, which is 82.1% of £60,000.

However, the company will enjoy less tax relief on the salary if its marginal rate of CT is lower, for example 25%, or partly only 19% (see Section 2.1). This will, in turn, increase the overall cost of paying the salary.

For example, let's say your company would enjoy CT relief at 25% on a salary of £60,000 and the accompanying employer's National Insurance of £7,024. The CT relief would now be £67,024 x 25% = £16,756.

Hence, the salary will effectively cost the company £50,268: £67,024 – £16,756. The true cost of the salary is now 83.8% of the £60,000 quoted salary.

At the other end of the scale, smaller companies will only enjoy CT relief at 19% on some or all of their salary costs, including cases where the payment of the salary itself reduces the company's taxable profits below £50,000.

For example, let's say your company has taxable profits of £100,000 before paying a salary of £60,000 to an employee. As we know, including the accompanying employer's National Insurance bill creates a total cost of £67,024. This will enjoy CT relief as follows:

| | |
|---|---|
| First £50,000 @ 26.5% | £13,250 |
| Remaining £17,024 @ 19% | £3,235 |
| Total | £16,485 |

This time, the salary will effectively cost the company £50,539 (£67,024 – £16,485) and the true cost of the salary is 84.2% of the £60,000 quoted salary.

So, with a few variations for different sizes of company and different salary levels, salaries generally have a true cost in the range of 80% to 85% of the quoted amount.

That cost comes down a little in some cases for lower salary levels of less than £25,000, or where the employment allowance or other exemptions are available (as examined below). However, it will rarely be less than 75%, and never less than 73.5%.

In theory, the cost could be up to 90% for a small company paying CT at 19%, although the employment allowance and other exemptions will generally restore the position to a similar cost range to other companies.

But all this is before taking account of another cost the Government has chosen to burden employers with: compulsory pension contributions. We will examine the impact of this additional tax in Section 6.3. (At Taxcafe, we regard any compulsory payment as a tax!)

### Young Employees
Employers don't always have to pay National Insurance on employees' salaries. There is generally no employer's National Insurance on salaries paid to any employee *under* age 21 or apprentices *under* age 25. In both cases the National Insurance exemption applies on salaries up to the £50,270 upper earnings limit.

So, if you employ someone who is 19 years old and pay them £15,000 per year there will not be any employer's National Insurance payable. If you pay the same salary to someone who is 30 years old there will be a National Insurance bill of £814.

The exemption is not lost if the employee is paid more than £50,270, but employer's National Insurance is payable on the excess. Hence, if one of these younger employees were paid £51,000, employer's National Insurance would only be payable on the final £730, resulting in a total bill of just £101.

### Older Employees
If an employee is over state pension age the employee does not have to pay National Insurance on their salary. This does NOT extend to employer's National Insurance, which continues to be payable on the salaries of older employees.

### Special Cases
There are also special exemptions for former members of the armed services in their first year of civilian employment and for employees based in Freeports or Investment Zones.

## Employment Allowance

As stated earlier, most businesses qualify for the employment allowance, which provides a £5,000 annual saving in employer's National Insurance.

### *Example*

*Chicken Brothers Ltd employs four warehouse workers (all aged 21 or over) and pays them each £20,000 per year. Thanks to the employment allowance the company has to pay just £1,016 in employer's National Insurance:*

| | |
|---|---|
| *£20,000 – £9,100 = £10,900 x 13.8% =* | |
| *£1,504 x 4 =* | *£6,016* |
| *Less employment allowance* | *£5,000* |
| *Total* | *£1,016* |

*(Note, this example ignores any National Insurance payable on the directors' own salaries: see Section 6.4.)*

This example shows that a company with just a few low paid employees will pay only a small amount of employer's National Insurance, possibly none at all in some cases.

### Other Employment Allowance Rules

The employment allowance is not available to 'one man band' companies where a single director is the only employee. HMRC interprets this rule as meaning there must be at least one other employee paid in excess of the secondary threshold.

The employment allowance is only given to employers whose National Insurance bill was less than £100,000 in the previous tax year. Fortunately, most small companies are unaffected and can continue enjoying this tax break.

The allowance can only be used against Class 1 National Insurance and not against Class 1A National Insurance. Class 1A is due on most taxable benefits provided to employees, e.g. company cars.

If your company belongs to a group of companies, only one can claim the allowance. If your business runs multiple PAYE schemes, the allowance can only be claimed against one scheme.

The allowance is claimed as part of the payroll process. The full £5,000 can be claimed in month one of the tax year if your employer's Class 1 National Insurance exceeds £5,000 per month.

You can start claiming the allowance after the tax year has started and make a catch-up claim which can also be offset against your other PAYE costs.

If you claim the allowance at the end of the tax year and your remaining PAYE costs are not sufficient to use the entire allowance, the unclaimed balance can be carried forward to the next tax year.

### Connected Companies

A company cannot claim the employment allowance if a connected company already claims it. The definition of a connected company for this purpose is the same as the definition of an associated company for CT purposes (which we will cover in detail in Section 12.3): they are effectively one and the same thing.

For example, if you own all the shares in two companies you will only be entitled to one employment allowance, even if the two companies are completely separate businesses, with separate premises and staff. If the company that claims the employment allowance has employer's Class 1 National Insurance of less than £5,000, the balance cannot be claimed by the other company.

Another important issue arises for married couples (or other close relatives). For example, if you own all the shares in company X and your spouse owns all the shares in company Y, your spouse's holding in company Y is attributed to you and you are treated as controlling company X and Y, as is your spouse.

However, in this case, the two companies will only be treated as connected companies if there is substantial commercial interdependence between them. If the two companies are completely unrelated, two employment allowances can be claimed. If there is substantial commercial interdependence between the companies then only one allowance can be claimed.

This arises because spouses, close relatives, and certain other persons are classed as your associates. We will cover the definition of associates, as well as substantial commercial interdependence, in detail in Section 12.3.

### National Insurance Saving Strategies

Once the company's £5,000 employment allowance has been used up there are a few things it can do to cut its National Insurance bill. Some of these strategies will not always be practical or work in all businesses:

### Employ Low Earners

It is cheaper from a National Insurance perspective to employ two people earning, say, £25,000 each, instead of one person earning £50,000.

This is because there is no National Insurance payable on the first chunk of every employee's salary (£9,100 at present). So, the more employees you have, the more tax-free chunks you can enjoy!

The total maximum saving is £1,256 this year for each additional employee: £9,100 x 13.8% = £1,256

Similar savings can be enjoyed every year.

Of course, it may not be practical to replace one high earning (high skilled) employee with two or more low earning (low skilled) employees.

Nevertheless, when the founders of a company start employing people to take on some of the duties they currently perform, it may be a good idea to employ people to take on the less skilled tasks first (e.g. admin, secretarial, customer service). This could result in a lower wage bill and lower National Insurance costs.

From the standpoint of saving National Insurance it may also pay to hire part-time workers wherever possible.

For example, hiring one person to work mornings and another person to work afternoons could result in a lower National Insurance bill than hiring one person to work the whole day.

### Employ Youngsters

It is more tax efficient to employ under 21s because there will be no employer's National Insurance payable on their wages.

For example, if a business employs ten under 21s earning £20,000 each per year, it will save £15,042 in employer's National Insurance this year.

Of course, 20 year olds eventually become 21 year olds, so this strategy will only generate long-term savings in a business with high staff turnover, i.e. where a fresh batch of under 21s is continually recruited!

### *Hire in Outside Help Where Possible*

The simplest way to avoid employer's National Insurance (and some of the other responsibilities that come with employing people) is to have fewer employees.

For some business tasks it may be cheaper to hire in outside help from other business owners occasionally instead of employing people.

These days it's possible to find people all over the world who can perform various tasks for your business. There are many websites where self-employed individuals offer their services for very modest fees.

While some tasks may have to be carried out on site at your company's premises (if the company has premises), there may be many other tasks that can be carried out remotely. After all, remote working is all the rage these days!

If you find someone in another country to do work for your company no UK employment taxes are payable, even if that person is an employee of your company.

However, employment taxes may be payable in the country where the employee lives. The last thing any small company wants is to become subject to payroll taxes and compliance regulations in another country, with all the additional time and cost this could entail.

If you use a self-employed person in the UK to do some work for your company there are also no employment taxes payable.

The idea here is that you hire genuine third-party businesses. What we're not talking about is hiring people who are for all intents and purposes employees of your company and pretending they are self-employed!

In some cases, contractors are treated as 'disguised employees' and Income Tax and National Insurance is payable on their income as if they had earned employment income.

Contractors will often operate through their own companies. If a contractor would be regarded as an employee of your company, were it not for the fact that they provide their services through their own company, a set of rules known as IR35 applies. This results in Income Tax and National Insurance being payable on the contractor company's income.

From April 2021, private sector employers are responsible for deciding whether the IR35 rules apply to a contractor's pay and have to deduct the correct Income Tax and National Insurance and pay it over to HMRC.

The good news is that small companies are exempt from this rule. Small companies are defined in the Companies Act as those that meet at least two of the following conditions:

- Turnover not more than £10.2 million
- Balance sheet total (total assets before deducting liabilities) not more than £5.1 million
- Not more than 50 employees

In summary, it is possible for small company owners to use self employed people to do work for the company and no employer's National Insurance will be payable.

### *Salary Sacrifice Schemes*
Some payments made to employees are exempt from National Insurance. The most valuable one is employer pension contributions.

These days employers are forced to contribute to their employees' pensions. The compulsory contributions are relatively modest but there's nothing to stop the employer and employee agreeing to a pay cut in return for a bigger employer pension contribution.

Every extra £1,000 paid into the employee's pension pot instead of taken as salary will save the employer £138 in National Insurance.

In recent times the Government has clamped down on most salary sacrifice arrangements, which allow employees to give up salary in return for benefits-in-kind that are taxed more favourably. Fortunately, pension contributions are one of a handful of benefits that are not affected: see Section 7.1 for details.


## 6.3    AUTO-ENROLMENT PENSIONS

A system of compulsory pensions, known as 'auto-enrolment', forces employers to enrol nearly all their staff into a pension and make contributions. Whether you view this as good or bad probably depends on your political leanings... and whether you are an employer or employee. Our view is that many small business owners cannot afford to save for their own retirements let alone those of their entire workforce.

### Which Employees Are Exempt?

Only employees earning more than £10,000 and aged from 22 to state pension age need to be *automatically* enrolled into a pension. However, some older and younger employees and those who earn less than £10,000 also have workplace pension rights:

- If an employee earns less than £6,240 this year (2024/25) they don't need to be automatically enrolled but the employer has to give them access to a pension if they request it and they are aged 16 to 74. However, the employer is not required to contribute.
- If an employee earns between £6,240 and £10,000 and their age is between 16 and 74 they don't need to be automatically enrolled but do have the right to opt in. If they do decide to join the pension scheme the employer will have to contribute as well.

- If an employee earns more than £10,000 but is aged 16 to 21 or between state pension age and 74 they don't need to be automatically enrolled but do have the right to opt in. If they do decide to join the pension scheme the employer will have to contribute as well.

### Company Directors

According to the Pension Regulator a company does not have any automatic-enrolment duties when:

- It has just one director, with no other staff
- It has a number of directors, none of whom has an employment contract, with no other staff
- It has a number of directors, only one of whom has an employment contract, with no other staff

A contract of employment does not have to be in writing. However, according to the Pension Regulator, if there is no written contract of employment, or other evidence of an intention to create an employer/worker relationship between the company and the director, it will not argue that an employment contract exists.

If a director does not have an employment contract they are always exempt from automatic enrolment. If a director has a contract of employment and there are other people working for the company with an employment contract, they are not exempt.

Depending on their age and earnings, they may qualify for automatic enrolment but the company can decide whether to automatically enrol them into a pension.

However, the director has the right to join a pension scheme at any time and the company cannot refuse to enrol them (although in practice this issue will not arise in most owner-managed companies).

If the company decides not to enrol any employed director who is eligible for automatic enrolment, and it has no other eligible staff, it does not need to set up a pension scheme. However, it will need to make a 'declaration of compliance'.

## Pension Schemes
A state-sponsored pension scheme called NEST (National Employment Savings Trust) is available for employers who do not have their own pension scheme. You can use another scheme if you prefer but it must be a qualifying scheme. The pension provider will be able to tell you if the scheme is qualifying or not.

## Employees Can Opt Out
Employees must be automatically enrolled into a pension scheme but employers can postpone this by up to three months. The three month period is designed to make life easier for businesses that employ lots of temporary and seasonal workers.

It is important to note that employees can opt out of compulsory pensions if they choose. Some employees may choose to opt out because they don't want to make any pension contributions themselves. The contributions employees have to make are higher than the contributions employers have to make.

Some employees may choose to spend their earnings rather than save for the future, especially those in their twenties, thirties and forties, faced with paying off student loans, climbing the housing ladder and bringing up children.

Note, however, employers are prohibited from inducing or encouraging employees to opt out. Any decision to opt out must be taken freely by the staff member without influence from the employer. If the employee does freely opt out the employer doesn't have to make any contributions.

Employers have to automatically re-enrol eligible employees back into the pension scheme roughly every three years.

## How Much Do Pensions Cost?
Generally speaking, contributions are a percentage of 'qualifying earnings' (see below). The total minimum contribution is 8% with at least 3% coming from the employer.

The total minimum contribution can be paid by the employer but in practice many small firms will insist that the employee makes up the required balance. This means that employees will typically contribute 5% and employers will typically contribute 3%.

Employees' contributions enjoy basic-rate tax relief, which means 4% will come from them personally and the extra 1% will be added by the taxman in the form of basic-rate tax relief.

**Qualifying Earnings**
Contributions are not based on the employee's total earnings but instead on a chunk of their earnings.

The lower and upper thresholds for 2024/25 are £6,240 and £50,270 respectively. What this means is that pension contributions are typically based on earnings of up to £44,030 (£50,270 - £6,240).

For example, if an employee earns £20,000 the employer has to make a contribution of: £20,000 – £6,240 = £13,760 x 3% = £413.

If an employee earns £75,000 the employer has to make a contribution of: £50,270 – £6,240 = £44,030 x 3% = £1,321.

Note, contributions do not have to be made on earnings above £50,270. So once the employee's earnings exceed £50,270 the employer's compulsory contribution is capped at £1,321 this year.

Table B shows the total net cost of employer pension contributions at various salary levels. Pension contributions are a tax-deductible expense so the true net cost is less than the actual contribution.

For example, for an employee earning £50,270 or more, the required employer contribution is £1,321, but this will attract CT relief of up to £350 (at 26.5%), so the true net cost may be just £971 (although this depends on the company's marginal CT rate: see Section 2.1). This is the maximum compulsory pension contribution your company has to make at present for any employee.

Table B also reveals that the total net cost is far less than the 3% headline rate. For example, for an employee earning £20,000 it could be just 1.52% (£303/£20,000).

## TABLE B
## Total Net Cost of Pension Contributions 2024/25

| Salary | Pension Contribution | CT Relief @ 26.5% | Actual Cost |
|---|---|---|---|
| £15,000 | £263 | £70 | £193 |
| £20,000 | £413 | £109 | £303 |
| £25,000 | £563 | £149 | £414 |
| £30,000 | £713 | £189 | £524 |
| £35,000 | £863 | £229 | £634 |
| £40,000 | £1,013 | £268 | £744 |
| £45,000 | £1,163 | £308 | £855 |
| £50,000 | £1,313 | £348 | £965 |
| £50,270+ | £1,321 | £350 | £971 |

As usual, where your company has a lower marginal CT rate, the actual cost will be slightly higher. However, even at the lowest CT rate of 19%, the actual cost of the £413 contribution for an employee earning £20,000 is still only £335, or 1.68%.

Table C shows the actual net cost of various salaries and includes the salary itself, employer's National Insurance and compulsory pension contributions and the reduction thanks to CT relief at 26.5%. For example, if you pay someone a salary of £30,000, the actual net cost (the amount of money that will flow out of the company's bank account) is £24,694:

| | |
|---|---|
| Salary | £30,000 |
| Employer's National Insurance | £2,884 |
| Employer's pension contributions | £713 |
| Total | £33,597 |
| Less: CT relief @ 26.5% | £8,903 |
| Actual net cost | £24,694 |

Of course, if the company's marginal rate of CT is lower than 26.5%, it will enjoy less tax relief and the net cost of the salary will be greater. For example, if the company enjoys only 19% tax relief on the entire salary cost, the total net cost will increase to £27,214.

## TABLE C
## Actual Net Cost of Salaries 2024/25

| Salary | Employer NI | Pension Contribution | Total Cost | CT Relief | Actual Cost |
|---|---|---|---|---|---|
| £15,000 | £814 | £263 | £16,077 | £4,260 | £11,817 |
| £20,000 | £1,504 | £413 | £21,917 | £5,808 | £16,109 |
| £25,000 | £2,194 | £563 | £27,757 | £7,356 | £20,401 |
| £30,000 | £2,884 | £713 | £33,597 | £8,903 | £24,694 |
| £35,000 | £3,574 | £863 | £39,437 | £10,451 | £28,986 |
| £40,000 | £4,264 | £1,013 | £45,277 | £11,998 | £33,279 |
| £45,000 | £4,954 | £1,163 | £51,117 | £13,546 | £37,571 |
| £50,000 | £5,644 | £1,313 | £56,957 | £15,094 | £41,863 |
| £55,000 | £6,334 | £1,321 | £62,655 | £16,604 | £46,051 |
| £60,000 | £7,024 | £1,321 | £68,345 | £18,111 | £50,234 |
| £65,000 | £7,714 | £1,321 | £74,035 | £19,619 | £54,416 |
| £70,000 | £8,404 | £1,321 | £79,725 | £21,127 | £58,598 |
| £75,000 | £9,094 | £1,321 | £85,415 | £22,635 | £62,780 |
| £80,000 | £9,784 | £1,321 | £91,105 | £24,143 | £66,962 |
| £90,000 | £11,164 | £1,321 | £102,485 | £27,159 | £75,327 |
| £100,000 | £12,544 | £1,321 | £113,865 | £30,174 | £83,691 |
| £110,000 | £13,924 | £1,321 | £125,245 | £33,190 | £92,055 |
| £120,000 | £15,304 | £1,321 | £136,625 | £36,206 | £100,419 |

## Conclusion

Salaries, employer's National Insurance and employer pension contributions are all expenses that can be put through the company.

As a general rule of thumb, for companies that enjoy 26.5% CT relief, the actual after-tax cost of employing someone is usually around 80% to 84% of their quoted salary.

For example, if you employ someone on a salary of £40,000, the actual net cost (the amount that will ultimately flow out of the company's bank account) is £33,279, which is 83.2% of £40,000.

For companies with a lower marginal CT rate, the cost is slightly higher. For example, for a company that enjoys 25% tax relief, the after-tax cost of employing someone is usually around 82% to 85.5% of their quoted salary.

For smaller companies paying CT at just 19%, the cost could theoretically be as much as 92%, but this will generally be reduced due to the employment allowance and other reliefs (see Section 6.2), and the fact these companies usually only pay lower levels of salary.

## 6.4 PAYING DIRECTORS

We mentioned the tax-saving potential of taking a salary out of your company in Section 5.2. It's now worth returning to the subject in the light of some of the issues covered in this chapter.

### Is the Employment Allowance Available?
There are some situations where the employment allowance may be used to reduce or eliminate the employer's National Insurance on the directors' own salaries. These include where the company:

- Doesn't have any employees other than the directors
- Has only a few low paid employees
- Has only one or two moderately well-paid employees (see below for some examples)
- Only, or mostly, employs people aged under 21 or apprentices aged under 25

Unfortunately, however, the employment allowance is not available to 'one man band' companies where there is just one director who is the only employee.

According to HMRC guidance, the employment allowance also cannot be claimed if there are other employees BUT the director's salary is the only one on which employer's National Insurance is payable. This is to prevent directors of one-man band companies employing friends or family and paying them a token amount in order to claim the employment allowance for their own salaries.

At least one of the additional employees must be paid more than the secondary threshold. For example, a company that employs a seasonal worker who earns above the secondary threshold in a week (£175 for 2024/25) will be eligible for the employment allowance for the whole tax year.

The second employee can be another director (e.g. your spouse) provided both directors' salaries exceed the annual secondary threshold (£9,100 for 2024/25 or pro rata if the directorship begins after the tax year has started).

If circumstances change during the tax year and the director becomes the only employee paid above the National Insurance threshold, the employment allowance can still be claimed for that tax year.

If a company with just one director who earns less than the National Insurance threshold employs just one other person (not a director), the company can claim the employment allowance if the employee earns more than the National Insurance threshold.

It should be pointed out that several expert commentators, including the Institute of Chartered Accountants, believe HMRC has not interpreted the law correctly and that it should be possible to claim the employment allowance even if the second employee receives a small salary on which no employer's National Insurance is payable. However, to be safe and avoid problems, it may nevertheless be sensible to pay a second employee a salary slightly higher than the National Insurance threshold.

See Section 6.2 for other restrictions on the employment allowance applying to large companies.

**How Far Does the Employment Allowance Go?**
To pay a single director a salary equal to the Income Tax personal allowance (£12,570 this year) free from employer's National Insurance, you only need £479 of the employment allowance to be available after any amounts used on other employees' wages.

Looked at another way, the director's salary will be free of employer's National Insurance if no more than £4,521 of the employment allowance is used on other wages (that would cover two employees paid £25,480 each).

For two directors taking a salary of £12,570 each, you will need £958 of the employment allowance to be available to fully cover the employer's National Insurance arising. In this case you could have two other employees being paid up to £23,745 each, or a single employee being paid up to £38,390.

Remember, you can effectively discount employees aged under 21 and apprentices under 25, unless they're paid more than £50,270.

Where none of the employment allowance has been used on salaries paid to other employees, two directors could take salaries of up to £27,216 each in 2024/25 free from employer's National Insurance.

A single director with one other employee being paid just a bit more than the £9,100 secondary threshold can take a salary of around £45,000 free from employer's National Insurance.

## Negative Cost Salaries

As discussed in Section 5.2, where a salary has an overall negative cost, it is always worth taking, even if the director doesn't need the cash. Where a shareholder/director has no taxable income from outside their company, a salary up to the personal allowance (currently £12,570) will be free from both Income Tax and *employee's* National Insurance. Salaries at this low level can easily be justified for any working director and hence will nearly always attract CT relief.

*Employer's* National Insurance at 13.8% may be due on any salary in excess of the £9,100 secondary National Insurance threshold but, where this is the only cost, it is outweighed by CT relief.

For a salary of £12,570, the maximum National Insurance cost, where none of the employment allowance is available, will be just £479 (£12,570 – £9,100 = £3,470 x 13.8%), but the CT relief will amount to at least £2,479 (at 19%). Hence, where the director has no income from outside the company, there is an overall negative cost, or benefit, of at least £2,000. This benefit will be increased if the company's CT rate is higher (see Section 2.1), or it has any spare employment allowance available.

For directors over state pension age (who are exempt from employee's National Insurance), any salary covered by the employment allowance will be *completely free* of National Insurance. This means, if the director is a basic rate taxpayer, and the company has a marginal CT rate of 25% or 26.5%, any salary covered by the employment allowance will have an overall negative cost.

In practice, however, most shareholder/directors need, or want, to take more income out of their company than the negative cost or tax-free amounts available. This can sometimes alter the question of what represents the most optimal, or tax-efficient salary.

## Optimal Salaries for Directors

A salary of £12,570 is usually most tax-efficient for directors who do not have any taxable income from outside the company. This is generally the same whether employer's National Insurance is payable on the salary or not and, as discussed above, will yield an overall net saving of at least £2,000.

But, where a director either has other income from outside the company (for example rental properties), or will have total taxable income (including dividends from their own company) of more than £100,000, a small saving can often be achieved by taking a salary of £9,100 instead.

Conversely, there are also a number of exceptions where it is tax efficient to pay yourself a salary *higher* than the £12,570 personal allowance (including the additional negative cost salaries for directors over state pension age discussed above). For more information on these special cases, see the Taxcafe guide *Salary versus Dividends*.

### The National Minimum Wage

The national minimum wage and living wage do not apply to directors unless they have an employment contract with the company (this is pretty rare for small company owner/directors). Hence, you will not generally be forced to pay yourself more salary than is optimal for tax purposes.

### Other Ways to Take Money Out of Your Company

Dividends can only be paid if the company's accounts show there are profits available to distribute (even if the profits were made in previous years).

Companies that do not have distributable profits cannot pay dividends, but the owners may still be able to extract money from the company without resorting to paying salaries.

One option may be to borrow money from your company. However, it is important to remember, as a director, you have a duty to act in the company's best interests. One of the main aspects of that duty is to ensure the company remains solvent, so you must bear this in mind before you borrow any money from the company.

As we saw in Section 4.3, a loan may have tax consequences for both the director and the company. However, few things are more unattractive from a tax standpoint than a fully taxed salary payment subject to Income Tax, employee's National Insurance, and employer's National Insurance.

For a more detailed examination of this subject see the Taxcafe guide *Salary versus Dividends*. See also Section 5.4 regarding interest payments and Section 10.4 regarding rent.

## 6.5    PAYING FAMILY

Many small companies are owned and run by a couple. Where there are two shareholder/directors, all the same considerations regarding paying salary, dividends, etc, apply equally to both of them. You can, of course, double the amounts taken out and double any overall tax savings that arise.

For those not already in this situation, you can easily make your spouse, partner, or adult children directors of the company. Shares can also be transferred to your spouse free from CGT. In other cases, there may be a CGT cost, as the transfer will be deemed to take place at market value for CGT purposes.

However, where the company is a trading company, the gains arising can usually be 'held over', thus deferring any CGT until the transferee disposes of the shares themselves.

To be a trading company for this purpose, the company's underlying business must not include any substantial element of non-trading activities. This is usually taken to mean non-trading activities amount to no more than 20% of the company's activities. For more information on passing company shares to children, see the Taxcafe guide *How to Save Inheritance Tax*.

Dividends can be paid to any shareholder (according to the rights attaching to their shares) as long as the company has sufficient distributable profits. Such arrangements are not usually challenged by HMRC except where a complex share structure is put in place.

Even then, careful planning can usually avoid any problems: generally the key is to ensure shares carry rights to assets as well as income.

For any family member, a salary must be justified by the work the recipient carries out for the company. Subject to this crucial point, the considerations for a spouse, partner, or adult child are the same as we have looked at previously in this chapter.

### Younger Children
Children generally need to be at least 13 or 14 (depending on the local authority) before they can legally be employed.

Salaries paid to children under 16 are exempt from all classes of National Insurance.

As usual, payments made to family members must be justified by the work they do and there are restrictions on the hours and type of work children under school leaving age can do.

Children aged at least 13 or 14 (depending on local by-laws), but under school leaving age may do 'light work' (e.g. office work) provided it does not interfere with their education or affect their health and safety.

Certain types of work (e.g. factory work) are prohibited and any business employing children under school leaving age should obtain a permit from the local authority.

Subject to these points, children still attending school can work up to two hours most days. On Saturdays and weekdays during school holidays this increases to eight hours (five hours if under 15). Working hours must fall between 7 am and 7 pm and are subject to an overall limit of 12 hours per week during term time or 35 hours during holidays (25 hours if under 15). The child must also have at least two weeks uninterrupted holiday each calendar year.

16 and 17 year olds over compulsory school age can generally work up to 40 hours per week and can do most types of work, although some additional health and safety regulations apply. However, it should be noted that in England children must remain in some form of education or training until they reach 18 years old. This could be through part-time education or training while they are working; or through an apprenticeship.

In essence, therefore, you can generally employ any of your children aged 13 or more and pay them a salary which is deductible from the company's taxable profits.

**How Much Can You Pay?**
A salary paid to a child must be justified by the amount of work they actually do for the company. If you employed your 15-year old daughter to answer your office phone one hour each evening, you could not justify paying her a salary of £30,000, but a salary of, say, £1,500 should be acceptable.

If your children are below the compulsory school leaving age, the national minimum wage does not apply. The national minimum wage applies to employees aged 16 to 20 and the living wage applies to those aged 21 and over.

While there is an exemption for relatives living in the employer's household, this does not apply where the employer is a company, so the national minimum wage or living wage continues to apply to family members working for your company (unless they are directors: see Section 6.4).

The hourly rates applying from April 2024 are as follows:

- £11.44    Living wage, 21 and over
- £8.60    age 18-20
- £6.40    age 16-17
- £6.40    apprentices under 19 or in their first year

Subject to the national minimum wage (where it applies), there is no fixed rate of pay which applies to children. The rate paid must, however, be commercially justified: in other words, no more than you would pay to a non-family member with the same level of experience and ability in the job. For a child below school leaving age with no experience carrying out unskilled work, the national minimum wage for 16 to 17 year olds (currently £6.40 per hour) represents a good guide. Where the child has some experience, or the role requires some skill, a higher rate will often be justified.

Assuming a rate of, say, £8 per hour can be justified, the maximum salaries a child could earn (based on an estimated 13 weeks of school holidays per year) would be approximately as follows:

| | |
|---|---|
| 13/14 year olds: | £5,944 |
| 15+ but still school age: | £6,824 |
| Over school age but under 18: | £16,640 |

Subject to this (and the national minimum wage), a salary of up to £12,570 could be paid tax-free to any child aged under 21 with no other income. For those aged 16 or more, any salary in excess of £12,570 will be subject to 8% *employee's* National Insurance (as well as Income Tax, of course).

For children aged under 21, *employer's* National Insurance at 13.8% will only be payable on any salary in excess of £50,270.

**How Much Could You Save?**
Despite all the restrictions and formalities involved, paying your children tax-deductible wages is a great deal better than giving them pocket money out of your own after-tax income.

### Example

*Ian is a higher rate taxpayer. He owns Fleming Publications Ltd, which makes annual profits of around £150,000 and draws up accounts to 31ˢᵗ March each year.*

*Ian has three children: Jimmy, born in July 2005, currently at university; Vesper, born in 2007, currently at sixth form college studying for her A levels; and Felix, born in 2010, who is still at school.*

*Previously, in 2023/24, Ian was giving £150 per week to Jimmy to help with rent and food, pocket money of £60 per week to Vesper, and £40 per week to Felix. This totalled £250 per week, or £13,000 per year. To fund this expenditure, Ian had to take additional dividends out of Fleming Publications Ltd.*

*If Ian carries on the same way in 2024/25, he will need to take additional dividends of £19,623, which will cost him £6,623 in Income Tax, to leave him with the net sum of £13,000 he needs.*

*Instead, Ian offers to pay each of the children 50% more if they work at Fleming Publications Ltd during their holidays. They all go for it and the total wages he pays them amount to £19,500. This saves the company £5,168 in CT (at 26.5%) and also means Ian saves £6,623 in Income Tax: a total saving of £11,791, which more than covers the extra £6,500 paid to the children.*

*There is no National Insurance on the children's wages since they all earn less than the National Insurance primary threshold and are all aged under 21.*

In summary, this strategy has produced three major benefits:

- Tax savings totalling £11,791
- The children are all 50% better off
- Ian has got his children to do some work for his company

That last one may seem a little tongue in cheek, but not only is it saving tax now, it may help with succession planning in the future.

Payments to children aged 16 or more will need to be timed carefully to ensure the National Insurance primary threshold is not exceeded in any of the relevant pay periods (see Section 6.2).

# Chapter 7

# Tax-Free Benefits

## 7.1 THE BENEFITS OF BENEFITS

A company can give its employees (including the directors) various benefits-in-kind that are either tax free or taxed less heavily than regular salary payments.

This includes any of the shareholder/directors' family who work for the company, subject to the overriding principle that the total value of the recipient's pay package must be justified by the work they do for the company.

To understand what sort of tax savings are possible you have to remember that a salary payment potentially suffers three different taxes, two paid by the employee and one paid by the company:

- Income Tax
- Employee's National Insurance
- Employer's National Insurance

Some benefits-in-kind are exempt from ALL three taxes, so there are significant savings to be had by both the employee and company.

With other benefits-in-kind, the employee has to pay Income Tax and the company has to pay employer's National Insurance, but there is no *employee's* National Insurance payable. So most benefits-in-kind provide at least one tax saving: employee's National Insurance.

There may be further savings in the form of group discounts. If an employer has a significant number of employees, it may be possible to negotiate discounts with suppliers of employee benefits.

Like salary payments, the cost of providing benefits-in-kind to employees is almost always a tax-deductible expense for the company.

The deductibility of the expense is rarely an issue when the expense is of a 'revenue' nature. This is because it is viewed as part of the employee's remuneration package and therefore incurred wholly and exclusively for the purposes of the company's business.

When capital expenditure is involved, there may be a question mark over whether the company can obtain tax relief in the form of capital allowances.

The main tax issue in most cases, however, is whether the employee has to pay Income Tax and the company has to pay National Insurance on the value of the benefit.

One of the most heavily taxed benefits is company cars, although there are some important exceptions. Apart from cars provided to disabled employees, which we will look at in Section 7.6, we will leave company cars to one side in this chapter and take a detailed look at them in Chapter 9.

### Salary Sacrifice
Salary sacrifice arrangements (also known as optional remuneration arrangements) have allowed employees to give up salary in return for tax-free benefits.

The Government was concerned about the amount of money lost from these schemes and as a result the Income Tax and employer's National Insurance advantages of many salary sacrifice schemes have been removed.

Some benefits are not affected and continue to enjoy Income Tax and National Insurance relief. These include employer pension contributions, employer-provided pensions advice, employer-supported childcare, cycle to work schemes, and ultra low emission cars (although a small benefit in kind charge does apply to low emission and electric cars: see Sections 9.2 and 9.5).

Other benefits that would otherwise be exempt are subject to Income Tax and employer's National Insurance (but generally not employee's National Insurance) if provided under a salary sacrifice arrangement.

### The Premier League
Subject to the rules regarding salary sacrifice arrangements, there are a host of benefits that are exempt from both Income Tax and National Insurance, i.e. they are completely tax free. As the cost will usually also attract CT relief, these benefits are hugely beneficial.

The tax-free benefits are all subject to detailed rules of their own, which we will cover in the remainder of this chapter. They cover a bewildering array of different things. If there is any logic to them, it is that they either reflected Government policy at the time they were introduced, or follow long-standing practice; but it is still difficult to discern any sort of pattern. In some cases, you will be astounded that there was ever any need for an exemption, but you have to understand that HMRC are phenomenally petty and out to take every penny they can get from you and your employees.

**Missing the Net**

If a benefit isn't covered by one of the exemptions in Sections 7.2 to 7.32, it is probably subject to both Income Tax and employer's National Insurance, although employee's National Insurance can usually be avoided. Such benefits may still yield some savings and we will take a closer look at these in Section 7.33.

Sometimes, as an employer, you may prefer it if your employees are not directly taxed on a non-exempt benefit. We'll look at what to do in that situation in Section 7.34.

## 7.2    PENSION CONTRIBUTIONS

We saw in Section 6.3 that employers are forced to make pension contributions for their employees these days. The contributions required by law are fairly small, but there's nothing to stop the company making far bigger contributions, especially if the employees agree to sacrifice some salary in return.

Like salary payments, employer pension contributions are a tax-deductible expense for the company: however, pension contributions carry the advantage that there is no employer's National Insurance payable.

So, if a company makes a £1,000 pension contribution for an employee instead of paying them salary, this will typically save £138 in employer's National Insurance.

The employee will also save £420 Income Tax and National Insurance as a higher-rate taxpayer or £280 as a basic-rate taxpayer (from 6$^{th}$ April 2024).

The employee will eventually pay Income Tax when the money is withdrawn from the pension scheme but up to one quarter can be taken as a tax-free lump sum. Most people are basic-rate taxpayers when they retire and will pay no more than 20% tax on the remaining taxable part of their pension income.

With many salary sacrifice arrangements some or all of the employer's National Insurance saving is added to the employee's pension pot.

The employer doesn't necessarily lose out in this situation because the extra £138 can be seen as a free pay increase for the employee, paid for by the taxman!

Pension contributions are also a tax efficient way for directors to take money out of their own companies. As a higher-rate taxpayer, the total tax on £1,000 of pre-tax profit paid out as a dividend could be up to £513 (up to 26.5% CT plus 33.75% Income Tax on the balance). However, with a pension contribution, the whole £1,000 will go straight into the director's pension pot.

When the money is eventually withdrawn from the pension, one quarter can be taken as a tax-free lump sum and the rest may be taxed at no more than the 20% basic rate.

We'll take a more detailed look at pension contributions for directors in Section 11.4. For further information on salary sacrifice arrangements and directors' pension contributions, see the Taxcafe guide *Pension Magic*.

### 7.3    PENSIONS ADVICE

There is an exemption of £500 per tax year for employer-arranged pension advice. The exemption covers pension advice and general financial and tax advice relating to pensions.

The exemption is available if the employer pays for the advice or reimburses the employee.

The exemption is allowed if the advice is made available to employees generally or at a particular location. It is also available when the pensions advice is tailored to the employee's specific personal circumstances of nearing retirement either due to age or ill health.

### 7.4    WORKPLACE PARKING

There is no tax payable if a parking space is provided to a director or employee at or near their place of work.

Note, the exemption doesn't just cover parking at your workplace, i.e. a car park attached to the company's premises. It also covers parking spaces 'near' the employee's workplace.

The word 'near' is not defined in the legislation and HMRC will allow the exemption where parking facilities are within a reasonable distance. They will not deny the exemption simply because there is another car park nearer the employee's place of work.

Parking costs can be paid directly by the company or reimbursed.

The legislation does not mention any restriction of the exemption or any benefit in kind charge if the parking space is used for private purposes outside working hours (for example, shopping at the weekend).

## 7.5    LATE NIGHT TAXIS

A company can pay for a taxi to take an employee home with no benefit in kind charge arising if:

- The journey is from the employee's workplace to their home,
- The 'late working conditions' or the 'car-sharing failure conditions' are met, and
- The company provides late-night taxis no more than 60 times per tax year (if the limit is exceeded, that does not disqualify the first 60 journeys)

### The Late Working Conditions
The late working conditions are that:

- The employee is required to work later than usual and until at least 9pm
- This does not happen on a regular basis
- When the employee stops work public transport has ceased for the day or it would not be reasonable to expect the employee to use it
- The transport is by taxi or similar private road transport

### *The First Condition*
An office worker who normally works from 9am to 5pm, but is required by the boss to work late one evening until 10pm, will satisfy the first condition. If the employee decided *voluntarily* to work late, the condition would not be satisfied.

What about an employee whose contract says they must work from midday to 8pm but often works until 10pm? Such an employee has established a pattern of working late at night.

If their employer pays for a taxi to take them home one night when they work until after 9pm, but no later than 10pm (their established working pattern), the exemption will not apply because they are not working later than usual. But if one night they unusually worked until after 11pm the exemption would apply.

What about restaurant/pub workers, often expected to work later than 9pm? A restaurant employee who normally works until closing time at 10:30pm and is provided with a taxi home will not qualify for the exemption because it is usual for the employee to work until this time. However, if the employee is required one night to work until midnight this will satisfy the condition.

### The Second Condition

The second condition is that the employee works later than usual *irregularly*. This means there must not be an established pattern of working later than usual. An employee who works later than usual once a week will not satisfy the condition... even if the day of the week varies. An employee who works later than usual once a month also will not satisfy the condition.

An employee who normally works from 9am until 5pm, but is required to stay until after 9pm once a month to help with the company's payroll, cannot be provided with a tax-free taxi. The late night working is a regular part of their employment.

An IT expert who normally works from 9am until 5pm but is required to work until 11pm for several days to fix the company's new server satisfies the second condition and may therefore qualify for a late-night taxi. The late working is not a regular occurrence (as long as it's not likely to become a regular event).

### The Third Condition

The third condition is that by the time the employee stops work either public transport is not available or it would not be reasonable to expect the employee to use public transport.

It is a matter of fact whether public transport has stopped for the day. If more than one form of public transport is needed and one has ceased to be available, HMRC accepts that public transport is not available for the whole journey.

The second part of this condition is more vague and each case will depend on its own facts.

HMRC does not accept that a taxi can be provided solely because the employee has to travel in the dark or has had a long day and is tired or is travelling to an unmanned station or because public transport services are reduced.

Employers may consider some or all of these factors together but none is sufficient on its own to warrant a taxi.

HMRC accepts that reduced availability/reliability of public transport is a sufficient excuse if this means the journey time is significantly longer, for example if it involves an extra hour or more of travelling time.

The employer may also consider the employee's perception of personal safety when deciding whether it is reasonable to expect them to use public transport. However, for the exemption to apply there must be a significant difference from the normal situation where people continue to use public transport after 9pm.

### Record Keeping
The employer must have the necessary management checks in place and keep sufficient records to be able to show the late night working conditions set out in the legislation are satisfied in all cases.

### Failure of Car Sharing Arrangements
The exemption for journeys paid for by the employer applies if:
- The employee regularly travels to work with another employee in a shared car, and
- The car sharing arrangement is unavailable because of unforeseen and exceptional circumstances

Circumstances will be unforeseen only if the car sharing arrangement fails after the employees arrive at work, for example if the car breaks down at work, or if the driver has to leave during the day, leaving the other employees without transport to get home.

### In Summary
If all that leaves you feeling HMRC are mind-bogglingly petty and have little regard for taxpayers' personal safety, dignity, or just about anything else, we can only say, somewhat sympathetically, we agree!

### 7.6    TRANSPORT FOR DISABLED EMPLOYEES

No Income Tax charge arises when a disabled employee has the cost of their home to work travel paid for or reimbursed.

This exemption does not apply when a car is provided to a disabled employee for home to work travel. There is a separate exemption for that (see below).

A disabled employee is someone who has a physical or mental impairment that has a substantial and long-term adverse effect on their ability to carry out normal day to day activities. However, an employee who is able to carry out normal day-to-day activities, or is receiving treatment that alleviates or removes the effects of the disability, will not qualify for the exemption.

## Cars Provided to Disabled Employees

Normally employees have to pay an Income Tax benefit in kind charge when they are provided with a company car. However, if certain conditions are met, disabled employees are exempt from having to pay tax on the car or for fuel provided by their employer. The three conditions are:

- The car must be adapted for the employee's special needs or is an automatic if the employee can only drive an automatic because of their disability
- The car can only be used for business travel, ordinary commuting or travel to a place which falls within one of the training exemption provisions
- During the tax year the car is only used in accordance with these terms

If the conditions are not met the car and car fuel benefit will be taxed in the usual way (which is usually heavily).

## 7.7    INCIDENTAL OVERNIGHT EXPENSES

When an employee is away from home for at least one night on business the company can cover the cost of small amounts of personal expenditure, such as private telephone calls, newspapers and laundry.

Payment can be made in lots of different ways, for example the employee can use their own card and ask the employer to reimburse them, or the employee can use the company's credit card, cash or the company can pay the bill directly.

The maximum amount that can be paid is:

- £5 per night for UK business trips
- £10 per night for overseas business trips

If the maximum is exceeded the whole amount becomes taxable. The limit is applied to the whole trip and not to each night separately.

## 7.8    BICYCLES

Where employees use *their own* bicycles for business journeys the company can pay them 20p per mile tax free. This is fairly generous but excludes commuting from home to work.

Alternatively, the company can buy bicycles and safety equipment and lend them to the directors and other employees.

Bicycles include electrically assisted pedal cycles. Safety equipment includes things like helmets, bells, child safety seats, panniers, locks, pumps, repair kits and reflective clothing.

The company will be able to treat the cost as capital expenditure and qualify for 100% tax relief thanks to either the annual investment allowance or full expensing. For new cycles and equipment purchased before 1$^{st}$ April 2023, the 130% super-deduction may be available, provided the bike is simply provided to the employee and not leased or hired to them. See Chapter 8 for full details of capital allowances available to a company.

The benefit will also be exempt from Income Tax and National Insurance providing:

- The bicycles and equipment are available generally to all employees, and
- The employees use them mainly for 'qualifying journeys'

Bicycles don't have to be actually provided to every employee but the offer must be open to all employees to take up if they wish.

The company does not have to make bicycles available in exactly the same way to all employees. For example, the choice of model can be more restricted for some employees than for others.

Qualifying journeys are journeys between home and the workplace and between workplaces. They also include journeys on a normal working day from the workplace to shops and other amenities where the return journey is no more than 20 miles.

The bicycle can also be used for pleasure purposes, including by family members, providing this is not the main use of the bicycle.

Employees are not expected to keep detailed records of their journeys and HMRC will not challenge whether you are entitled to the exemption, unless there is clear evidence to suggest that less than half the use of the cycle or equipment is on qualifying journeys.

Note, to be tax exempt, the bicycle must be loaned and not given to the employee. This would make the benefit taxable.

### Salary Sacrifice

The company can simply buy bicycles and lend them to employees without adjusting their salaries.

Alternatively, the company can recover the cost through salary sacrifice. This is still tax efficient for the employees because the payments come out of their gross (before tax) earnings. The company also saves 13.8% National Insurance on the reduced salary payments.

Several companies such as Cyclescheme offer 'Cycle to Work' schemes that operate through a salary sacrifice arrangement.

When a company offers bikes through a salary sacrifice arrangement it may be subject to consumer credit legislation unless the total expenditure is less than £1,000 per employee.

However, it is possible to spend more than this and avoid the regulations by using suppliers who are authorised by the FCA (Financial Conduct Authority) to run the scheme for the company.

Any employee who cannot participate in the arrangement (for example, because sacrificing salary will take their income below the national living wage) will still need to be offered a bike without salary sacrifice. Otherwise the tax exemption will not be available to the other employees: to qualify for the exemption bikes must be available generally to all employees.

Although bicycles have to be offered to all employees, they don't have to be offered on the same terms. For example, employees participating in a salary sacrifice arrangement may be offered more expensive bicycles than those who are not.

There is also no requirement that all employees have access to a bike that is solely for their personal use. A pool of bikes can be made available to employees, as long as they are provided in sufficient numbers so that there is genuine availability.

Finally, please note that one complication with salary sacrifice arrangements is VAT. The salary sacrificed is regarded as consideration for the equipment and VAT is due on the amount of salary sacrificed.

## 7.9    WORK BUSES

No tax is payable by the employees if the company lays on a bus or minibus for travel between home and work. The exemption also covers trips from work to shops and other amenities as long as the journey is no more than 10 miles each way. To qualify for the exemption:

- The vehicle must be able to seat nine or more people
- The bus must be available to all employees
- The use of the service is nearly all by employees and their children

Employers can band together to provide a works bus service.

It's fine for children to use the bus to get to school and for employees to use the service to go shopping, as long as the main use of the service is to transport employees between home and work.

The company can also pay a subsidy to a public bus service so that the employees travel free or at a reduced cost, provided the service on that route is available to all employees.

## 7.10   MOBILE PHONES

Mobile phones are a tax-free benefit that can be provided to directors and employees. The exemption covers the phone itself, line rental, and the cost of private calls paid for by the employer on that phone.

The exemption is limited to one mobile phone per employee. Phones supplied to family members do not qualify, unless the family members are also employed by the company.

After some initial reluctance, HMRC now accepts smart phones are mobile phones and not computers. Thus, you can get your company to provide you with an iPhone, say, and this will not give rise to a taxable benefit. The company must retain ownership of the device, however.

The contract must be in the company's name, not your own, and the company must pay the bills directly. This may cause difficulty when you walk into the average high street phone shop.

Most sales staff have experience dealing with business customers who are sole traders, with contracts in their personal names, but are not used to dealing with small companies.

However, the sales staff will have business support teams they can call for advice and direction. You must stick to your guns and make it clear you are a limited company director, not a sole trader. You may have to bring in company documentation of various types, so don't be surprised if you end up making more than one visit to the shop!

The restriction of the exemption to one mobile does not alter the treatment of mobile phones provided solely for business use, which continue to be exempt as long as any private use is not significant.

Tablets and laptops are excluded from this exemption (but see Section 7.11).

## 7.11    EQUIPMENT AND SUPPLIES USED AT HOME

There is no Income Tax or National Insurance payable if the company provides directors and employees with equipment and supplies to use at home (or while travelling away from the office). The sole purpose must be to enable the director or employee to perform their duties and any private use must not be significant.

Not only is the benefit tax free in the hands of the directors and employees, the company will be able to claim tax relief on these expenses too.

The exemption would cover things like office furniture and equipment, stationery, office supplies, computers, laptops and tablets.

The exemption does not cover motor vehicles and, for the tycoons among us, yachts or helicopters.

Whether the staff member works at home full time or part time, the tax position is mostly the same.

The equipment has to be provided by the company: the exemption does not apply to reimbursements of employees' expenses or if the company pays invoices in the employee's name. The invoices/contracts must be in the employer's name.

Whether private use is not significant can be a bit of a grey area. However, HMRC's own manuals state it should be accepted private use is not significant where:

- The company clearly explains the circumstances in which private use can be made (for example in the employment contract or a signed statement setting out the company's policy), and
- Any decision by the company not to recover the cost of private use is a commercial decision (for example, based on the impractical nature of doing so) rather than a desire to reward the employee.

It is not necessary to keep detailed records of private use. The 'not significant' condition should not be based solely on the amount of time spent using equipment or services for private or business purposes. It should be considered in the context of the employee's duties and how necessary it is for them to have the equipment or services in order to do their job. Private use may even exceed business use.

The employer's sole reason for providing equipment or supplies must be to enable the employee to do their job, not to reward them. If there is a mixed motive, for example to enable the employee to do their job and so that the employee can use the equipment or service privately, the exemption will not apply.

### Example

*A company provides a computer to an employee who works at various clients' premises, so that she can log in each morning and download details of the jobs that need done each day. The computer is also used for online shopping and for other private purposes. The employer gave the employee the computer, not as a reward, but to download the work roster each day. This is an essential duty the employee has to carry out as part of her job and the sole reason the computer was provided. Private use of the computer is secondary, even though the time spent using the computer for private purposes exceeds the business use. Thus, private use is not significant and the exemption should apply.*

### Example

*A computer programmer who works for an internet company decides to work at home one day each week. It is not an essential part of her job to do this but the company agrees to this arrangement and provides a computer to use at her house. The computer is required to enable the employee to do her job and the sole reason it has been provided. It is therefore essential for work purposes. Even if the employee spends, say, the same amount of time using the computer for private purposes private use is still secondary to the primary purpose: to enable the employee to work from home once a week. Thus, the exemption should apply.*

### Example

*An employee who handles admin at an insurance broker is provided with a computer for private use at home. The employee is not required to work at home, although some work is done on the computer. Because the sole purpose for providing the computer was not for business purposes and private use is significant relative to business use, the exemption will not apply.*

If an employee buys home office equipment and the employer reimburses them, the amount reimbursed is taxable. There was a temporary relaxation of these rules for the 2020/21 and 2021/22 tax years, but this has now ceased to apply. However, there will be no charge where the employee continues to use equipment purchased during this period under the terms of the relaxation. This means the equipment must have been purchased for the sole purpose of enabling the employee to work from home because of the pandemic and the equipment would have been exempt if it had been provided directly by the employer. Any private use should not be significant and the benefit must have been made available to all employees that needed to work from home.

See also Section 7.19 regarding payments to employees for business use of their home and Section 10.7 for payments to directors.

### 7.12   MEDICAL TREATMENT

Medical treatment paid by the company that helps an employee return to work is tax free up to £500 per tax year per employee. The treatment must be recommended by a healthcare professional. According to HMRC, recommendations for treatment can be provided by either 'Fit for Work' (a Government service that has now been disbanded), or any employer-arranged occupational health service.

The employee must have been absent from work for at least 28 days due to ill health or injury. Alternatively, a healthcare professional must have assessed the employee as unfit to work for at least 28 days.

The employer can pay for the treatment directly or reimburse the employee.

### Medical Treatment Abroad

No tax liability arises when the company pays for, or reimburses the employee for, necessary medical treatment abroad, where the employee falls ill or suffers injury while working outside the UK. The exemption does not cover other household members.

The cost of providing insurance for overseas medical treatment is also covered by the exemption. (Medical insurance paid by the company is a tax-deductible expense, but directors or employees are normally taxed on the benefit when not covered by this exemption.)

## 7.13   MEDICAL CHECK UPS

The company can pay for one health screening and one medical check-up per year. To be eligible for the tax exemption, health screenings must be available to all employees. Medical check-ups must be available to either all employees or those who require one following a health screening.

A 'health screening' is an assessment to identify employees who might be at particular risk of ill-health.

A 'medical check-up' means a physical examination by a health professional to determine the employee's state of health. This exemption doesn't cover medical treatment (but see Section 7.12).

## 7.14   EYE TESTS AND GLASSES

Employers are obliged to pay for an eye test if an employee asks for one and uses display screen equipment at work. Display screen equipment includes pcs, laptops, tablets, smartphones etc. Employers must also pay for glasses if an employee needs special glasses prescribed for the distance the screen is viewed at.

The company can claim tax relief for the expense and there is no Income Tax or National Insurance payable.

If an ordinary prescription is suitable, employers do not have to pay for glasses.

If an employer pays for glasses that are not related to computer use, the cost must be declared on form P11D, the employee will pay Income Tax on the benefit, and the company will pay Class 1A National Insurance.

## 7.15   WELFARE COUNSELLING

Welfare counselling provided to employees and paid for by the company is exempt from tax, as long as it is available to all employees.

The types of counselling covered include: stress, problems at work, debt problems, alcohol and other drug dependency, career concerns, bereavement, equal opportunities, ill-health, sexual abuse, harassment and bullying and personal relationship difficulties.

The exemption does not cover any medical treatment, advice on finance or tax (other than debt counselling), advice on leisure or recreation, or legal advice.

### 7.16   HEARING AIDS & OTHER EQUIPMENT

Certain equipment, including hearing aids, can be provided tax free to employees with a disability. The company should be able to obtain CT relief for the purchase and there will be no Income Tax or National Insurance payable by either the employee or the company.

Hence it is much more tax efficient for a company owner to get their company to pay for their hearing aid instead of paying for it personally out of taxed salary or dividend income.

Anyone who has experience purchasing a top quality hearing aid privately will appreciate this is an extremely valuable concession: the cost can run to thousands of pounds.

The main purpose of providing the benefit must be to help the employee carry out their duties. However, no taxable benefit will arise even if there is significant private use of the equipment (which, of course, there will be in most cases).

The benefit must be made available to the company's employees generally on similar terms, although in most small companies there may be only one member of staff with hearing loss and that may be one of the directors.

### 7.17   GYMS & SPORTS FACILITIES

If a company gives an employee an extra £40 per month to pay for a gym membership the amount will be fully taxed as earnings.

If the company pays the gym membership, this will count as a taxable benefit in kind. This sort of arrangement may still carry some advantages, and we will take a closer look at the potential savings arising in Section 7.33.

If a company sets up its own gym, however (for example by putting a running and rowing machine, exercise bike and weight lifting equipment into a spare room at the office) the benefit will be tax free… providing a couple of conditions are met. It's not just gyms that qualify but also other qualifying sports and recreational facilities (for example, table tennis and pool tables). A qualifying facility is one that is:

- Available generally to all employees
- Not available generally to members of the public
- Used mainly by people who are employees or former employees and members of their families or households

Employers can group together to provide facilities and the benefit will still be exempt, as long as the facilities are not available to the public generally.

Sports facilities can be opened to a restricted section of the public (for example, those who live in the immediate vicinity) without the exemption necessarily being lost.

Some facilities are specifically excluded. These include:

- Use of mechanically propelled vehicles (boats, planes, cars). Sailing yachts do not fall into this category unless they also have an engine
- Holiday accommodation
- Facilities provided on domestic premises

### 7.18   LIFE INSURANCE

Many life insurance companies sell 'relevant life' policies. These are marketed as allowing your company to pay for directors' or employees' life insurance or terminal illness insurance with the following tax benefits:

- The premiums are typically viewed as a tax-deductible expense for the company as part of the employees' remuneration
- Payment of the premiums by the company does not give rise to a taxable benefit (i.e. no Income Tax or National Insurance)
- Any payout from the policy to your family will be free from Income Tax and typically not form part of your estate for Inheritance Tax purposes

These policies do not have any investment value ('surrender value').

There is some uncertainty as to whether the premiums will always be an allowable expense for the company. One insurer has a brochure with the bold title: 'Put Life Cover on Expenses'. However, most of the literature we have read is a bit vague on the deductibility of the premiums. For example, another insurer says in its sales literature:

*"So long as the company's accountant and the local inspector of taxes are happy that the premiums are 'wholly and exclusively for the purpose of trade' as part of the employee's remuneration, they can be treated as a trading expense. It's difficult to be precise about this because different inspectors and accountants have different views. And there's no HMRC precedent on this that we're aware of."*

This type of insurance should be distinguished from 'key person' insurance, where *the company* receives the payout on death, not your family. With key person insurance, the premiums are generally tax deductible, but the proceeds are taxed in the hands of the company.

According to HMRC guidance the premiums on key person policies will be an allowable expense if the sole purpose for taking out the policy is to protect against a loss of trading income and not to protect against a capital loss.

A non-trade purpose for taking out a key person policy might include taking out a policy for directors who are major shareholders, but not for other employees. Where the key person is a director whose death would affect the value of the company's shares, one of the purposes for taking out the policy may be to protect the value of the director's shares (a non-trade purpose).

### 7.19    EMPLOYEES WORKING FROM HOME

A company can make tax-free payments to directors and employees to cover the additional costs they incur from working at home under a 'homeworking arrangement'.

A homeworking arrangement is an arrangement between the company and the employee whereby the employee must regularly work at home.

The arrangement does not have to be in writing but this is advisable. The exemption is not granted if the employee works at home informally and not by arrangement with the employer (but see Section 10.7 regarding owner/directors working from home). It is not good enough to simply take work home in the evenings.

'Regularly' means frequently or following a pattern: for example, where an employee agrees to work one day each week at home.

Where an employee works from home, it is advisable to agree with the employee in writing that homeworking arrangements exist.

Additional costs would typically include increased gas and electricity costs and metered water, additional insurance costs and in some cases internet access charges.

Excluded are costs that would be the same whether or not the employee works at home, for example mortgage interest, rent and Council Tax.

Also excluded here are expenses that put the employee in a position to work from home, such as furniture or equipment, or building alterations (but see Section 7.11 regarding equipment).

With respect to internet access, if an employee who begins working from home is already paying for broadband there is no additional expense, so if the employer reimburses the expense, the amount paid will be taxable. But, if the employee does not already pay for internet access at home (unlikely in this day and age) and needs it to work from home under a homeworking arrangement, the cost of broadband would be an additional expense that the employer can reimburse tax free.

To avoid the hassle of reimbursing the precise additional expenses the employees incur it is possible for the company to pay a fixed amount of £26 per month to employees who work at home regularly, without having to justify the payment. The employee also does not have to keep records or receipts. The amount is £6 per week for employees paid weekly.

This amount can be paid even if the employee is part time and it is not necessary to reduce it if the employee does not work from home all the time.

The employer can pay more than this as long as the employer keeps records to show how the payments are calculated. This will require the employee to keep evidence of the additional costs.

**Employee Pays, Company Does Not Reimburse**

If the employer does not reimburse the employee's additional homeworking expenses, the employee may be able to claim them as a tax deduction against their earnings when they complete their personal tax return. This is only possible if the costs are incurred wholly, exclusively, and necessarily for the employee's work.

This is a far more stringent test and would typically only be met where the company does not have the appropriate space or facilities at its premises (or the employee lives too far away) and the employee is forced to work at home (i.e. does not work from home out of choice).

For owner/directors, however, it is better to use one of the alternative methods to claim tax relief for home working and we will return to this subject in Section 10.7.

## 7.20   RELOCATION COSTS

The company can pay some relocation costs of up to £8,000 with no tax consequences for the company or the employee. The costs that qualify include:

- The cost of selling an old home and buying a new one
- Moving costs
- Travel and subsistence
- The cost of replacing domestic goods

Interest on a bridging loan is also exempt if the loan is needed to bridge the gap between buying the new house and getting the money for the old one. The money must be used to pay off the mortgage on the old home or buy the new house. The loan cannot exceed the market value of the old house at the time the new house is bought.

These costs can only qualify when:
- A new employee moves area to work for your company
- An existing employee changes their place of work within your company
- The employee's old home is not reasonably close to work but their new one is reasonably close

## 7.21   JOB-RELATED ACCOMMODATION

Where an employer provides an employee with living accommodation the employee generally has to pay tax on the value of the benefit. However, no tax is payable if:

- The accommodation is 'necessary' for the proper performance of the employee's duties. This would cover employees who are required by their employers to live on site to do their job (caretakers for example).
- The accommodation is provided for the better performance of the employee's duties and it is customary for employees in that line of work to be provided with accommodation. This would include vicarages, publicans, and teachers at boarding schools.

There is also no tax payable in respect of Council Tax or water or sewerage charges for the accommodation.

The rules are stricter for company directors. The accommodation will only be tax free if the director:

- Does not have a material interest in the company (i.e. does not own more than 5% of the shares), and
- Is employed as a full-time working director or the company is a non-profit-making organisation

There is also no tax payable if the accommodation is provided for security reasons. Both 10 and 11 Downing St are job-related accommodation and tax free for the occupant (despite all the money they take off us, the Government is clearly a non-profit-making organisation).

## 7.22   CHILDCARE

Childcare voucher schemes are closed to new entrants. However, employees who were signed up before 4th October 2018 can continue to benefit, as long as the company continues to offer the scheme. The same goes for childcare that is directly contracted for by employers.

For new entrants, the current alternative is Tax-Free Childcare. The idea here is that for every 80p paid in by parents, the Government will top up their account with 20p of basic-rate tax relief. While this may be of benefit to many employees on a personal level, it does not provide the type of tax advantages we are looking at in this chapter.

## 7.23   WORKPLACE NURSERIES

Workplace nurseries are where an employer provides places for employees' children in an employer-managed and financed nursery. Provided certain qualifying conditions are met the benefit is completely tax free.

For example, the nursery must be registered appropriately and be available to all employees. The nursery can be in another place, not necessarily at the workplace, but not a private residence.

### 7.24  WORK RELATED TRAINING

Your company can pay for or reimburse the cost of 'work-related training' and there will be no Income Tax payable by the employee or director.

Work-related training is training that is likely to prove useful to the employee when performing his or her duties or make them better qualified to do their job.

The training must relate to the employee's current job or a future job with the same employer. The intention is to include all genuine training the employee needs to advance their career or to achieve a career move within the same company.

The range of skills that qualify for exemption is pretty wide. It includes developing leadership and team skills, first aid and health and safety courses and safe driver training for employees with company cars.

The exemption covers distance learning, computer-based training, work placements, traditional classroom-based training and can be full time or part time.

The exemption also covers related costs such as childcare, travel and subsistence costs, including normal meals, refreshments and leisure activities offered within a training course.

However, the training will not be exempt if it is given as a reward to the employee or is entertainment or recreation disguised as training.

Where there is a combination of training and recreation the costs can be apportioned. Only the extra cost of the recreation is taxable. For example, if a training course is held in a hotel and afterwards the employees enjoy a golfing weekend, the cost of travel to and from the hotel and the costs incurred during the course are not taxable. Only the added cost of the golfing weekend is taxable.

## 7.25  RETRAINING COSTS

There is a tax exemption for training courses paid for by the company, or reimbursed by the company, to help an employee obtain another job or become self employed. To qualify all of the following conditions have to be met:

- The opportunity must be offered to all employees or to a particular class of employees (i.e. it must not be restricted to, say, relatives of directors).
- The employee must have been employed for at least two years before the course begins or, if it is earlier, at the time the employment ceases.
- The course must begin while the employee is still working for the company or within one year of leaving.
- If the employee is still working for the company, they must leave within two years of finishing the course.
- The employee must not be re-employed within two years

The course must also provide or improve skills or knowledge that can be used in another job or to become self-employed, and must last no longer than two years.

The exemption extends to fees for the course, essential books, examination fees and the cost of travelling to the course, plus subsistence expenses.

## 7.26  PERSONAL GIFTS

The general rule is that gifts made by employers to employees are taxed as earnings when they arise from the employment.

However, HMRC will accept that a gift does not count as earnings if it is made for personal reasons (for example, a wedding present) or as a mark of personal esteem or appreciation. In the latter case, however, it would be difficult to say with certainty whether a gift is taxable as earnings or tax free. Similar problems still arise, even with the introduction of the trivial benefits exemption (Section 7.32).

## 7.27  GIFTS FROM THIRD PARTIES

If a business makes gifts to, say, the employees of its customers, those employees will not have to pay any tax on the value of the gift, providing the gift:

- Costs £250 or less
- Consists of goods or a voucher to buy goods (the voucher must not be convertible into cash)
- Is not made by the individual's employer or someone connected to the employer
- Is not made in recognition, or in anticipation, of particular services performed by the employee
- Is not directly or indirectly paid for by the employer or someone connected to them

The total cost to the donor of all eligible gifts to the employee in a tax year must not exceed £250. The cost to the person making the gift includes any VAT paid, whether or not it is reclaimable.

Where the cost of gifts received by an employee from the same third party exceeds £250 in a tax year, tax will be payable on the full amount of the gifts.

### 7.28   LONG SERVICE AWARDS

Long service awards made to both directors and employees to mark long service are covered by a statutory exemption and are therefore tax free, providing the following conditions are met:

- An award can only be made once the director or employee has worked for the company for 20 years or more
- The award cannot take the form of a cash payment. National saving certificates and premium bonds also do not qualify. Tangible assets like watches and paintings do qualify.
- The cost of the award must not be more than £50 for each year of service. So an award given just after 20 years of service (the minimum period) cannot cost more than £1,000. If it costs more, it is only the excess that is taxable.

If a director or employee receives a second award after, say, 30 years the tax-free amount of the award is calculated without regard to the first award.

In other words, a company director can receive a long service award worth £1,000 after 20 years (20 x £50) and then another award worth £1,500 after 30 years (30 x £50).

However, there must be a gap of at least 10 years between awards. You cannot receive a tax-free award after 25 years and then another one after 30 years.

## 7.29  STAFF SUGGESTION SCHEMES

Suggestion scheme awards are also covered by a statutory exemption and are therefore tax free. To qualify:

- The scheme must be open to all employees or a 'particular description of them' (e.g. all employees in a particular location)
- The suggestion must relate to the activities carried on by the employer
- The suggestion must not fall within the normal duties of the employee who makes the suggestion
- The suggestion must not be made at a meeting for making suggestions
- The award must be an 'encouragement award' or a 'financial benefit award'

An encouragement award is given for 'a suggestion with intrinsic merit or showing special effort'. The maximum for a tax-free encouragement award is £25. There is no need for the suggestion to be adopted.

A financial benefit award is made for a suggestion that:

- The employer has decided to adopt,
- Relates to an improvement in efficiency or effectiveness, and
- The employer reasonably expects will result in a financial benefit

Financial benefit awards are for suggestions that will save the company money or make it money. The maximum that can be given tax free is £5,000. Subject to this overriding limit, the maximum tax-free award is calculated as the *greater* of:

- 50% of the money the company expects to make or save in the first year after the suggestion has been adopted, or
- 10% of the money the company expects to make or save in the first five years after the suggestion has been adopted

If two or more employees jointly submit a suggestion, the award is split between them. The overall maximum tax-free amount is still £5,000.

If an award exceeds the maximum, only the excess is subject to Income Tax and National Insurance.

If an employee makes more than one successful suggestion, he or she can receive more than one tax-free payment of up to £5,000 for each suggestion.

## 7.30   FREE OR SUBSIDISED MEALS

This is the exemption that allows your company to provide you and your employees with free tea, coffee, and biscuits and also fully-fledged meals. As long as the rules are followed, the cost will be a tax-deductible expense for the company and there will be no Income Tax or National Insurance payable by the employee or employer.

There is no tax payable when a company provides free or subsidised meals and light refreshments to directors or employees, as long as the meals are provided:

- In a canteen *or*
- On the company's premises

The following conditions must also be met:

- The meals must be provided on a 'reasonable scale'
- The free or subsidised meals must be available to all employees (hence why things like working lunches during a business meeting are not generally covered in their own right: but see further below)
- If the meals are provided in the restaurant or dining room of a hotel or catering business at a time when meals are being served to the public, part of the room must be designated for the use of employees only

### What is a Canteen?
Somewhere that serves meals to the public at large (e.g. a pub, restaurant or cafe) is not a canteen.

The meals can be provided in any canteen: it does not have to be on the employer's premises. It also does not have to be restricted to just your company's employees.

For example, a single canteen located on an industrial estate and serving all those who work on the estate would qualify.

### What is on a Reasonable Scale?
Just how good can the meals be? This is a grey area. According to HMRC, "*In general, you should only assess a benefit in those cases where the provision is clearly unreasonable.*

*For example, where it involves the provision of an elaborate menu, fine wines, and cigars. The provision of a glass of wine with an otherwise modest meal is not unreasonable."*

## Available to All Employees
If the opportunity to obtain a free or subsidised meal is not open to all employees (for example, if it is only available to directors or to senior staff) the exemption does not apply.

Note also that there is no need for all the employees to get the same level of subsidy. Provided a free or subsidised meal is available to all employees, the exemption applies.

The exemption covers meal vouchers if they are for use on the company's own premises or for a canteen open to the employees generally. It does not apply to vouchers used to get meals elsewhere.

According to HMRC guidance: *"If the exemption applies then all meals on a reasonable scale provided on the employer's premises are exempt from tax. This means that if all employees may get a free or subsidised meal on the employer's premises or in a canteen, or meal vouchers, then working lunches on a reasonable scale, provided on the employer's premises, will also be exempt even if not all of the employees get the working lunches."*

### Example 1
*Louis has a boat building business with 20 employees working on an industrial estate and another five employees at an office a couple of miles away. There's a canteen on the industrial estate where all employees can get a free meal, although the office workers hardly ever make the journey.*

*Every now and then the office staff have a working lunch in the office which the industrial estate workers never attend.*

*The tax exemption applies to the canteen meals because all employees can have them if they wish. Because the exemption applies, the working lunches are also exempt even though the workers on the industrial estate do not attend them.*

### Example 2
*Three Brambles Ltd has two directors and two employees. Once a week they all have a working lunch in the office where they discuss various ways to grow the business. They order in food from a local Nepalese restaurant. The lunch is on a reasonable scale and paid for by the company.*

*The meals are covered by the exemption and tax free because they are available to all of the employees and take place on the company's premises.*

*If, however, they went to the Nepalese restaurant for the working lunch the exemption would not apply because the meal is not on the employer's premises or in a canteen.*

### Example 2 continued
*Let's say the company takes on a third employee as a receptionist. If the receptionist is not invited to the weekly lunches, the exemption will no longer apply: all employees must be able to get a free or subsidised meal.*

*The company gives the receptionist a free meal voucher which they can use at the local greasy spoon. The exemption now applies to the working lunches because all of the employees can now get a free meal or meal voucher. The exemption does not apply to the receptionist's meal vouchers because the meal is not obtained on the company's premises or in a staff canteen.*

If an employee brings food into the workplace purchased from an outside supplier (for example if they are working late), any reimbursement by the company is not covered by this exemption and will be taxed as earnings.

## 7.31 CHRISTMAS PARTIES AND OTHER ANNUAL FUNCTIONS

If your company holds an annual staff function (typically a Christmas party) the directors and other employees will not have to pay any Income Tax and the company will not have to pay any employer's National Insurance, providing the cost does not exceed £150 per person. The party will also, of course, be a tax-deductible expense for the company.

The exemption covers not just the direct costs of the party (food, alcohol, etc) but also incidental costs like transport and overnight accommodation (e.g. taxis and hotels).

£150 used to be fairly generous but the exemption has been fixed at this level since 2003. Nowadays, it's unlikely to be enough to cover many incidental costs, like hotel rooms (unless employees are bunking together).

The cost per head is calculated by dividing the total cost of the event by the number of people attending, including spouses and other guests. Sometimes this could mean that increasing the size of the event reduces the cost per head to the point where the exemption applies.

150

There doesn't have to be just one staff function during the year. Several events can be covered by the exemption, as long as the total aggregate cost per head over the tax year does not exceed £150.

There are a few pitfalls to watch out for:

- The exemption only covers *annual* events. A Christmas party or summer barbeque would qualify because they would be something that happens once a year. The exemption does not cover 'casual hospitality', like taking the staff for a drink on a Friday night, or one-off events such as celebrating the company's 20th anniversary.
- The event must be open to all members of staff. It can be restricted to staff working at a particular location, such as a branch or regional office, but it cannot be restricted to staff of a particular grade, such as management or directors.
- Where the total cost of the event including VAT (regardless of whether the business can recover it) exceeds £150 per head, **none** of the expenditure is covered by the exemption.
- Where there are two or more functions during the year, the exemption can be used as long as the total aggregate cost is no more than £150 per head. If the total cost per head goes over £150 then whichever functions best utilise the £150 are exempt, the others will be taxable.

### Example 1
*Jack Ltd spends £160 per head on a Christmas party. None of this is covered by the exemption.*

### Example 2
*Jill Ltd spends £60 per head on a summer ball in August and £80 per head on a Christmas party. The exemption can be used to cover both functions (total cost £140 per head).*

*If the Christmas party cost £100 per head then the aggregate cost would be £160 which would exceed the £150 limit. The best way to utilise the exemption in this case would be to have the Christmas party covered by the exemption. The summer ball would then be taxable.*

### Example 3
*Hill Ltd spends £45 per head on a summer barbecue and £120 per head on a Christmas party. The exemption cannot be used to cover both functions (total cost £165 per head).*

*The Christmas party can be covered by the exemption and although the barbecue cannot be covered by this exemption, it can be covered by the trivial benefits exemption (Section 7.32) because the cost does not exceed £50.*

### Example 4
*Pail Ltd holds a Christmas party for all of the staff and the cost per head comes to £50. The party is exempt from tax. The directors then decide to have another director-only Christmas party which costs £100 per head. This party is not covered by the exemption because it is not open to all employees. The directors will pay Income Tax on the £100 benefit and the company will pay Class 1A National Insurance.*

### 7.32   TRIVIAL BENEFITS

Most benefits given to employees are taxable. This means the employee has to pay Income Tax and the employer has to pay National Insurance. No employee's National Insurance is due on benefits in kind.

However, when the benefit is small enough it does not have to be reported and is tax exempt. The trivial benefits exemption covers things like Christmas presents and birthday presents. There are, of course, some rules that have to be followed to keep the benefit out of the tax net:

- The cost of providing the benefit must not exceed £50
- The exemption does not cover cash (gift vouchers are, however, acceptable)
- The employee must not be contractually entitled to the benefit
- The benefit must not be provided in recognition of particular services performed by the employee

The company can provide trivial benefits as many times as it likes (even to the same employee) as long as the cost each time does not exceed £50. If the benefit costs more than £50, the whole amount is taxable, not just the excess.

To calculate the cost of the benefit, the VAT inclusive amount is used: this is the general rule for benefits provided to employees.

When a benefit is given to several employees (such as a restaurant meal), the average cost per person should be used to decide if the £50 limit has been breached.

## Company Owners and Trivial Benefits

Small company owners can give themselves tax-free trivial benefits but the exemption is capped.

If the company is a close company, the exemption is capped at £300 per tax year per director. (Most family and small owner-managed companies are close companies: see Section 12.6.)

Where the cost of a benefit results in the £300 annual limit being exceeded, none of that benefit is exempt. The tax treatment of earlier benefits is not affected.

### *Example*

*Sophie's company provides her with eight benefits during the tax year. The first six cost less than £50 each and take her annual total to £275. The first six are all tax exempt.*

*The seventh costs £40 and brings the total cost to £315, which exceeds the annual exempt amount. Therefore the £40 benefit is not tax exempt. However, it does not count towards the annual exempt amount, which means there is still scope for Sophie to give herself a benefit costing £25 to use up the last of her annual exempt amount.*

Where a benefit is provided to a close family member of the director, the benefit counts towards the director's own annual exempt amount. For example, if a company provides a director with a £30 Christmas gift and also gives their son (not a director or employee) a separate £30 gift, the total cost of £60 counts towards the director's annual exempt amount.

However, this is not the case if the family member is also a director: family members who are employees of the same close company are each subject to their own £300 cap. Thus, a couple who are both directors of the same company can each enjoy £300 worth of tax-free benefits every tax year.

## Not for Services Performed

The key point about the exemption is that the benefit must be given as a gift and not as a reward for work carried out.

For example, if you ask some employees to work through their lunch hour and order in some pizzas, the food will not be covered by the trivial benefits exemption as it is provided because of the work they are doing, i.e. in recognition of particular services performed by the employees.

If the company gives one of its employees a gift voucher for £30 as a small thank you for doing good work, the gift will not be covered by the exemption because it is provided in recognition of their services.

But if the company gives the same employee a £30 gift voucher because it's their birthday the amount will be covered by the exemption.

Most employers will only very occasionally give their employees gifts that are not linked in any way to services performed. You can expect HMRC to consider whether regular or frequent benefits are actually linked to the employee's work in some way.

Of course, in a small company set up, the directors probably only want to give themselves numerous £50 gifts. However, they are prevented from doing this by the £300 per year cap.

**Interaction with Other Exemptions**
Where a benefit is covered by the trivial benefits exemption and another exemption, you can apply the exemptions in the way that provides the best outcome for the employee.

### *Example*
*Dominy Ltd has two annual functions for employees, a Christmas party and a summer barbeque. The Christmas party costs £130 per head and the barbeque costs £40 per head.*

*The Christmas party is covered by the £150 exemption for annual parties and functions (Section 7.31). However, the barbeque is not covered by the annual parties exemption, because the total cost per person of both events comes to £170.*

*However, the barbeque can be covered by the trivial benefits exemption because the cost does not exceed £50.*

### 7.33   TAXABLE BENEFITS

If a benefit falls through the net and isn't covered by any of the exemptions we have looked at in this chapter then, as explained in Section 7.1, it will generally still be free from one tax: employee's National Insurance.

To achieve this saving, it is essential that the employer company contracts directly with the benefit provider and pays them directly. If the company settles an employee's contractual liability, this will be fully taxable.

(Apart from expenses incurred wholly, exclusively and necessarily in the performance of the employee's duties, like travel and subsistence, as explained in Chapter 4.)

Admittedly, the employee's National Insurance saving doesn't amount to much if the employee is a higher-rate taxpayer. Higher-rate taxpayers only pay 2% National Insurance.

However, for basic-rate taxpayer employees, the saving is more substantial because they pay 8% National Insurance.

### Example
*Fremah is the receptionist at Bigship Ltd. She is a basic-rate taxpayer and a keen fitness enthusiast. She would like a membership at the top local gym, but it would cost £900 per year, including VAT. She's a good receptionist and the company's directors want her to stay, so they offer to pay for her gym membership and she accepts.*

*Bigship Ltd contracts directly with the gym and pays the £900 annual cost. Adding 13.8% employer's National Insurance means the total cost to the company is £1,242. This amount is fully tax deductible, just like cash salary.*

*How much better off is Fremah? She still faces an Income Tax charge of £180 but saves £72 of National Insurance (£900 x 8%).*

The tax saving is not large, but it is an annual saving, so the same saving may be reaped in future years. What is more, this is just one of many benefits-in-kind that could be offered to Fremah, so the total annual saving could be significant.

For the company, the cost of providing a benefit is generally allowed as a tax-deductible expense because it is provided for the benefit of employees.

If the company has a significant number of employees, it may be possible to negotiate discounts with suppliers when contracting to provide employee benefits. Furthermore, as we saw in Section 3.5, where a benefit is available to *all* employees, VAT can usually be recovered.

Let's suppose Bigship Ltd has ten employees and the company negotiates a corporate gym membership at a rate of £810 per person per year (i.e. a 10% discount). The company will suffer employer's National Insurance at 13.8%.

This is based on the VAT-inclusive cost, even though the company is able to recover the VAT. It will also enjoy CT relief on the overall net cost. Let's assume the company's marginal CT rate is 26.5%, so this is how it all works out:

| | |
|---|---|
| Ten gym memberships | £8,100 |
| Employer's National Insurance | £1,118 |
| VAT recovered | (£1,350) |
| Net cost before tax relief | £7,868 |
| Corporation Tax relief | (£2,085) |
| Final net cost | £5,783 |

To enable those ten employees to each purchase an individual gym membership out of their after-tax income, the company would have had to pay each of them additional salary of £1,250. Adding employer's National Insurance, multiplying by ten, and deducting CT relief gives a final net cost of £10,455.

The corporate gym membership could be said to have saved the company almost £5,000. However, the employees might not be so happy, as not all of them might value the gym membership as much as Fremah. That's not a problem from the company's point of view, the benefit only needs to be *available* to employees generally to enjoy VAT recovery, it does not matter how many of them take up the offer.

A £900 gym membership is not worth as much as £900 cash in the hand unless you really want that membership. Nonetheless, there may be situations where this type of approach can be used to yield major savings for the company which can, of course, eventually be fed back into more income for the shareholder/directors.

### Benefits for Directors
As far as taxable benefits provided to directors themselves are concerned, we saw in Sections 1.3 and 4.1 that these are not generally worthwhile. However, where the director participates in a wider benefit available to employees generally, so that corporate discounts can be negotiated, and VAT can be recovered, savings may be possible.

### Example
*Maxwell is the owner/director of Bigship Ltd and takes one of the corporate gym memberships discussed above. He's a higher rate taxpayer by virtue of dividends he takes out of the company, so his benefit in kind suffers overall Income Tax of £365 (at 45%: 20% on the benefit itself and an extra 25% on dividends taxed at 33.75% instead of 8.75%).*

*The position for the company is the same as with all the other employees, so the final net cost of Maxwell's benefit is £578 (£5,783/10). However, to compensate Maxwell for his Income Tax cost, the company will also need to pay him an extra dividend of £551, meaning the ultimate cost is £1,129.*

*Nonetheless, to get an extra £900 into Maxwell's hands to enable him to buy an individual gym membership would require a dividend of £1,358, so there is still a saving of £229.*

In fact, even without the 10% corporate discount applied in the example, this approach still yields a small saving thanks to the VAT recovery and CT relief. In Maxwell's case, the saving with no corporate discount would be £105, or 11.7% of the cost of the benefit.

This saving is reduced if the company has a lower marginal CT rate, but a small saving persists even if the company has the lowest tax rate of 19% (there would be a saving of £39 in Maxwell's case).

So, it's well worth looking out for these opportunities: but remember the benefit has to be available to all employees.

**Time Cost and Compliance Costs**
Although benefits-in-kind can provide attractive tax savings for the company and its employees, the time cost should also be factored in. Setting up a gym membership is more time consuming than paying a salary.

Taxable benefits must also be reported annually on Form P11D (one for each employee concerned), so most small companies will have to pay additional fees to their accountant, which will obviously eat into the available savings. That said, an annual saving of almost £5,000 would cover a lot of accountancy fees.

### 7.34  PAYE SETTLEMENTS

As we have observed throughout this chapter, HMRC are mindbogglingly petty when it comes to charging tax on benefits in kind. Many benefits can be covered by the exemptions we have seen in previous sections, but there are still gaps, and these gaps are often the kind of things the company might not want its employees to be taxed on.

Some good examples we have cited a number of times are working lunches and food provided to employees required, or volunteering, to work late.

These might sometimes be covered by the exemption in Section 7.30, but in other cases, for the sake of staff morale, the company will often want to pick up the tax bill.

There may also be cases where staff entertaining cannot be covered by the exemptions for annual functions (Section 7.31), or trivial benefits (Section 7.32), but the directors do not want all the positive, morale-boosting, teambuilding benefits of their efforts undone by the nasty surprise of a tax bill for the employees: there's nothing worse ("I only went to show my face"; "I only drank water"; "But I left early"; "I wasn't even there, what am I supposed to do, provide an alibi?!?!")

Thankfully, there is a way to prevent morale-shattering tax charges falling on the staff under these circumstances, but it comes at a cost.

The employer company can enter into a PAYE Settlement Agreement and pay all the Income Tax and National Insurance. This payment is usually tax deductible. For information about arranging a PAYE Settlement Agreement see: www.gov.uk/paye-settlement-agreements

PAYE Settlement Agreements no longer have to be renewed annually. Agreements can now be arranged that remain in place for subsequent tax years. Under these agreements, costs are grossed up to allow for the fact the employer is settling the staff's Income Tax liability. Class 1B National Insurance will also be payable at 13.8% (it's basically the same as Class 1A but has a different name).

### Example

*PNCF Ltd spends £4,800 (including VAT) on a staff party, which is not covered by the annual party exemption. The company advises HMRC that it wishes to enter a PAYE settlement agreement rather than allow its staff to be taxed on this benefit.*

*Half of the staff at the party were basic rate taxpayers, so the grossed-up cost of their benefit is £2,400 x 100/80 = £3,000. The other half were higher rate taxpayers, producing a grossed-up cost of £2,400 x 100/60 = £4,000. The total grossed up cost is thus £7,000, giving rise to a tax charge of £2,200 (£7,000 – £4,800) plus Class 1B National Insurance of £966 (£7,000 x 13.8%).*

*The company's PAYE settlement is £3,166 (£2,200 + £966). This is 66% of the cost of the party, but at least the company can claim CT relief on this cost.*

The company may be able to reclaim some or all of the VAT cost of the party (see Section 3.5). Assuming all the associated costs were standard-rated, the company is entitled to full recovery, and its marginal CT rate is 26.5%, this would reduce the net cost to £5,267, as follows:

| | |
|---|---|
| Cost of party | £4,800 |
| PAYE Settlement | £3,166 |
| VAT recovery | (£800) |
| Net cost before tax relief | £7,166 |
| Corporation Tax relief | (£1,899) |
| Final net cost | £5,267 |

If the company had instead given each employee a bonus sufficient to leave them with enough cash after tax to cover the cost of the party, it would have paid out a total of £7,471 plus £1,031 in employer's National Insurance. After CT relief, the final net cost would have been £6,249.

So, it could be said the party saved the company almost £1,000. Which is why we say, 'Party on Dudes'.

# Chapter 8

# Capital Expenditure

## 8.1    WHAT IS CAPITAL EXPENDITURE?

As explained in Section 2.2, where something is deemed to be capital expenditure, it is subject to different rules. Here, we need to think about a few key issues:

- What is capital expenditure?
- Has that expenditure been incurred for business purposes?
- What allowances or reliefs are available?

I will look at each of these issues in detail over the next few sections. However, it is worth pointing out at this stage that, **subject to the exceptions noted below, most items of capital expenditure incurred by small companies are fully allowable in the period they are incurred**. This is because of the annual investment allowance, which we will be looking at in Section 8.4, and full expensing, which we will look at in Section 8.5.

Nonetheless, there are some important exceptions to this general conclusion, including:

- Land and buildings (see Chapter 10)
- Cars (see Chapter 9)
- Expenditure over £1 million per year (see Section 8.4); although not in all cases
- Expenditure by companies renting out residential property (see Section 8.3)

Certain expenditure incurred by companies on the purchase of new assets before 1st April 2023 was eligible for a super-deduction of up to 130%. We'll take a closer look at this in Section 8.5, as it is still relevant for those who have not yet finalised their accounts or submitted their CT returns for periods beginning before 1st April 2023.

### What is Capital Expenditure?
In the world of tax and accounting, expenditure is either 'capital' or 'revenue'. So far in this guide, we have mostly talked about revenue expenditure and the general principles covered in Section 2.2 apply.

160

Revenue expenditure comes in many varieties, including expenditure on consumable items, goods for resale, raw materials, wages and salaries, utility supplies, rent, interest, repairs and maintenance, and many others. Revenue expenditure is claimed as it is incurred, under the principles covered in Chapters 2 and 4.

Expenditure is generally revenue in nature if the goods or services being purchased:

- Are intended to be consumed in the business (e.g. buying office stationery or diesel for a company van)
- Cover a defined period (e.g. wages, insurance premiums, utility bills, office rent, business rates)
- Are intended for resale (e.g. trading stock or raw materials to be used in a manufacturing process)
- Have no enduring benefit (e.g. advertising): but see further below
- Need to be purchased at regular intervals (e.g. repairs and maintenance expenditure)

The question of whether there is any enduring benefit is a tricky one sometimes, but I use advertising as an example because no asset is acquired and, without repetition, the impact the advertising has on the company's business will fade over time. Perhaps it might be more accurate to say any enduring benefit is only incidental, or only created indirectly.

Which brings us back to the question: 'What is Capital Expenditure?' Because it is the creation of an enduring benefit that lies at the heart of the matter.

Expenditure will be capital expenditure if it is incurred to acquire, create, or enhance an asset of enduring benefit to the business. The asset can be either tangible, such as machinery, computers, cars, land and buildings; or intangible, such as software, websites, or business goodwill.

Generally, the asset is of enduring benefit if it is intended to be used in the business for at least two years, although this guideline can be overridden. For example, a construction company may buy land for development and hold it for many years before building work commences. However, the land was always intended to be sold, so it remains part of the company's trading stock.

A lot of capital expenditure is pretty obvious, of course, like buying business premises, machinery, equipment, vehicles, computers, furniture, and most other tangible assets. Less obvious are some of the other items that need to be treated as capital expenditure, such as:

- Incidental purchase costs (e.g. legal fees and Stamp Duty Land Tax on a property purchase)
- Intangible items like software and websites: but only if an enduring asset is purchased or created; often it isn't, and we will look at this issue in more detail in Section 11.3
- Improvement or enhancement expenditure (e.g. building an extension onto your business premises, acquiring the freehold of a property where you already have the leasehold, or having the company van strengthened to increase its payload). The most significant items of improvement expenditure generally relate to property, so we will return to this subject in more detail in Chapter 10.

### Has the Expenditure been Incurred for Business Purposes?

Once we have established that expenditure is capital in nature, we will need to consider what allowances are available, and we will turn to that issue in the next section. However, before we do that, we also need to establish whether the expenditure has been incurred for business purposes. In other words, being capital in nature changes the way in which we are able to claim relief for the expenditure, but we still need to ensure the expenditure meets our general principles in Section 2.2.

So, for example, a company car is capital expenditure and, thanks to the 'employee benefit override' it attracts tax relief in the form of capital allowances, as we shall see in Section 9.2.

On the other hand, a trading company whose activities have no connection with the art world, but which has spare cash available, might buy a Picasso painting and keep it in the company safe, or hang it in the boardroom. This is capital expenditure, but it could not be said it had been incurred wholly and exclusively for the purposes of the business. Hence, there would be no tax relief for this expenditure. (Although any gain arising on a subsequent sale of the painting will be subject to CT.)

## 8.2 INTRODUCTION TO CAPITAL ALLOWANCES

In Section 8.1, we looked at how to determine when an item of expenditure is capital expenditure. We also considered the question of whether it represented qualifying business expenditure under general principles.

Tax relief is available on certain types of capital expenditure where the asset purchased, created, or enhanced through the expenditure is used in a 'qualifying activity'. A qualifying activity for this purpose is effectively the same as the different types of business we examined in Section 2.2.

Tax relief is given on capital expenditure through a system of reliefs known as capital allowances. For the purpose of capital allowances, we can effectively divide capital expenditure into three main types:

i)   Cars, covered in Chapter 9
ii)  Plant and machinery, covered in Sections 8.3 to 8.9
iii) Buildings and structures, covered in Chapter 10

The boundary between 'plant and machinery' and 'buildings and structures' is a complex area, and we will look at this further in Chapter 10.

Many types of capital expenditure do not attract capital allowances. Some of the most important of these are:

*   Land
*   Residential property
*   Intangible assets (but software is treated as plant and machinery)

In other cases, the question of whether capital allowances are available depends on the type of business the company is carrying on and we will look at this further in Section 8.3.

## 8.3 WHAT IS PLANT AND MACHINERY AND WHAT ALLOWANCES ARE AVAILABLE?

It is tempting to say that if it's a tangible asset and it isn't land, a building, or a car, then it is plant and machinery. That's not totally accurate, but it's a good starting point.

163

Plant and machinery includes the following items:

- Motor vehicles, including vans and motorcycles (technically, cars are also included, but they are treated differently for capital allowances purposes, as we shall see in Chapter 9)
- Ships, aircraft, spacecraft, satellites, locomotives and carriages
- Tools, machinery and equipment
- Computers and associated equipment such as printers, etc.
- Mobile phones, tablets, and other similar devices
- Software
- Furniture and moveable furnishings
- Caravans and mobile homes (when let out as holiday accommodation)
- Fixtures and fittings: there is a defined list of items affixed to buildings or structures that qualify as plant and machinery. We will cover this in detail in Section 10.5.

**Plant and Machinery NOT Qualifying for Capital Allowances**

Just because something is plant and machinery, doesn't necessarily mean it qualifies for the plant and machinery allowances we will be looking at in this chapter. These are some of the important exclusions to be aware of:

- Companies renting out residential property cannot claim capital allowances on assets within a rented residential dwelling (but see Section 10.5 for some exceptions to this rule)
- Caravans and mobile homes do not qualify for capital allowances if they are not being rented out as holiday accommodation
- Decorative assets (paintings, sculptures, etc) only qualify for capital allowances where provided for public enjoyment in hotels, restaurants and similar establishments

In general, an asset can only qualify for capital allowances if it is being used for the purpose of a qualifying business activity.

**What Allowances are Available?**

The most important allowance for small companies purchasing plant and machinery is the annual investment allowance and we will look at this in Section 8.4.

For purchases of new plant and machinery, companies also have the option to claim full expensing. However, this allowance, which we will look at in Section 8.5, has some drawbacks, so the annual investment allowance is to be preferred whenever possible.

Other allowances for plant and machinery include enhanced capital allowances, writing down allowances, balancing allowances and, for expenditure incurred before 1$^{st}$ April 2023, the super-deduction. We will look at these in Sections 8.5 to 8.8. Other capital allowances issues for companies are covered in Section 8.9.

**Commercial Considerations**
Throughout most of this chapter, we will be looking purely at the tax consequences of your company's capital expenditure. In practice, commercial considerations should generally take precedence.

Nonetheless, it remains a fact that small timing differences could sometimes make a big difference to your CT bill: and that in itself may sometimes make the most sense commercially.

## 8.4    THE ANNUAL INVESTMENT ALLOWANCE

Qualifying companies are entitled to an annual investment allowance of up to £1m. The allowance provides 100% tax relief for qualifying expenditure on plant and machinery up to the specified limit in each accounting period.

**Restrictions**
The annual investment allowance is not available for:

- Cars
- Expenditure incurred in earlier accounting periods where allowances were not previously claimed
- Assets transferred to the company by a connected person (see Appendix C), for example the company owner

The annual investment allowance is restricted where a company has an accounting period of less than twelve months' duration (see Section 8.9 for an illustration).

The annual investment allowance must be shared between companies that are members of the same group, or which are otherwise closely related to each other. This would include associated companies under the control of the same persons (see Section 12.3). The allowance can be shared in any proportion the companies agree. Hence, for example, where the same person owns both a trading company and a property investment company, the trading company could claim an annual investment allowance of, say, £900,000 for the year ending 31$^{st}$ December 2023, while the property investment company claims an annual investment allowance of £100,000 for the same period.

However, where a company owner also operates as a sole trader, an individual landlord, or is a member of a partnership, that other business activity attracts its own annual investment allowance and does not need to share the company's allowance.

**Interaction with Other Allowances**
Expenditure on which full expensing, the super-deduction, or the 50% first year allowance is claimed, or which qualifies for enhanced capital allowances (Section 8.6), does not use up any of the company's annual investment allowance for the relevant period.

However, there are many types of expenditure that will qualify for the annual investment allowance, but cannot qualify for either full expensing or the super-deduction. These include:

i)    Used and second-hand assets
ii)   Assets held for leasing (see Section 8.5)
iii)  Ships and railway assets
iv)   Assets (other than cars) falling into the special rate pool (see Section 8.7)

In the March 2024 Budget, the previous Conservative Government proposed extending full expensing to assets held for leasing. However, it isn't clear if the new Labour Government will carry on with this proposed change.

Any expenditure on the above assets in excess of the maximum annual investment allowance available for the relevant period will not qualify for full expensing, but will qualify for:

* The 50% first year allowance for most new assets falling into the special rate pool (see Section 8.5 for details)
* Writing down allowances at just 6% for other assets falling into the special rate pool, including used or second-hand integral features (see Section 10.5)
* Writing down allowances at just 18% in all other cases

In contrast to the immediate 100% relief provided by the annual investment allowance, expenditure attracting writing down allowances at 18% may take twelve years to achieve even 90% relief. For assets falling into the special rate pool, it may take almost forty years; although this is reduced to twenty-seven years where the 50% first year allowance is available.

**Summary**

Most small companies have an annual investment allowance of £1m available for each accounting period and are unlikely to spend more than this on qualifying plant and machinery. Hence, for expenditure after 31st March 2023, the simple answer in most cases is to claim the annual investment allowance on all qualifying expenditure and thus obtain immediate 100% tax relief.

For expenditure incurred before 1st April 2023, it is generally worth claiming the super-deduction where it is available (see Section 8.5) as this provides relief at more than 100%.

We will return to the subject of choosing the best allowances to claim on qualifying plant and machinery in Section 8.10. Cars and expenditure on buildings are subject to special rules, which we will look at in Chapters 9 and 10 respectively.

## 8.5    ADDITIONAL ALLOWANCES FOR NEW PLANT AND MACHINERY

Expenditure on new, unused plant and machinery, incurred by companies is eligible for some additional allowances. Anything that qualifies for one of these additional allowances would also, alternatively, qualify for the annual investment allowance. The same expenditure may only be claimed once, however.

The allowances covered in this section are subject to a number of exclusions, including:

- Cars
- Used and second-hand assets
- Assets held for leasing (see further below)
- Acquisitions during the accounting period when the qualifying activity ceases
- Gifted assets or other transfers from a connected person (see Appendix C)
- Ships and railway assets

Assets held for leasing means assets purchased with the main purpose of hiring or leasing them out (e.g. vans purchased by a van hire company, machinery purchased by a plant hire company, or bicycles purchased by a company that hires out bicycles: including hiring them to staff, as discussed in Section 7.8).

In addition to the exclusions listed above, assets falling into the special rate pool (see Section 8.7) are also excluded from both the 100% full expensing allowance and the super-deduction, but may, in some cases, qualify for the 50% first year allowance (see below).

**Rental Property**
Fortunately, most fixtures and fittings within rental property are excluded from the definition of 'assets held for leasing' for the purposes of the allowances covered in this section. This means landlord companies will be able to claim these allowances on most new fixtures and fittings (subject to the restriction on assets within residential dwellings discussed in Sections 8.3 and 10.5).

However, the exemption for fixtures and fittings in rental property only covers items that are affixed to, or otherwise installed in, the property, and does not cover movable items. Hence, landlord companies will not be able to claim either the 100% full expensing allowance or the super-deduction on most furniture and free-standing, movable equipment within rental properties.

**Full Expensing**
Qualifying expenditure on new, unused plant and machinery incurred after 31$^{st}$ March 2023 is eligible for a 100% first year allowance. In other words, the entire cost may be claimed for CT purposes in the accounting period in which the asset is purchased. For ease of reference, we will refer to this as full expensing throughout the rest of this guide. This allowance was initially due to run only until 31$^{st}$ March 2026, but has now been extended indefinitely.

Unlike the annual investment allowance, full expensing has no monetary limit and hence will greatly benefit large companies. However, there is generally no benefit to small or medium-sized companies spending less than £1m on qualifying plant and machinery in any accounting period, and full expensing even has some disadvantages, which we will examine later.

Nonetheless, for companies spending in excess of £1m, full expensing is highly beneficial.

**The Super-Deduction**
Qualifying expenditure on new, unused plant and machinery incurred between 1$^{st}$ April 2021 and 31$^{st}$ March 2023 is eligible for the super-deduction. For accounting periods ending before 1$^{st}$ April 2023, the super-deduction was given at the rate of 130%.

For accounting periods straddling 1$^{st}$ April 2023, the super-deduction remains available for expenditure incurred before that date, but is given at a reduced rate. For example, the super-deduction for expenditure incurred between January and March 2023 by a company with a twelve-month accounting period ended 31$^{st}$ December 2023 is: 30% x 90/365 = 7.4% + 100% = 107.4%.

Generally speaking, it is worth claiming the super-deduction on any qualifying expenditure incurred before 1$^{st}$ April 2023. There may, however, be a few exceptions due to the way disposal proceeds received for such assets are taxed and we will look at this further in Sections 8.8 and 8.10.

It is worth noting the general rule applying for capital allowances purposes is that expenditure is treated as incurred as soon as there is an unconditional commitment to pay. In some cases, this commitment may have arisen by 31$^{st}$ March 2023, even if qualifying plant and machinery was not physically acquired until later. It's worth looking out for opportunities to claim the super-deduction under these circumstances.

**The 50% First Year Allowance**
Subject to the exclusions listed above, this allowance is available for expenditure on:

- Integral features (see Section 10.5)
- Thermal insulation of an existing building (except residential property, but currently including furnished holiday lets: see Section 1.6)
- Expenditure of £100,000 or more on plant and machinery with an anticipated working life of 25 years or more (long life assets)

As for the other allowances covered above, the assets must be new and unused. In the case of long-life assets, the expenditure must be incurred after 31$^{st}$ March 2023.

Where the first year allowance is claimed, the remaining unrelieved 50% of the expenditure falls into the special rate pool and will attract writing down allowances at 6% from the following accounting period onwards. There is no writing down allowance available in the period in which the first year allowance is claimed and nor can the annual investment allowance be claimed on the unrelieved 50% falling into the pool.

While the 50% first year allowance is much better than the 6% writing down allowance, it is nowhere near as good as the 100% relief available under the annual investment allowance. Hence, most small and medium-sized companies will be better off claiming the annual investment allowance on any expenditure that might otherwise qualify for the 50% first year allowance.

However, companies spending in excess of £1m on assets not eligible for full expensing may face a more complex decision, and we will look at this in Section 8.11.

## 8.6    ENHANCED CAPITAL ALLOWANCES

As an alternative to the allowances covered in Section 8.5, certain spending on new, unused plant and machinery incurred by 31st March 2025 is eligible for 100% enhanced capital allowances. These enhanced capital allowances are available for:

- Installation of electric vehicle charge-points
- Gas refuelling stations
- Zero emission goods vehicles

Enhanced capital allowances are not generally subject to any monetary limits and claims do not use up any of the company's annual investment allowance (the same expenditure can only be claimed once though). Zero emission (all electric) cars are also eligible for a 100% first year allowance: we will look at this in Section 9.5.

## 8.7    WRITING DOWN ALLOWANCES

Qualifying expenditure on plant and machinery that is not eligible for any of the allowances covered in Sections 8.5 and 8.6, and which is not covered by the annual investment allowance, is eligible for writing down allowances. The rate of writing down allowances on most plant and machinery is 18%, although a reduced rate of 6% applies to expenditure falling into the special rate pool (see further below).

Writing down allowances also apply to expenditure on qualifying plant and machinery that is not eligible for the annual investment allowance, including cars and assets purchased from connected persons.

## Pooling

Technically, what actually happens is that all of a company's qualifying expenditure on plant and machinery is placed in one of two 'pools', known as the main pool and the special rate pool. There are three exceptions to this:

- Assets on which either full expensing or the super-deduction is claimed are not placed in a pool, but are held as separate assets
- Only the unclaimed 50% of assets on which the 50% first year allowance has been claimed goes into the special rate pool (see Sections 8.5 and 8.8 for further details)
- Assets subject to a short life asset election are held as separate assets (this option is currently of little practical use due to full expensing and the £1m annual investment allowance)

The company then deducts its annual investment allowance claim from the amount in the pools. It's worth noting the annual investment allowance may be allocated to expenditure falling into the special rate pool in preference to expenditure falling into the main pool (except the unrelieved 50% of expenditure where the 50% first year allowance has been claimed). This is extremely beneficial in most cases.

The company would then also deduct any claim for enhanced capital allowances (Section 8.6) and the lower of disposal proceeds or original cost for any 'pooled' assets sold during the period (see Section 8.8).

The remaining balance is treated as follows:

- If it exceeds £1,000, the company may claim writing down allowances at the appropriate rate (18% or 6%) and carry the remainder of the balance forward to the next accounting period
- If it is between £1 and £1,000, the full balance may be claimed immediately
- If it is negative, the company is subject to a balancing charge equal to the negative balance: this is an addition to the company's taxable profits for the period

## The Special Rate Pool

The following expenditure must be allocated to the special rate pool:

- Cars with $CO_2$ emissions over a specified threshold (in effect, this is most petrol or diesel cars: but see Section 9.2 for details)
- Integral features (see Section 10.5)
- Expenditure of £100,000 or more on plant and machinery with an anticipated working life of 25 years or more

- Thermal insulation of an existing building (except residential property, but currently including furnished holiday lets)

Where the assets acquired are new and unused, most of this expenditure (apart from cars), also qualifies for the 50% first year allowance that we looked at in Section 8.5.


## 8.8    ASSET DISPOSALS

As we saw in Section 8.7, the normal rule is that any sale proceeds received on the disposal of plant and machinery are deducted from the balance on the main pool or special rate pool, as appropriate. This includes disposal proceeds for company cars. Where this gives rise to a negative balance, a balancing charge will arise.

However, the amount to be deducted is restricted to the lower of the amount of expenditure originally 'pooled' and the sale proceeds received. Remember, for this purpose, claiming the annual investment allowance or enhanced capital allowances effectively means the expenditure has been pooled.

Sadly, while the deduction from the pool is restricted, any gain arising on the disposal of qualifying plant and machinery (whether capital allowances have been claimed or not) is subject to CT (except gains on cars, which are exempt).

### *Example*
*Alltrades Ltd is a small building contractor. In the year ended 31ˢᵗ December 2022, the company purchased a second-hand van for £12,000 and claimed a full deduction under the annual investment allowance. On 31ˢᵗ December 2024, the company sold the van for £15,000. The balance on the company's main pool is nil, so it is subject to a balancing charge on the sale of the van.*

*The balancing charge is restricted to the £12,000 of expenditure pooled in 2022, but the company will also be taxed separately on its gain of £3,000.*

The restriction to the lower of the amount of expenditure originally 'pooled' and sale proceeds received is done on an item by item basis.

### Example Continued

*Let us now suppose Alltrades Ltd also bought a cement mixer for £10,000 in 2022 and again claimed a full deduction under the annual investment allowance. The cement mixer is sold for £6,000 in 2024. The amounts to be deducted from the company's main pool are thus:*

*Van            £12,000 (cost is lower than sale proceeds)*
*Cement mixer   £6,000  (sale proceeds are less than cost)*

*The total deduction is £18,000, giving the company a balancing charge of that amount.*

There is no separate deduction for the £4,000 loss on the cement mixer, as relief has already been given through the capital allowances system. In other words, losses on qualifying plant and machinery are effectively relieved via capital allowances, whereas gains are taxed separately in their own right (except gains on cars).

For assets acquired before December 2017, the position on any gains arising is a little better, as indexation relief will be available. This will be a pretty rare occurrence on a plant and machinery disposal though.

Since the advent of the annual investment allowance, most small companies have little or no balance of unrelieved expenditure left in their main or special rate pools. Hence, there is a strong chance of a balancing charge arising whenever any asset is sold: unless it is replaced by another qualifying asset of equal or greater value within the same accounting period. This makes the timing of replacement expenditure very important.

### Example Part 3

*In January 2025, Alltrades Ltd buys a new van for £60,000 and is able to claim full relief under the annual investment allowance. However, if the company had purchased the new van on or before 31ˢᵗ December 2024, it could have avoided the £18,000 balancing charge it suffered, claiming a net sum of £42,000 in capital allowances for 2024 instead.*

### Super-Disposals

Special rules apply to assets on which the allowances in Section 8.5 have been claimed. Disposal proceeds for these assets lead to an immediate balancing charge equal to the proceeds multiplied by:

- 50% for assets on which the 50% first year allowance has been claimed (the other 50% is deducted from the special rate pool any may lead to further balancing charges if this exceeds the pool balance)

- For assets on which the super-deduction has been claimed and which are disposed of in an accounting period beginning before 1st April 2023, the same percentage as would be available as a super-deduction for a new asset acquired in the same accounting period (e.g. 107.4% where the asset was disposed of during the year ending 31st December 2023). See Section 8.5 for details.

For assets on which either full expensing or, where the asset is disposed of in an accounting period beginning after 31st March 2023, the super-deduction, was claimed, the balancing charge is simply equal to the disposal proceeds.

The key point for a disposal of any asset on which any of the allowances in Section 8.5 has been claimed is that there is an immediate balancing charge on disposal (if there are any disposal proceeds), regardless of whether the company has any balance on its capital allowances pools.

### VAT and Disposal Proceeds

The disposal proceeds to be used in calculating balancing charges or capital gains should exclude any VAT the company has to account for on the disposal.

## 8.9    MORE POINTS ON PLANT AND MACHINERY ALLOWANCES

Where VAT is recovered on the purchase of an asset, only the net cost after VAT recovery is eligible for capital allowances.

Both the annual investment allowance and all writing down allowances, are restricted if the company draws up accounts for a period of less than twelve months. For example, if a company draws up accounts for the nine months ending 31st December 2024, it will be entitled to:

- A maximum annual investment allowance of £753,425 (£1m x 275/365)
- Writing down allowances at 13.56% on its main pool (18% x 275/365)
- Writing down allowances at 4.52% on its special rate pool (6% x 275/365)

Similar restrictions may apply in the period a company commences business (see Section 2.6 regarding accounting periods applying for CT purposes in the period of commencement).

Writing down allowances may be claimed on assets a company owner (or other connected person) transfers into the company. Such claims are generally based on the asset's market value at the date of transfer, except that:

- Fixtures and fittings (including integral features) are subject to the rules on second hand property (see Section 10.5)
- Where an individual or a partnership transfers an existing business to a company, they may elect to transfer the plant and machinery used by the business at its tax written down value for capital allowances purposes

None of the usual allowances on plant and machinery are available in the accounting period a business ceases. A balancing allowance or charge will apply instead, based on the difference between the unrelieved balance of expenditure and the market value of the remaining assets at the date of cessation (or the amount of expenditure originally 'pooled' in respect of each asset, if lower: see further below).

While a furnished holiday letting business carried on by a company will be deemed to cease on 1$^{st}$ April 2025 (see Section 1.6), no balancing allowances or charges will arise as a result of this in itself: the 'pooled' expenditure will simply transfer to the company's ongoing 'normal' property business.

The general rule applying for capital allowances purposes is that expenditure is treated as incurred as soon as there is an unconditional commitment to pay. However, assets bought on extended credit terms of more than four months are treated as if they were purchased on the date payment is due.

Despite this last rule, assets bought on hire purchase continue to be eligible for capital allowances as normal, but must be brought into use in the business before the end of the accounting period for full relief to be allowed in that period.

Subject to the above points, the full allowance due is available on any asset purchased part-way through the accounting period, even on the last day.

## Capital Allowance Disclaimers

Apart from balancing allowances and charges, capital allowances are not mandatory. The amount of allowance available is effectively a maximum that may be claimed and the company may claim any amount between zero and that maximum for each accounting period. Any amount not claimed (or 'disclaimed') will increase the tax written down value carried forward in the relevant pool, thus increasing the allowances available in future periods. However, where other, more generous allowances are disclaimed, the expenditure will only attract writing down allowances at the appropriate rate in future periods.

The facility to disclaim capital allowances in one period might perhaps be useful where it will lead to a reduction in a balancing charge (or, more rarely, an increase in a balancing allowance) in a subsequent period when the company has a higher marginal CT rate.

## Late Claims

The annual investment allowance and the allowances covered in Sections 8.5 and 8.6 can only be claimed in the period the qualifying expenditure is incurred. However, writing down allowances may be claimed at any time, provided the relevant asset is still in qualifying use. Hence, it is often possible to claim writing down allowances on assets purchased in earlier years where a claim was not originally made: provided the assets qualified in the first place. This is particularly relevant to property purchases.

## Notifying Expenditure

The company must notify HMRC of new expenditure on which it is claiming capital allowances (or which it is pooling in other words) each accounting period. This is generally done through the usual tax return process, including the facility to make amendments within twelve months of the normal filing date (see Section 2.5).

## 8.10   CHOOSING THE BEST ALLOWANCES

The introduction of the additional allowances covered in Section 8.5 has left companies facing a choice over which allowances to claim on many new, unused assets. In this section, I will guide you through the alternatives.

I will not repeat the qualifying criteria for the different allowances discussed, as we have already covered these, except to say there are no choices when it comes to cars, or expenditure on land and buildings not qualifying as plant and machinery: these types of expenditure can, of course, be ignored when it comes to considering whether the company has spent in excess of the available annual investment allowance.

In this section, I will assume the company has the maximum annual investment allowance of £1m available: but see Section 8.4 for details of potential exceptions.

## The Super-Deduction

In the vast majority of cases, the super-deduction will be the best allowance to claim where it is available, as it provides relief at a rate of more than 100%. However, there may be a few exceptions where a disposal of an asset is anticipated in the near future, for a high proportion of its original cost, and the company will have a higher marginal CT rate at that time.

## The Annual Investment Allowance

For anything that doesn't qualify for the super-deduction, the annual investment allowance is the 'go to' allowance for most small or medium-sized companies. The annual investment allowance provides immediate 100% relief without any of the strings attached to full expensing, or even enhanced capital allowances. Hence, provided the company's total expenditure on plant and machinery not qualifying for the super-deduction does not exceed £1m, the annual investment allowance is the best allowance to claim.

## Enhanced Capital Allowances

Where total expenditure not qualifying for the super-deduction exceeds £1m, it will generally make sense to claim enhanced capital allowances where they are available. This is because enhanced capital allowances do not automatically trigger balancing charges in the same way as assets on which full expensing is claimed.

However, in the case of plant and machinery purchased for use in a designated investment zone or freeport tax site, full expensing may be preferable as enhanced capital allowances are clawed back if the assets are moved out of the tax site within five years.

## Full Expensing

Once expenditure not qualifying for the super-deduction or enhanced capital allowances exceeds £1m, full expensing is the best allowance to claim where available. However, if, having allocated the annual investment allowance first to anything not qualifying for full expensing, the super-deduction, or enhanced capital allowances, some of the annual investment allowance remains available, it makes sense to allocate what remains to items qualifying for full expensing, prioritising items likely to be disposed of in the near future.

**50% First Year Allowances**

The only virtue of 50% first year allowances is they are better than writing down allowances at 6%. Hence, where all of the company's expenditure on qualifying plant and machinery can be covered by some combination of the other allowances discussed in this section, the annual investment allowance should be allocated to items where the only other choice, apart from writing down allowances, is the 50% first year allowance.

In other cases, the position is more complex and we will look at the choices available to the company in this scenario in Section 8.11.

## 8.11 ALLOCATING THE ANNUAL INVESTMENT ALLOWANCE

Utilising the annual investment allowance in the most beneficial way can lead to substantial CT savings, but there are sometimes conflicting factors to consider where new, unused assets are being acquired. We'll look at that a little later, first let's start with the simpler position where only used or second-hand assets are purchased.

### Example

*During the year ending 31st March 2025, Star Ltd spends £1.25m on integral features and £1m on other qualifying plant and machinery. All the company's expenditure is on second-hand assets, so the only capital allowances available are the annual investment allowance or writing down allowances.*

*At first, the company draws up a draft CT computation claiming a £1m annual investment allowance on the assets falling into the main pool and writing down allowances at 6% on the integral features. This results in a total claim of £1.075m (£1m + £1.25m x 6%), saving the company £268,750 in CT (at 25%).*

*However, before submitting the final computation, the company's accountant revises the capital allowances claim by allocating the annual investment allowance to the integral features instead of assets falling into the main pool. The company may now claim an annual investment allowance of £1m **plus** writing down allowances at 6% on the remaining £250,000 of integral features **and** at 18% on the other qualifying plant and machinery. This produces a total claim of £1,195,000 (£1m + £250,000 x 6% + £1m x 18%), saving the company £298,750 in CT, or £30,000 more than the original computation.*

Furthermore, the company will continue to benefit from greater writing down allowances in future years, as illustrated below:

| Year end 31st March | Allowances Claimed Original Method | Revised Method | Extra CT Saving |
|---|---|---|---|
| 2025 | £1,075,000 | £1,195,000 | £30,000 |
| 2026 | £70,500 | £161,700 | £22,800 |
| 2027 | £66,270 | £134,286 | £17,004 |
| 2028 | £62,294 | £111,706 | £12,353 |
| 2029 | £58,557 | £93,094 | £8,634 |

The total **additional** CT saving achieved in the year of expenditure and the following four years amounts to over £90,000. Hence, as we can see, allocating the annual investment allowance to integral features and other assets falling into the special rate pool can prove hugely beneficial.

### Expenditure on New Integral Features
The example above shows the benefit of allocating the annual investment allowance to expenditure on used or second-hand integral features. The position for expenditure on new integral features is more complex, however, as such expenditure is eligible for either the annual investment allowance or the 50% first year allowance.

Generally speaking, these complications only arise where the company is spending more than £1m on a combination of used, second-hand assets and other items not qualifying for full expensing or the super-deduction. Where such expenditure is less than £1m, it remains better to claim the annual investment allowance on integral features, and thus get immediate 100% relief. This will be the position for the vast majority of small or medium-sized companies. For some larger companies, however, there may be a difficult choice to make.

### *Example*
CSSG Ltd has annual profits of around £1.5m. During the year ending 31$^{st}$ December 2024, it spends £400,000 on new integral features and £900,000 on second-hand vans and machinery. Whatever the company does, it will be able to claim an annual investment allowance of £1m, but which assets should the allowance be allocated to?

***Scenario 1:*** *The company claims the annual investment allowance on the vans and machinery plus £100,000 of the new integral features. It can claim the 50% first year allowance on the remaining £300,000 of expenditure on integral features. CSSG Ltd's total capital allowances claim is thus:*

First year allowance: £300,000 x 50%      £150,000
*Annual investment allowance:*      £1,000,000
*Total*      £1,150,000

**Scenario 2:** *The company claims the annual investment allowance on the integral features plus £600,000 of the vans and machinery. It can claim writing down allowances at 18% on the remaining £300,000 of expenditure on vans and machinery. CSSG Ltd's total capital allowances claim is thus:*

*Writing down allowances: £300,000 x 18%*      £54,000
*Annual investment allowance:*      £1,000,000
*Total*      £1,054,000

*The extra tax saving for the year ending 31st December 2024 produced by Scenario 1 is £24,000 (£1.15m – £1.054m = £96,000 x 25%).*

Clearly, claiming the annual investment allowance on the assets not qualifying for the 50% first year allowance produces the better result in the first instance. However, the unrelieved expenditure carried forward will attract writing down allowances at different rates in the following year, ending 31st December 2025, as follows:

Scenario 1: £150,000 at 6% =      £9,000
Scenario 2: £246,000 at 18% =      £44,280

The writing down allowances over the next three years under the two scenarios will be:

| Year Ending | Scenario 1 | Scenario 2 |
|---|---|---|
| 31st December 2026 | £8,460 | £36,310 |
| 31st December 2027 | £7,952 | £29,774 |
| 31st December 2028 | £7,475 | £24,415 |

By this point, the benefit produced by Scenario 1 will reverse, as the additional CT savings produced by Scenario 2 in the subsequent period (2025 to 2028) will total £25,473, putting the company an overall net £1,473 better off than under Scenario 1.

The additional savings produced by Scenario 2 will continue to accumulate thereafter until reaching a total of £36,163 after twelve years, putting the company an overall net £12,163 better off than under Scenario 1 (assuming its marginal CT rate remains 25% throughout this period).

Things then reverse again with the writing down allowances under Scenario 1 starting to exceed those under Scenario 2.

However, the differences by this point are small and the company is still an overall net £9,717 better off under Scenario 2 after twenty years.

In summary, where there is a choice between allocating the annual investment allowance to assets that would otherwise qualify for the 50% first year allowance, or to assets falling into the main pool, but not qualifying for full expensing or the super-deduction:

- Allocating the annual investment allowance to assets falling into the main pool produces greater savings in the first instance, but
- Allocating it to assets that would otherwise qualify for the 50% first year allowance will produce greater cumulative savings within four years, although
- You may decide it is better to take the immediate saving, as the additional long-term savings produced are not great

## 8.12  FUTURE CHANGES TO CAPITAL ALLOWANCES

The capital allowances regime has seen numerous changes in recent years. In its election manifesto, the new Labour Government promised: *"We will retain a permanent full expensing system for capital investment and the annual investment allowance for small business. And we will give firms greater clarity on what qualifies for allowances to improve business investment decisions."*

So, while further changes are perhaps inevitable, it would appear that small and medium-sized companies will continue to be able to claim most of their capital spending on qualifying plant and machinery immediately, thanks to the annual investment allowance and full expensing: for the foreseeable future at least!

# Chapter 9

# Motoring

## 9.1 VEHICLE VAT

In this chapter, we will be discussing the tax issues relating to vehicles owned by the company, or used for the purposes of its business. As far as the VAT aspects of this are concerned, we will generally assume, throughout most of this chapter, that the company is not in the flat rate scheme. We will then look at the impact of the flat rate scheme on company vehicles and motoring costs in Section 9.8.

### VAT on Fuel

Where the company only meets the cost of fuel for business use, it may claim the VAT cost in full (assuming it is registered for VAT, fully taxable, and not in the flat rate scheme).

Where the company also (or only) meets the cost of fuel for private use, there are four options available:

i)   Claim VAT in full on all fuel costs and account for VAT (as output tax) on supplies of fuel for private use
ii)  Claim VAT in full on all fuel costs, apply the fuel scale charge (see below) in respect of any cars for which fuel is provided for private use, and account for VAT (as output tax) on supplies of fuel for private use in any other vehicles (vans, pickups, etc.)
iii) Only claim VAT in respect of business use
iv)  Do not claim VAT on fuel

Again, this is assuming the company is registered for VAT and not in the flat rate scheme. Further restrictions would apply if the company was not fully taxable.

The VAT fuel scale charge under option (ii) is a fixed amount of additional output VAT that must be accounted for in each VAT period in respect of fuel provided for private use. The scale charge can only apply to cars (not vans, etc) and, like most tax rules, is based on the car's $CO_2$ emissions. You can find the applicable charge by visiting: www.gov.uk/fuel-scale-charge

The scale charge makes option (ii) a good choice for cars where there is extensive private use, but a bad choice for cars with low private mileage. But you can't pick and choose, because the critical point to understand at this stage is that the company *must follow the same method in respect of all vehicles* for which fuel is provided, or fuel costs are being met.

Hence, where the fuel scale charge is applied to one car, it must be applied to all cars where fuel is provided for private use; if the company chooses not to claim VAT on fuel for one vehicle, it cannot claim VAT on any vehicle fuel costs at all!

Options (i) and (iii) will effectively produce the same overall result and require detailed mileage records in respect of all vehicles in order to support the claim for business use (or the amount of output VAT accounted for in respect of private use).

Option (ii) will only require detailed mileage records for vehicles other than cars. In practice, many companies will claim VAT on fuel for cars in full and apply the scale charges, while only claiming VAT for business use of other vehicles (rather than claiming it in full and then accounting for output tax in respect of private use). This is not strictly correct but, as it still produces the same overall result, it will usually be acceptable.

For vans, pickups, etc, it is only necessary to restrict VAT claims where the private use is significant: see Section 9.6 for further details. For cars (but not vans, etc), travel between home and the director's (or other employee's) permanent workplace is classed as private use.


### 9.2    COMPANY CARS

You can get your company to buy a car for your personal use. The company will be able to claim tax relief on the running costs and capital allowances on the cost of the car.

That's the good news. The bad news is you the director will have to pay Income Tax each year on the benefit in kind and your company will have to pay employer's National Insurance on that benefit. In many cases these charges are so high that most small company owners are put off going down the company car route.

Exceptions are company-owned vans, motorbikes, and electric cars, which are taxed much more generously and covered in Sections 9.5 to 9.7.

As well as the tax issues involved, there are also non-tax factors such as consumer rights (see Section 1.5) to consider before buying any vehicle through your company, and it's worth bearing these in mind.

**Capital Allowances**

The company enjoys tax relief on the purchase price of the car by claiming capital allowances. This applies whether the car is bought outright or using hire purchase.

The amount of capital allowances that can be claimed depends on the car's $CO_2$ emissions. From 1st April 2021, the emission thresholds for capital allowances are as follows:

- Over 50g/km    6% per year
- 1 to 50g/km    18% per year
- Zero           100%

The car must be purchased new for the 100% rate to apply. A second-hand zero emission car will only attract the 18% rate.

The average car has $CO_2$ emissions of well over 50g/km, so most companies will only be able to claim capital allowances of just 6% per year on 'regular' petrol or diesel cars. You can check car $CO_2$ emissions easily using websites such as: https://carfueldata.vehicle-certification-agency.gov.uk

The $CO_2$ emission thresholds were higher in previous tax years. In other words, it has become harder and harder to qualify for the better capital allowance rates.

As expenditure on company cars is 'pooled' (see Section 8.7), there is no adjustment to the rate of writing down allowances applying if the car qualified for the 18% rate under a higher $CO_2$ emission threshold when it was first purchased in the past: the expenditure will continue to enjoy that writing down allowance rate, even if the car's $CO_2$ emissions now exceed the current threshold.

**The 100% first-year allowance for new electric cars is only available until 31st March 2025**. This relief allows your company to claim the whole cost of the car as a tax-deductible expense in the year of purchase.

Electric cars have to be new to qualify for the 100% first-year allowance. The car doesn't have to be new to qualify for the 6% or 18% writing down allowances. In other words, you can claim these smaller capital allowances on second-hand cars.

184

If a loan is taken out to buy the vehicle the interest costs are also an allowable expense, as are the running costs such as repairs, insurance and road tax.

Unlike vehicles bought for use by sole traders or business partners, there is no restriction to capital allowances or other costs to reflect private use by company directors or employees, as this is taxed through the benefit in kind system instead.

## VAT
VAT cannot be recovered on the purchase price of company cars in the vast majority of cases. There are a few, limited exceptions including cars owned by taxi firms, driving schools, and car-hire companies.

You can, in theory, recover the VAT if your intention is to use the car exclusively for business purposes and it is not available for any private use. However, generally speaking, it is extremely difficult, almost impossible, to convince the taxman that a company owned car is not available for any private use. Remember, it's not just that there isn't any private use; it must not be possible to use the car privately.

If VAT cannot be recovered then capital allowances are claimed on the total cost of the car including VAT.

One way to avoid or reduce the amount of irrecoverable VAT is to buy a second-hand car. If the car is purchased from a private individual who is not VAT registered then no VAT is payable. If the car is purchased from a dealership the sale is likely to fall under the second-hand margin scheme. Here VAT is levied only on the dealer's *profit*, not the overall price of the car. The VAT is passed onto the customer but is not itemised on the purchase invoice. However, the total VAT paid is likely to be much lower than on a fully taxed sale.

If the car is used for business purposes, the company can reclaim all the VAT it pays on repairs and maintenance.

## How to Calculate Capital Allowances
Technically, the purchase price of the car is added to one of the company's capital allowances pools (see Section 8.7) and writing down allowances are claimed on the pool balance. Cars with $CO_2$ emissions over 50g/km are added to the special rate pool, other cars are added to the main pool. This includes new electric cars on which 100% enhanced capital allowances have been claimed although, in this case, the balance added to the pool is effectively nil.

This pooling of expenditure generally only makes a difference to the tax relief obtained by the company when the car is sold, and we will look at this shortly.

While the car is held by the company, we can calculate the effective amount of tax relief obtained in most cases by applying the 6% and 18% writing-down allowance rates to the cost of the car. These writing down allowances are rather stingy, not just because the rates themselves are low, but also because they're calculated using the 'reducing balance' basis instead of the more generous 'straight line' method.

For example, if your company buys a second-hand car for £15,000 that qualifies for a 6% writing down allowance, it can claim £900 in year 1. This will save the company between £171 (£900 x 19%) and £239 (£900 x 26.5%) in CT (see Section 2.1).

In year 2 the company can claim £846, calculated as follows:

£15,000 – £900 = £14,100 x 6% = £846

Thus, the company will save between £161 (£846 x 19%) and £224 (£846 x 26.5%) in CT in year 2.

Each year the amount that can be claimed gets smaller, so it takes many years to recover all the tax relief. After five years, the company will have claimed capital allowances of £3,991, possibly saving as little as £758 in CT (if the company's CT rate remains 19% throughout this period).

**Selling the Car**
When cars used by sole traders or business partners are sold for less than their written down value, it is usually possible to claim a balancing allowance, albeit with a restriction to reflect private use.

Sadly, this is not the case for companies because of the way company cars are pooled for capital allowances purposes (see Section 8.7 for how capital allowances pools work).

For example, after five years, our car discussed above will have a written down value of just over £11,000. Let's say the company then sells it for £3,000.

If such a car was owned and used by a sole trader, he or she would be able to claim a balancing allowance of £8,000 (£11,000 – £3,000), subject to an adjustment for private use. In other words, their taxable profits could be reduced by up to £8,000 in the year the car is sold.

Companies cannot do this. A company effectively has to claim writing down allowances at 6% per year on the £8,000 balance, meaning it will usually take many, many years to claim all the tax relief to which it is entitled.

If the company sells the car for more than its written down value, but less than the purchase price, the sale proceeds are deducted from the relevant pool (usually the special rate pool). This may lead to a balancing charge, depending on the pool balance

In the rare case that a company makes a profit on the sale of a car, the amount deducted from the capital allowances pool is restricted to the purchase price. The profit, or gain, is usually exempt from CT and is, in effect, a tax-free windfall (make the most of it, you don't get many of these). Profits on other company vehicles (vans, motorbikes, etc) will, however, be subject to CT, as explained in Section 8.8.

As far as VAT is concerned, if a VAT-registered business sells a car on which no VAT was recovered because the vehicle was available for private use, no VAT has to be charged when the company sells the vehicle. It is an exempt supply.

If VAT was not charged when the car was purchased and the business chooses to use the second-hand margin scheme, VAT is only due on any profit margin made on the sale. If no profit is made, there is no VAT due (most cars are sold for a loss).

**Taxable Benefit in Kind**
If your company buys a car for your personal use you will have to pay Income Tax on the benefit and your company will have to pay employer's National Insurance.

The taxable benefit is found by multiplying the manufacturer's list price (also known as the P11D value) by a percentage that depends on the car's $CO_2$ emissions and the type of fuel it uses.

Note, the list price is not necessarily the price your company pays for the car. The list price will probably be higher and will almost certainly be much higher if the car is second hand.

For the highest emission cars, the taxable percentage is 37%. The various taxable percentages can be found under 'Company car tax' at: https://tinyurl.com/cartax24

Note, the taxable percentages for cars powered solely by diesel are 4% higher than the rate given by the table, unless they meet the Real Driving Emissions Step 2 ('RDE2') standard. The rate cannot go higher than 37%, however.

Let's say our company car that cost £15,000 second hand is a petrol car with $CO_2$ emissions of 129g/km. The taxable percentage is therefore 30%. If the car has a list price of £30,000, this means £9,000 (£30,000 x 30%) will be added to the director's taxable income this year.

The taxable percentages for most cars will be 1% higher next year (2025/26) but capped at 37%. See Section 9.5 regarding the taxable percentages for electric cars, which are much lower.

### How Much Tax Do Company Car Drivers Pay?

It's important to point out that there is no *employee's* National Insurance payable on this or other benefits in kind.

As far as Income Tax is concerned, most articles on company car tax state that basic-rate taxpayers pay 20% tax and higher-rate taxpayers pay 40% tax.

It's not as simple as that if you're a company owner taking a small tax-free salary and the rest of your income as dividends. The amount of Income Tax payable on the car benefit depends on the level of salary and whether the director has income from other sources such as rental income.

Directors who are basic-rate taxpayers will effectively pay between 8.75% and 20% tax on the benefit, although they could, of course, be pushed into higher rate tax, which will increase the cost. Directors who are higher-rate taxpayers will effectively pay between 33.75% and 45% tax on the benefit.

The lower tax rates (8.75% and 33.75%) are payable to the extent the taxable benefit is covered by the director's personal allowance.

### Example
*Cameron is a company owner who pays himself a small salary that uses up his Income Tax personal allowance and takes his remaining income as dividends, for a grand total of £75,000 per year.*

*If his company provides a car with a £9,000 benefit in kind charge, Cameron will pay £1,800 Income Tax directly on the benefit (at 20%). The £9,000 taxable benefit uses up £9,000 of his basic-rate band. This means £9,000 of his dividend income which would have been taxed at 8.75% will now be taxed at 33.75%, resulting in extra tax of £2,250.*

*The total tax increase is £4,050, which is 45%. (Note, salaries and benefits are always taxed before dividends. Dividends are always treated as the top slice of income and taxed last.)*

### *Example*
*John is a company owner who pays himself a small salary that uses up his Income Tax personal allowance and takes his remaining income as dividends, for a grand total of £40,000 per year (making him a basic-rate taxpayer).*

*If his company provides a car with a £9,000 benefit in kind charge, Cameron will pay £1,800 Income Tax directly on the benefit (at 20%).*

*The £9,000 taxable benefit will use up £9,000 of his basic-rate band but, because his total taxable income (£49,000) is still less than the £50,270 higher-rate threshold, none of his dividend income will be taxed at 33.75%.*

*The total tax increase is just £1,800, which is 20%.*

### Employer's National Insurance
As a company owner you also have to take account of the tax your company pays. The employer's National Insurance cost on the above car benefit for 2024/25 will be £30,000 x 30% x 13.8% = £1,242.

Employer's National Insurance is a tax-deductible expense for the business, so the cost net of CT relief will be between £913 (relief at 26.5%) and £1,006 (relief at 19%).

### Private Fuel Costs
If the company pays for the car's fuel there is an additional fuel benefit charge which is £27,800 this year (the same as last year). This is not the amount that is added to the employee's taxable income. The taxable amount is found by multiplying £27,800 by the car's benefit in kind percentage.

For example, if the benefit in kind percentage for the car is 30%, the taxable amount is £8,340 (£27,800 x 30%). This amount is added to the employee's taxable income. Thus, a higher-rate taxpayer will pay up to £3,753 in extra Income Tax this year (at 45%, see above).

The company will pay £1,151 National Insurance (£8,340 x 13.8%), costing at most £932 net of CT relief.

Because the fuel tax charge is so high, most commentators agree it almost never makes sense to get your company to pay for fuel.

Where the company pays for fuel for a director's (or any employee's) private use, it must either restrict its VAT claim or account for extra output VAT, following one of the options described in Section 9.1.

If you have a company car but pay for your own fuel you can recover the cost of *business travel* from your company using the so-called advisory fuel rates: https://www.gov.uk/guidance/advisory-fuel-rates

You can currently pay yourself between 14p and 26p per mile (for petrol cars), although the rates are updated quarterly. No Income Tax or employer's National Insurance is due on these payments.

For a VAT registered company, VAT can be recovered on these payments in the same way as discussed in Section 9.4.

As always, it is important to remember travel from home to a permanent workplace is classed as a private journey for tax purposes. See Section 4.4 for further details regarding what can be classed as business travel.

### Is a Company Car Worth Having?
For the sample company car used in all the examples, it has been shown that a director who is a higher-rate taxpayer could end up paying an extra £4,050 Income Tax this year, *with similar payments every year*. This is assuming the director pays for his or her own fuel and therefore avoids the additional fuel benefit charge.

The company will pay an extra £1,242 National Insurance this year, *with similar payments every year*.

The total tax bill is £5,292 this year alone... and the car only cost £15,000!

On the plus side, the company can claim capital allowances but these produce only a tiny CT saving each year if (as is most likely) the writing-down rate is just 6%.

The company can also pay for most of the car's running costs, such as its annual service and MOT, other repair costs, insurance and road tax, and this is much more tax efficient than paying these expenses out of your own after-tax income. The company can also recover all the VAT on the car's maintenance costs.

Weighing up the benefits and drawbacks, it is difficult to conjure up a scenario where a company owner will be better off getting their company to buy a regular petrol or diesel car, rather than buying the car personally using his or her own money.

Even if you have to extract additional dividend income from your company to buy your own car, this will almost always be more tax efficient than getting the company to pay for the car. You may have to pay 33.75% or 39.35% Income Tax on the additional dividend, but this will be a one-off tax charge compared with the company car tax charges that have to be paid every year.

### Leased Cars
Of course, many individuals and businesses prefer to lease their cars these days. If your company leases a car, the monthly payments are a tax-deductible expense. For new leases commencing after 31$^{st}$ March 2021, however, if the car has $CO_2$ emissions greater than 50g/km, 15% of the lease payments are disallowed.

Most cars have $CO_2$ emissions greater than 50g/km so, in most cases, the company will only be able to claim 85% of the lease payments as a tax-deductible expense.

Where the rental agreement separates out maintenance costs, these costs are not subject to the 15% disallowance and can be claimed in full.

Note, with leasing the company does not claim capital allowances, just the lease payments.

The 50g/km threshold was higher in the past. If the lease commenced before 1$^{st}$ April 2021 and the car's $CO_2$ emissions are below the threshold that applied at the time, the 15% disallowance does not apply.

### VAT on Lease Payments
Generally speaking, 50% of the VAT on the lease payments can be recovered (where the car is used partly for business and partly for private purposes).

VAT can be recovered in full if the car is exclusively for business use and the intention is that it will not be available for any private use. In practice for most businesses it would be almost impossible to convince HMRC this test has been met.

All of the VAT on maintenance charges included in a lease agreement can be recovered, as long as they are shown separately.

The benefit in kind charges are exactly the same as for cars purchased by the company and discussed in the previous paragraphs. The benefit in kind tax charge is not affected by the method used by the company to provide the car to the employee.

## 9.3    POOL CARS

If employees have access to a company owned pool car, rather than having a car for their exclusive use, there is no Income Tax benefit in kind charge.

Some company owners may thus attempt to treat company owned cars as pool cars, even though they are used by the directors individually. This is a dangerous mistake to make because, as we saw in Section 9.2, benefit in kind charges on petrol and diesel cars can be extremely high and are based on the car's list price, even if the vehicle was purchased second-hand for a fraction of the list price.

There are strict rules to be satisfied to qualify as a pool car:

- The car must be made available to, and actually used by, more than one employee
- The car must be made available to each of those employees by reason of their employment
- The car must not ordinarily be used by one employee to the exclusion of others
- Any private use must be merely incidental to business use
- The car must not normally be kept overnight at or near where any of the employees live, unless they live near the employer's premises.

The rule that private use must be merely incidental to business use may cause confusion. Using a car for what is primarily a business journey, but includes some limited private use, would satisfy the condition.

HMRC gives the example of an employee who is required to make a long business journey and, so as to make an early morning start, takes a pool car home the previous evening. The office to home journey is classed as private use of the car but in these circumstances is undertaken to facilitate the business trip. It is thus merely incidental to the business use.

But if it happens too often, the car could fail the fifth condition that it must not normally be kept overnight at an employee's home. In these circumstances the car would not be treated as a pool car.

The fact that the director or employee has another car for their private use does not prevent the pool car being available for their private use too.

HMRC will usually accept that a car is not normally kept overnight at employees' homes if the total number of nights on which it is taken home, for whatever reason, is less than 60% of the year.

This is just a rule of thumb, however, and cannot be relied on in all circumstances. If a car is taken home enough times, even if within the 60% limit, HMRC is unlikely to accept all the home to work journeys will satisfy the fourth test that any private use must be merely incidental to business use (remember, travel between home and a permanent workplace is classed as private use for tax purposes).

If the car is normally taken home by an employee because there are inadequate parking facilities at the company's premises, or there are security concerns, this is not a good enough reason to pass the 'not normally kept overnight' condition.

Even if all the conditions are met, it is important to be able to demonstrate this to HMRC. A company should keep sufficient evidence, for example evidence demonstrating how the car is used by employees and mileage logs showing the car is only used for business journeys. It may be helpful to expressly prohibit employees from using the car privately in writing. The car's insurance must also allow business use.

Where HMRC has accepted a car is a pool car it may check every three or four years whether all the conditions are still being met.

## 9.4    USING YOUR OWN VEHICLE FOR BUSINESS

Because it is not very tax efficient in most cases to get your company to buy a regular petrol or diesel car, most company owners buy their cars personally. These personally owned cars will then often be used for both business and private travel.

When you use your own vehicle for business journeys, your company can pay you back using the following mileage rates:

|  | **First 10,000 miles** | **Above 10,000 miles** |
|---|---|---|
| Cars and vans | 45p | 25p |
| Motorbikes | 24p | 24p |
| Bicycle | 20p | 20p |

If you take one of your employees (including another director) in your car on a business journey you can claim an extra 5p per mile.

These are known as the approved mileage allowance payment (AMAP) rates. They are supposed to cover not just your fuel costs but also wear and tear on the vehicle. The 10,000 mile limit applies for each tax year ended 5th April (as this is effectively an Income Tax relief).

The amount your company pays you will be tax free in your hands and a tax-deductible expense for the company.

For example, if you rack up 5,000 business miles in your own car this tax year, your company can pay you £2,250 tax free (5,000 x 0.45). The company can also claim the expense, saving it CT of at least £428 (£2,250 x 19%).

If your business mileage comes to 12,000 your company can pay you £5,000 tax free (10,000 x 0.45 + 2,000 x 0.25) and the company will save at least £950 in CT.

Business mileage does not include travel from your home to your permanent place of work. See Section 4.4 for further details of what may be classed as a business journey for tax purposes.

Using the above mileage rates is a simple way to obtain tax relief for your business travel, although it is necessary to keep a record of your business journeys (using a mileage log or app, for example).

Generally speaking, neither you nor the company can claim tax relief for any other costs relating to the vehicle under these circumstances, and capital allowances are not available.

## Recovering VAT on Business Mileage

If your company is VAT registered it is also possible to recover the VAT element of your business fuel costs. The portion of the 45p/25p mileage rate that is for fuel is generally calculated using HMRC's advisory fuel rates. These are updated quarterly and can be found at: https://www.gov.uk/guidance/advisory-fuel-rates.

For example, if your car has a two-litre diesel engine, the rate at the time of writing is 15p per mile, and the VAT element would be 2.5p (15p x 20/120). So, for each business mile, the company can recover 2.5p in VAT. If you drive 1,000 miles on business during the period, your company can recover £25 of VAT (1,000 x 2.5p).

You will have to keep VAT fuel receipts that contain enough VAT to cover the claimed mileage for the relevant period (the simplest solution is to keep every fuel receipt).

Naturally, where any VAT is recovered, the tax-deductible cost that may be claimed for CT purposes is reduced accordingly.

## National Insurance Confusions

Payments to directors and employees using the AMAP rates are exempt from Income Tax and National Insurance. Payments at a lower rate continue to be exempt from Income Tax (and the employee may claim tax relief for the underpayment).

The situation with National Insurance is a bit more complex and has led HMRC to charge National Insurance on payments at a lower rate in some situations. This mainly arose where the company was also paying a lump sum car allowance to the employees. Affected companies and employees are being given the opportunity to reclaim any excess National Insurance paid.

In the simple situation, where the employees only receive mileage payments and there is no lump sum car allowance, payments at less than the AMAP rates should not attract any National Insurance. However, employees cannot claim National Insurance relief for underpayments of business mileage in the same way they can claim Income Tax relief.

Another bizarre twist is that the 10,000 mile limit does not apply for National Insurance purposes, so the higher 45p rate can be paid on further business mileage over the limit free from National Insurance, but partly subject to Income Tax. For a small company owner/director, this is a more tax efficient form of profit extraction than dividends, so it could be worth considering in some cases.

## 9.5 ELECTRIC CARS, ELECTRIFYING TAX BREAKS

At present, it is extremely tax efficient to get your company to purchase a new electric car for your personal use, instead of buying it yourself out of your after-tax income. Not only is the cost of the car a fully tax-deductible expense for the company, the director and the company only have to pay a tiny amount of Income Tax and National Insurance on the benefit in kind.

This makes electric cars one of the most tax efficient ways to take money out of your company for your personal benefit. Electric vehicles also come with other financial benefits and incentives including:

- No road tax: however, this exemption will be scrapped from April 2025. Electric cars will then also potentially be subject to the £355 expensive car supplement
- Exemption from London's congestion charge (until 25th December 2025)

Although buying electric cars is extremely tax efficient, this does not necessarily mean buying one makes *overall financial sense*. For example, the correct question could be: Is it more cost effective overall for a company owner to buy a second-hand petrol or diesel car *personally* if the price tag is much lower than a brand new electric car?

We don't know the answer to that question. What we can say is, if you are planning on buying an electric car anyway, putting it through the company currently makes a lot of sense from a tax saving perspective.

### 100% Enhanced Capital Allowances
When your company buys a new electric car, it can claim enhanced capital allowances: a type of first-year allowance that allows tax relief to be claimed on the whole cost of the car in the year of purchase.

So, if your company pays £30,000 for a new electric car it can claim CT relief of between £5,700 (£30,000 x 19%) and £7,950 (£30,000 x 26.5%).

Note the car has to be new: enhanced capital allowances cannot be claimed on second-hand cars.

This tax break is only available until **31st March 2025**. Cars bought after this date will only qualify for the more stingy writing down allowances, typically 18% per year for an electric car.

First year allowances on zero emission goods vehicles have also been extended until 31$^{st}$ March 2025 (although these will also qualify for the annual investment allowance or full expensing anyway).

Until fairly recently, cars with $CO_2$ emissions of 50g/km or less qualified for the 100% first-year allowance. From April 2021, only cars with zero emissions qualify (i.e. fully electric cars and not hybrids).

Sadly, when it comes to recovering VAT, electric cars are no different to other cars: VAT usually cannot be reclaimed.

## Selling the Car

When the company eventually sells the electric car on which the 100% first-year allowance has been claimed, there is likely to be a balancing charge, with an amount up to the entire sales proceeds potentially being added to the company's taxable profits.

A balancing charge arises when an asset is sold for more than the balance on the relevant capital allowances pool (see Section 8.7). In the case of electric cars, this will be the main pool.

Assets on which 100% tax relief has been claimed do not lead to any increase in the balance on the capital allowances pool, so there will often be a balancing charge when they are sold.

It's possible CT will be payable on this balancing charge at up to 26.5%, even if some or all of the CT relief enjoyed on the original purchase was at a rate of just 19% (see Section 2.1 and Chapter 12).

As far as VAT is concerned, the position on the sale of an electric car is the same as any other company car (see Section 9.2). In the vast majority of cases, no VAT will be payable by the company.

Take our new electric car which cost £30,000 and on which no VAT was reclaimed. CT relief was claimed on the whole £30,000 purchase price. If the car is eventually sold for £10,000, no VAT will be payable because it will be an exempt supply. However, up to £10,000 could be added to the company's taxable profits in the year of sale.

## Benefit in Kind Charges

As with other company cars, the director has to pay Income Tax on the benefit in kind and the company has to pay National Insurance. However, the taxable percentage is just 2% this year (2024/25). The taxable percentages will then increase as follows:

- 2025/26    3%
- 2026/27    4%
- 2027/28    5%

Let's say our brand new electric car that cost £30,000 also has a list price of £30,000. (Note, the list price may be different for various reasons.)

The benefit in kind charge will be £600 this year (£30,000 x 2%), rising to £1,500 by 2027/28. This means the company will pay National Insurance of just £83 (£600 x 13.8%) this year, rising to £207 by 2027/28. This is a tax-deductible expense, so the true cost, net of CT relief, will be no more than £67 at the most this year.

**Income Tax**
As explained in Section 9.2, the amount of Income Tax small company owners have to pay on benefits in kind depends on the amount of salary they take and whether they have income from other sources such as rental income.

If the director is a basic-rate taxpayer they will effectively pay between 8.75% and 20% tax on the benefit. If the director is a higher-rate taxpayer they will effectively pay between 33.75% and 45% tax on the benefit.

The lower tax rates (8.75% and 33.75%) are payable to the extent the benefit is covered by the director's personal allowance.

Sticking with the same £30,000 car, let's take the example of a director who takes a salary equal to the Income Tax personal allowance. If the director is a basic-rate taxpayer they will pay £120 in extra Income Tax this year, rising to £300 by 2027/28.

If the director is a higher-rate taxpayer they will pay £270 in extra Income Tax this year, rising to £675 by 2027/28.

The bottom line is this: regardless of whether the director is a basic-rate taxpayer or higher-rate taxpayer the amount of Income Tax and National Insurance payable is currently extremely modest: no more than £270 in Income Tax and no more than £67 employer's National Insurance (net of CT relief) for our car with a list price of £30,000.

That's a maximum total net tax cost of just £337, which is a mere 1.1% of the actual £30,000 purchase price.

## Leasing Electric Cars

Many individuals and businesses prefer to lease their cars. Some electric cars can be leased for between £200 and £300 per month.

The monthly payments you see advertised may be somewhat misleading because there may also be a significant initial rental payment at the start of the lease. This could be up to nine times the ongoing monthly payment.

If your company leases an electric car, the monthly payments are a fully tax-deductible expense. There is no restriction, as there is for cars with $CO_2$ emissions above 50 g/km.

Note, with leasing, the company does not claim the 100% first-year allowance, just the lease payments.

## VAT on Lease Payments

50% of the VAT on the lease payments can be recovered in most cases.

Business lease payments are often quoted excluding VAT altogether. So if a monthly payment of £250 per month excluding VAT is quoted, the total cost including VAT would be £300.

After recovering 50% of the VAT the total cost to the company would be £275. This is the amount that can be claimed for CT purposes, so the total cost to the business, net of CT relief would be no more than £223 at most (based on CT relief at 19%).

All of the VAT for repairs and maintenance costs can be recovered if these are shown separately.

The benefit in kind charges are exactly the same as for electric cars purchased by the company, as discussed above.

## Electricity for Electric Company Cars

If your company provides electricity to charge a fully electric company car, there is no benefit in kind charge, regardless of the level of private mileage the director or employee does, or where the car is charged. In practice, however, it may be difficult for the company to calculate the precise cost of charging the car at someone's home.

If the director pays for electricity personally but uses a fully electric company car for business travel, an advisory fuel rate of 8p per mile can be used to reimburse the director tax free for business mileage.

The company can also pay for a charging point for a fully electric car to be installed at the director's home without a taxable benefit arising.

**Electric Cars Owned by Employees (Including Directors)**
If a company provides electricity to charge electric or hybrid cars owned by employees there will not be any taxable benefit in kind. The charging facilities must, however, be provided at or near the company's workplace. There will be a benefit in kind charge if the company pays for an employee to charge their own car away from the workplace, for example at home or at a motorway service station.

Charging must be available to all employees or all employees at a particular location. If the company has multiple workplaces, charging facilities do not have to be available at all of them.

Remember also that, like other cars, the employee (or director) can claim business mileage using the approved mileage rates (i.e. 45p per mile for the first 10,000 miles and 25p thereafter: see Section 9.4 for further details).

## 9.6    BECOME A VAN MAN (OR WOMAN) AND SAVE THOUSANDS

Vans are treated much more favourably than petrol or diesel cars. For starters, the company may be able to reclaim some or all of the VAT on the purchase price. This is almost never possible with cars.

Second, the company can claim 100% CT relief on the purchase price thanks to the annual investment allowance or full expensing. Most cars only qualify for a stingy writing-down allowance of 6% per year. (See Chapter 8 for full details regarding capital allowances available on plant and machinery, including vehicles other than cars.)

Third, if the van is used privately, the benefit in kind charge is likely to be much smaller than it is for most cars. And if the company pays for the van's fuel as well, the additional benefit in kind charge is likely to be much, much smaller.

These tax breaks are worth noting because some of the vehicles classed as 'vans' by the taxman, such as double cab pick-ups, offer similar levels of comfort and convenience as the average 4x4.

In some cases, the amount of tax relief that can be claimed depends on how much the vehicle is used for business purposes.

For this reason, it is advisable to keep detailed mileage records as evidence of its use.

## VAT

If a company is VAT registered it may be able to claim back some or all of the VAT paid on a new van purchase.

Although vans are 'commercial vehicles', this does not automatically mean all the VAT can be recovered. VAT can only be reclaimed if the vehicle is used for business purposes.

If the vehicle is used solely for business purposes then all of the VAT can be reclaimed. If the vehicle is used, say, half of the time for business purposes then 50% of the VAT can be reclaimed.

Many commercial vehicles are not suitable for private use and HMRC will view any private use as insignificant and will not restrict the VAT reclaim.

However, some types of commercial vehicle (such as double cab pickups) are suitable for private use and where the private use is not insignificant the company must restrict its VAT claim accordingly.

One obvious example where one would expect HMRC to restrict the VAT claim is where the van is the only vehicle the director has available for private use. In such a case it is pretty obvious the director will be using the vehicle privately and HMRC will expect a suitable VAT apportionment.

### Example
*Vanessa gets her company to buy a new van costing £30,000, including VAT. The total VAT paid is £5,000 (£30,000 x 20/120). The van will have 50% business use and 50% private use by Vanessa. This means half the VAT (£2,500) can be reclaimed.*

When a van is purchased it may be difficult to determine how much business and private use there will be and therefore how much VAT should be reclaimed. An estimate will therefore be required. The key point is that the apportionment between business and private use must be 'reasonable' (perhaps based on mileage in a previous vehicle). It is also advisable to keep a record of how you came to your decision.

## Paying Less VAT
Where a van is expected to have significant private use one way to reduce or avoid paying VAT that can only be partially recovered is to buy a second-hand vehicle.

For example, where a van is purchased from a private individual who is not VAT registered no VAT is payable. If the van is purchased from a dealership the sale is likely to fall under the second-hand margin scheme. Here VAT is levied only on the dealer's *profit*, not the overall price of the van.

The VAT is passed onto the customer but is not itemised on the purchase invoice and cannot be reclaimed. However, the total VAT paid is likely to be much lower than on a fully taxed sale.

## Annual Investment Allowance

Vans qualify for 100% tax relief thanks to the annual investment allowance. New vans purchased after 31st March 2023 also qualify for full expensing although, as explained in Section 8.4, it is generally better for small companies to claim the annual investment allowance where it has not been exhausted on other purchases.

The company can claim CT relief on the total cost of the van after deducting any VAT that has been recovered.

It doesn't matter if the van will be used privately. In other words, private use does not restrict the amount of CT relief that can be claimed.

### *Example continued*

*Vanessa's company paid £30,000 for the van and recovered VAT of £2,500, so the total cost net of the VAT reclaim was £27,500. The purchase qualifies for tax relief under the annual investment allowance. This will result in CT relief of between £5,225 (£27,500 x 19%) and £7,288 (£27,500 x 26.5%). (See Section 2.1 regarding CT rates.)*

*Although the company paid £30,000 for the van, after claiming all the tax relief to which it is entitled, the van will only cost between £20,212 and £22,275. Up to 32.6% of the cost will be recovered in tax relief.*

The annual investment allowance is available regardless of whether the van is second hand or new. It does not allow for unlimited spending, but the annual spending limit is now £1 million, which is more than adequate for most small companies.

New zero emission goods vehicles also qualify for 100% enhanced capital allowances until March 2025, or for full expensing from April 2023. See Chapter 8 for details, including an examination of the comparative merits of each allowance.

## Selling the Van

When the company eventually sells a van on which capital allowances have been claimed, there will generally be a balancing charge added to the company's taxable profits. The amount of the charge depends on a number of factors, although, in many cases, it will be equal to the sale proceeds received for the van.

Where either full expensing or the 130% super-deduction have been claimed on the van, the balancing charge is a certainty. In most cases, the balancing charge will be equal to the sale proceeds, but see Section 8.8 regarding some potential exceptions.

Where either the annual investment allowance or enhanced capital allowances have been claimed, there is still likely to be a balancing charge, although this depends on the balance on the company's main pool (see Section 8.7).

Balancing charges arise when 'pooled' assets are sold for more than the remaining balance on the relevant pool. Because of the annual investment allowance, many small companies have a zero balance on their capital allowances pools, so the sale of a van will often still produce a balancing charge equal to the sale proceeds.

See Section 8.8 for full details of how balancing charges are calculated. As explained in Section 8.8, where the van is sold at a profit, the balancing charge will be restricted, but the profit will also be taxable as a capital gain.

Note that sales proceeds for the purposes of balancing charges or capital gains are net of any VAT the company has to account for on the sale. (Just as purchase cost is net of any VAT recovered for these purposes.)

As far as VAT is concerned, if a company sells a van on which VAT has been recovered, it will have to charge VAT when it sells the vehicle.

If the van was purchased second-hand from an unregistered business or under the margin scheme for second-hand vehicles, the company can also use the margin scheme when the van is sold. This means VAT will only be payable on any profit (there may not be any profit because most vehicles fall in value).

Returning to Vanessa, let's say the company eventually sells the van for £8,000 plus VAT. After paying the VAT to HMRC, the company will be left with £8,000.

Assuming (as is likely), the company has a zero balance on its main pool, the £8,000 net proceeds will be added to its taxable profits as a balancing charge.

## Benefit in Kind Charges

Where a van has significant private use by the director (or another employee) a taxable benefit will arise. Unlike cars, where the taxable benefit depends on the car's $CO_2$ emissions, for vans the taxable benefit is the same for every make and model: £3,960 in 2024/25.

One exception is electric vans. Vans that produce zero emissions are currently exempt from benefit in kind charges.

For other types of van, the company will pay National Insurance of £546 this year (£3,960 x 13.8%), or between £402 and £443 net of CT relief at between 19% and 26.5%.

As for the director, if they're a basic-rate taxpayer they'll effectively pay between 8.75% and 20% tax on the benefit. If they're a higher-rate taxpayer the tax rate is between 33.75% and 45%.

The lower tax rates (8.75% and 33.75%) are payable to the extent the van benefit is covered by the director's personal allowance.

These tax rates take account of the fact that the benefit in kind charge may push some of the director's dividend income into a higher tax bracket.

### Example continued

*Let's say Vanessa pays herself a salary of £12,570 (see Section 6.4) and takes her remaining income as dividends, for a grand total of £75,000 (making her a higher-rate taxpayer). We also know her company has provided a van that has a £3,960 benefit in kind charge.*

*Vanessa will pay £792 Income Tax directly on the benefit (at 20%). The taxable benefit uses up £3,960 of her basic-rate band. This means £3,960 of dividend income that would have been taxed at 8.75% will now be taxed at 33.75%, resulting in extra tax of £990.*

*The van increases Vanessa's Income Tax bill by £1,782, so the effective tax rate on the benefit is 45%.*

## Insignificant Private Use

The van will not be subject to benefit in kind charges if it is available for private use but that private use is 'insignificant'.

This is a bit of a grey area but HMRC would regard the following as examples of insignificant private use of a van:

- Taking household rubbish to the tip once or twice a year
- Regularly making a small detour to drop off a child at school or stopping at a shop on the way to work
- Calling at the dentist on the way home

Furthermore, no taxable benefit will arise just because the van is used to commute from home to work (this would be treated as private use if the vehicle was a car).

The following would count as significant private use leading to a benefit in kind charge:

- Using the van to do the weekly supermarket shop
- Taking the van away on holiday
- Using the van for social activities

**Company Pays for Fuel**
If the company pays for the van's fuel it can claim CT relief on the total cost, even if the vehicle is used privately. The company and the director/employee will then be subject to a benefit in kind charge but for vans this is extremely small: just £757 in 2024/25. Remember, for cars this charge can be as high as £10,286 (£27,800 x 37%).

For vans, this means the company will pay National Insurance of £104 this year (£757 x 13.8%), or between £77 and £85 net of CT relief.

The director/employee will pay Income Tax on the benefit. In Vanessa's case, the cost would be £341 (at 45%) this year.

Clearly, a combined net tax bill of £418 (£77 + £341) for potentially unlimited private fuel paid for by the company is extremely attractive for company owners who expect to do a lot of private mileage.

**VAT on Fuel**
Where a van is used exclusively for business purposes (or any private use is merely incidental) the company can reclaim all the VAT paid on fuel.

Where there is significant private use, either the VAT claim has to be restricted or additional output VAT will need to be accounted for, following one of the options described in Section 9.1.

## Other Running Costs

The company can pay for all of the van's other running costs, including servicing, repairs, road tax and insurance. VAT can be reclaimed in full, even if the vehicle has extensive private use. CT relief can be claimed on the balance.

## Summary

In summary, Vanessa's company paid £30,000 for a new van and recovered up to £9,788 in tax relief (£2,500 in VAT and up to £7,288 in CT relief).

This year, the company will pay an additional £546 in National Insurance on the van itself, which may cost as little as £402 net of CT relief. Vanessa will pay an additional £1,782 Income Tax.

If the company pays for fuel, it will pay a further £104 in National Insurance, costing perhaps just £77 net of CT relief. Vanessa will pay a further £341 Income Tax.

Similar charges will be paid every year.

The company can claim full tax relief on all the other running costs of the van.

## Is It a Car, Is It a Van?

The definition of a van varies from one tax to another. For capital allowances, a van is effectively a vehicle that is:

- Primarily suited for the conveyance of goods or burden of any description, or
- Of a type not commonly used as a private vehicle and unsuitable to be so used.

A vehicle only needs to meet one of these criteria to qualify as a van and be eligible for 100% relief under the annual investment allowance or full expensing.

For VAT purposes, a van is generally a vehicle that has:

- A payload of 1 tonne (1,000kg) or more, or
- No accommodation to the rear of the driver's seat fitted, or capable of being fitted, with side windows.

For benefit in kind purposes, a van is generally defined as a vehicle primarily suited for the conveyance of goods or burden.

Vehicles with a maximum laden weight over 3.5 tonnes are not classed as 'vans', but could provide even greater advantages. Not many people will want to use them for the school run though!

## Double-Cab Pick-Ups

One type of 'van' which is popular is the so-called double cab pick-up. An attractive alternative to a large car, they have enough seating space for the average family and often have removable canopies that effectively make them just like a large '4 x 4' with a lot of extra storage space in the back!

Several manufacturers produce these vehicles specifically designed to carry a payload of one tonne and thus meet the VAT definition of a van.

HMRC has for a long time stated it will accept double cab pick-ups with a payload of one tonne or more as vans for both benefit in kind and capital allowances purposes (this puts them in line with the VAT rules).

Where the payload area has a hard top canopy, the weight of the canopy must be deducted from the payload weight. For this purpose, HMRC will deem the weight of any hard top canopy to be 45kg. Many double cab pick-up models have a minimum payload of 1,045kg to allow for a canopy to be fitted without reducing the payload below the one tonne threshold.

Broadly speaking, as long as this rule is met, a double-cab pick-up attracts all the tax advantages of a van while providing all the comfort of a car.

## Recent Developments

In February 2024, HMRC issued new guidance, stating that double cab pick-ups would be classified as cars from 1st July 2024 for both benefit-in-kind and capital allowances purposes.

This bombshell caused huge anxiety in many important sectors of the economy, especially in the motor industry and the farming community, where double cab pick-ups are the vehicle of choice.

Fortunately, we can announce that HMRC has performed a spectacular volte face.

Double cab pick-ups with a payload of one tonne of more will continue to enjoy the favourable capital allowances and benefit-in-kind tax treatment enjoyed by vans. (Those with a payload of less than one tonne will continue to be treated as cars.)

In other words, double cab pick-ups continue to benefit from the 100% annual investment allowance and the £3,960 taxable benefit (£757 for fuel) described above.

The previous Government stated it would introduce legislation to ensure double cab pick-ups continue to be treated as goods vehicles rather than cars for tax purposes in future. As yet, there has been no word on the issue from the new Labour Government, and it was not mentioned in their election manifesto. Nonetheless, in view of the importance of the farming and motor industries, we would tend to expect they will honour this commitment, although we cannot be absolutely certain.

## 9.7   MOTORBIKES

If there's not enough room on your driveway for a double-cab pick-up, you might fancy a motorbike instead. Motorbikes attract many of the same tax advantages as vans but take up a lot less space.

### Business Use of Own Motorbike
When you use your own motorbike for business journeys, your company can pay you back at the rate of 24p per mile. The amount your company pays you will be tax free in your hands and a tax-deductible expense for the company.

### Company Motorbikes
Alternatively, your company can purchase a motorbike that can be used for both business and private purposes.

VAT can be reclaimed on the purchase of a motorbike used for business purposes. For example, if the bike has 60% business use and 40% private use then 60% of the VAT can be recovered.

The company can claim the annual investment allowance on the cost of the motorbike, thus providing immediate 100% tax relief in most cases. For example, if your company pays £5,000 for a second-hand bike it will enjoy tax relief of between £950 (£5,000 x 19%) and £1,325 (£5,000 x 26.5%).

For new motorbikes, full expensing is also available to provide 100% relief on purchases by companies.

## Benefit in Kind Charges
If the bike is used for private journeys, a taxable benefit will arise. The annual benefit in kind charge is equal to 20% of the *market value* of the motorbike (including VAT) when first provided to the employee.

Unlike cars, the charge is not based on the list price and can therefore be reduced considerably by purchasing a second-hand bike.

For example, if the company buys a second-hand bike for £5,000 the benefit in kind charge will be £1,000. This is the amount added to your taxable income.

As we saw in Section 9.2, company owners who are higher-rate taxpayers will typically pay between 33.75% and 45% Income Tax on such benefits: so between £338 and £450 per year for this bike.

Unlike cars and vans, the Income Tax benefit in kind charge is proportionately reduced to reflect any business use.

For example, if the bike has 40% private use the benefit-in kind charge will be £400 (£1,000 x 40%) and the resulting Income Tax bill will be £135 to £180 per year if you're a higher-rate taxpayer.

The company will pay National Insurance of £138 (£1,000 x 13.8%), or £112 at most net of CT relief. Employer's National Insurance is generally payable on the full annual value of assets that have both business and private use.

## Fuel, Maintenance etc
If the company pays for the bike's running costs (including fuel) these costs can be claimed as a tax-deductible expense. These costs are added to the taxable benefit (with a reduction for business use).

For example, if the running costs are £3,000 per year and the bike has 40% private use, £1,200 will be added to the director's taxable income (£3,000 x 40%).

## 9.8    MOTORING AND THE FLAT RATE SCHEME

Where the company is in the VAT flat rate scheme (Section 3.7), it cannot recover any VAT on:

- Fuel costs (the options in Section 9.1 become irrelevant)
- Repairs and maintenance
- Other vehicle running costs
- Lease payments

This, of course, is the same as the position for other expenses.

The company can, however, generally still recover VAT on the purchase of a vehicle for £2,000 or more (including VAT), but only where it would be able to recover VAT under normal principles (as detailed in previous sections).

Where VAT can be recovered, there is no restriction for private use where the flat rate scheme is being used. Hence, it will generally be possible to recover all the VAT on the purchase of a van, pickup, or motorbike.

However, where VAT has been recovered on the purchase of a vehicle, it must also be accounted for on the sale of the vehicle: and at the full standard rate of 20%.

That's probably fair enough, but the bad news is that, where VAT was not, or could not be, recovered on the purchase (e.g. a car with private use), the sale of the vehicle must be included in the company's taxable turnover under the flat rate scheme.

So, for example, if a company is in the flat rate scheme with an applicable rate of 14.5% and it sells an old company car for £5,000, it will have to pay £725 in VAT (£5,000 x 14.5%). The amount to be deducted from the relevant capital allowances pool would be the net proceeds of £4,275.


## 9.9    PARKING FINES

The position for parking fines is both complex and controversial. It is also dependent on whether the vehicle is registered in the company's name, or in the name of an employee (including a director).

Where the vehicle is registered in the name of an employee but the company pays the fine, or reimburses the cost to the employee, the cost is allowable for CT purposes. However, the payment represents a taxable benefit in kind for the employee. Furthermore, since the fine is the employee's liability, the benefit will generally be fully subject to Income Tax and National Insurance as if it were additional salary.

Where the vehicle is registered in the company's name, there will be no benefit in kind charge on the employee. In this case, it is important to ensure the penalty notice is affixed to the vehicle and not handed to the employee.

There is then the issue of whether a parking fine on a company vehicle can be claimed for CT purposes. Many people in the tax profession would argue there are circumstances where a parking fine is wholly and exclusively incurred for the purposes of the business and should therefore be allowed, and I have a huge amount of sympathy for this view. Take, for example, a plumber working on a job for their company at a city centre location where the only practical place to park the company van is on double yellow lines.

Many people would argue that, under these circumstances, the fine is wholly and exclusively incurred for the purposes of the company's business and therefore represents an allowable expense.

However, I am sorry to say HMRC disagree with this view and, sadly, their opinion is backed up by case law: although it is worth remembering case law always depends on the facts of the case and your circumstances may differ enough to enable you to mount a better argument than Group 4 Security did when they lost that particular case. It won't be easy though.

**Commercial Charges**
All of the above relates to parking fines imposed by the authorities. The position is different in the case of a so-called 'penalty charge' issued by a commercial organisation.

In these cases, we go back to basic principles: was the penalty incurred wholly and exclusively for the purposes of the business? If the vehicle was parked at the penalising entity's premises because the small company owner, or any other company employee, was there for business purposes, the penalty is allowable for CT purposes and no benefit in kind charge should arise, even if the vehicle is registered in the individual's name. Basically, it's just part of the cost of parking; it's part of travel and subsistence.

# Chapter 10

# Property

## 10.1 BUSINESS PREMISES

Is it better to rent or buy premises for your business? This is a very important issue, so we will take a look at some of the tax and non-tax issues to consider in the next section. Tax will usually have very little to do with this decision, however.

If you do decide to buy a property for your business, the next question is: should you buy the property *personally*, in your own name, or get the *company* to buy it? We'll try to answer this question in Section 10.3.

If you or your company *already* own a business property, there are still many tax issues to consider, including:

- The types of spending that can be put through the company
- The difference between spending on repairs and improvements
- How to obtain immediate tax relief when you spend money on integral features (plumbing, wiring, heating, etc)
- The structures and buildings allowance which, for the first time in a generation, provides tax relief on the purchase price of new commercial property, or improvements to existing properties
- CGT when the property is sold, including the special reliefs for property used in a trading business: business asset disposal relief (BADR), holdover relief, and rollover relief
- Inheritance Tax, in particular the availability of business property relief, which can shelter the whole property from this graverobbers tax

We will cover all these topics in this chapter. We also mustn't forget a great many small company owners work from home and have no need for standalone business premises: in Section 10.7, we explain what sort of tax relief is available in these circumstances.

## 10.2 IS IT BETTER TO RENT OR BUY?

Your company's business premises will often represent one of your most significant assets. Your premises will also give rise to substantial amounts of tax-deductible expenditure.

One of the most important decisions you will face is therefore whether to rent or buy your premises.

While 'rent or buy' is largely an investment decision, driven by non-tax factors, it remains important to understand the tax consequences of this decision. Furthermore, if you decide to buy your premises, the next decision is whether to buy them through the company or in your own name, personally.

Buying the premises personally then opens up more options, including the question of whether to charge your company rent, and how much, whether to invest in premises via a pension fund or 'SIPP' (self-invested personal pension), and whether to involve your spouse, or other family members, in the ownership of the premises. So, it's a complex question!

We'll return to the issue of **who** should buy the property in Section 10.3. For now, though, let's stick to the question of **whether** you should buy the property.

### Rent versus Interest

People often say that if you are paying rent to a landlord you are 'throwing money away'. However, if you buy a property using a mortgage, you are also arguably throwing money away: by paying interest to a bank. In a way, the bank becomes your landlord.

Rent and interest payments on business premises enjoy exactly the same tax relief. If your company rents a property, the rent payments will be a fully deductible business expense. If instead a commercial property is purchased using a mortgage, the interest payments will also be a fully deductible expense.

Unlike individuals who own residential property, owners of commercial property do not have the tax relief on their interest payments restricted (except in the case of some companies paying more than £2 million per year).

In terms of your ongoing monthly costs, it could be argued in very basic terms that it is cheaper to buy than to rent if the mortgage interest payments are lower than the rental payments on a similar property.

When interest rates were very low this was often the case. However, with interest rates having risen significantly in recent times it may now be cheaper to rent than buy some commercial properties (unless the properties have fallen in value significantly).

(Note, many commercial property mortgages are repayment mortgages, which means you also have to repay part of the loan each month. However, paying back a loan is effectively a form of saving, not an expense, although the extra payments will affect your cashflow. The capital portion of the loan repayments is not a tax-deductible expense.)

Whether it's cheaper to rent or buy is only one factor business owners have to consider. For example, renting arguably provides more flexibility, allowing you to relocate more easily. Buying may give your business more security.

**Lease Premiums**
You may have to pay a lease premium when you first rent commercial property. The CT treatment of a lease premium depends on the length of the lease. For a lease in excess of fifty years, the entire premium is treated as capital expenditure, like the purchase of an asset. This treatment also applies where the lease is assigned to you from a previous tenant.

Where a property owner grants you a lease for less than fifty years at a premium, only part of the cost is treated as capital expenditure and the remainder is treated like additional rent and is thus allowable for CT purposes. However, this allowable expense must be spread over the life of the lease.

The part treated as capital expenditure is 2% of the premium for each whole year of the lease, excluding the first year. Hence, for example, if your company takes out a lease for ten years at a premium of £100,000, the capital element will be 18%, or £18,000. The remaining £82,000 can be claimed over the ten years of the lease, or £8,200 per year.

**Upfront Costs**
Buying a commercial property may come with significant upfront costs. The mortgage deposit could be in the region of 20%-30% of the purchase price, although some mortgage brokers may be able to negotiate a smaller deposit.

It is this potentially large upfront cost that will make it impossible for many company owners to buy a property for their business, even if that is what they would prefer to do.

Whether you or your company purchases the property, the mortgage deposit will not be a tax-deductible expense.

However, one benefit of getting your company to buy the property is that you may not have to pay yourself additional dividend income (taxed at say 33.75%) to pay the deposit yourself.

## Stamp Duty Land Tax on Purchase

Another upfront cost is Stamp Duty Land Tax (SDLT). The rates for *non-residential* property are as follows:

| | |
|---|---|
| Up to £150,000 | 0% |
| £150,000 to £250,000 | 2% |
| Over £250,000 | 5% |

For example, if you buy a property for £250,000 there will be no tax payable on the first £150,000 and 2% on the final £100,000: total tax bill £2,000.

If you buy a property for £500,000 there will be £2,000 tax payable on the first £250,000 and 5% on the final £250,000: total tax bill £14,500.

Whether you or your company purchases the property the SDLT payment will not produce immediate tax relief. The SDLT can, however, be deducted from the capital gain when the property is eventually sold.

One benefit of getting your company to buy the property is that you may not have to pay yourself taxable dividend income to pay the SDLT yourself.

## Stamp Duty Land Tax on Leases

If your company rents a commercial property, instead of buying one, it may have to pay SDLT on the lease. Firstly, any lease premium will attract SDLT at the same rates as an outright purchase (see above).

Beyond that, there is generally no SDLT payable on short-term leases that have fairly modest rental payments. In other cases, however, SDLT is calculated by adding up all the rent payments your company will make over all the years of the lease. If the total is £150,000 or less, there is no SDLT payable. If the total exceeds £150,000, 1% tax is payable on the excess. The tax rate increases to 2% for amounts in excess of £5m. This is in addition to any SDLT due on a lease premium, where relevant.

For example, if your company takes a three year lease over a property with an annual rent of £24,000 the total rent payments will come to £72,000, which is less than £150,000, so no SDLT is payable.

Actually, the calculation is a bit more complicated than this. Instead of adding up the actual rental payments, you add up the 'net present value' of the rental payments, which will result in a smaller number.

For example, if your company takes a five-year lease at an annual rent of £36,000, the total rent payments will come to £180,000. The net present value of these rental payments comes to £162,541. SDLT is payable at 1% on the excess over £150,000, which comes to £125.

What this example shows is that, for those small companies that do have to pay SDLT, the total bill is likely to be relatively small.

The easiest way to calculate the net present value and SDLT payable on a lease is by using HMRC's SDLT calculator:
www.tax.service.gov.uk/calculate-stamp-duty-land-tax

Alternatively, if you want to see how to do it yourself, see the Taxcafe guide *Using a Property Company to Save Tax*.

Often a lease will be granted for a fixed term but the tenant will remain in the property after the lease period has ended, for example until a new lease is negotiated. This can have SDLT consequences. For example, a five-year lease may be treated as a six-year lease and then a seven-year lease, and so on. As a result, the SDLT threshold may eventually be breached, a tax bill will result and HMRC will have to be notified.

This is a complex area and professional advice may be required so that you do not incur penalties.

### SDLT: Owner Occupied Properties
If your company owns the property out of which it trades there will be no lease agreement and therefore no SDLT payable on any lease: the company cannot pay itself rent!

But if you *personally* own the premises out of which your company trades, the company can pay you rent. This is often extremely tax efficient. If there is a lease agreement between you and the company this may create a SDLT liability.

However, it is possible to avoid SDLT altogether by granting the company what is known as a *non-exclusive* licence to occupy the property. This is because a licence to occupy a property is exempt from SDLT.

A licence does not give the occupier any legal protection. The property owner can also occupy the property or grant a further licence to another business. However, this lack of legal protection doesn't really matter when you are the landlord and your company is the tenant.

It is very important that the document is drafted correctly and does not give the occupier exclusive possession of the property.

### Property in Scotland or Wales
Property in Scotland or Wales is not subject to SDLT. However, each country has a similar tax that operates in broadly the same way: Land and Buildings Transaction Tax in Scotland; Land Transaction Tax in Wales. The rates at which the taxes are levied are different, although the variations are not great. It is generally best to seek local advice when buying property in Scotland or Wales.

### Running Costs
Whether you rent or buy, there are a number of costs that will probably be the same. These include:

- Buildings insurance
- Repairs and maintenance
- Business Rates
- Electricity, gas, and other utility costs
- Cleaning

Provided the property is used exclusively for business purposes, these can be claimed for CT purposes. Any VAT arising can be claimed where the company is VAT registered, subject to the issues discussed in Chapter 3.

Business use of the property includes facilities provided for employee welfare, etc, e.g. kitchens, canteens, bathrooms, etc, even an inbuilt gym if it's available to all employees.

It will not, however, include any leisure or personal facilities provided exclusively for the company owner or their family: although the occasional night on a camp bed in the office does no harm.

If part of the property is in disuse (not used at all), this, in itself, will not lead to any restriction in tax relief. Furthermore, renting out surplus space will generally still count as business use, although:

- Rent received will be subject to CT as additional income
- To maintain full VAT recovery, you will need to exercise the option to tax and charge VAT on the rent
- If you are in the flat rate scheme (Section 3.7), the rent received will be included in the company's taxable turnover whether you exercise the option to tax or not (and there will be no VAT recovery on most of your costs)
- There may be an impact on the availability of some tax reliefs where a capital gain arises on a later sale of the property
- There may also be an impact on the company owner's CGT or Inheritance Tax position in respect of the company shares

You will probably also need the owner's permission if you are sub-letting part of a property that your company is renting itself.

Many commercial properties are rented with a 'full repairing and insuring' lease. This means the tenant, not the landlord, has to pay the building insurance and for all repairs to the property.

Often the landlord will arrange the insurance but invoice the tenant for the cost. When a property has multiple tenants, the landlord may recover these costs by levying a service charge. Either way the tenant ultimately pays, not the landlord. This is different to the world of residential property where landlords are responsible for building insurance and repairs.

What this means is that, if your company is renting premises from a third party landlord, it may still have to pay for the property's insurance and repairs. These costs will be allowable for CT purposes. If your company owns its own premises it will also have to pay these expenses and can claim tax relief.

If the property is owned *personally* by the directors and they pay these expenses, tax relief can be claimed against the rental income they receive from the company. (However, it may be the case that the company will still be liable for these expenses if there is a full repairing lease between the directors and the company).

Business Rates are a tax levied by the local authority, much like Council Tax. The company will generally be liable to pay this tax, although many smaller properties are exempt. Any Business Rates suffered will be an allowable expense for CT purposes.

## Flexibility and Security

What happens if you want to move your business to a different location, for example to a bigger or smaller property, or perhaps even a different part of the country?

If you are renting a commercial property, you may not be able to move out before the end of the lease unless the landlord agrees to it, you are able to pass the lease on to someone else, or you are allowed to sublet the property.

If you want to remain flexible, the key is to avoid a long-term lease. It may be better to negotiate a short-term lease lasting one, two, or three years, with a potential break clause that allows you to terminate the lease early. This will provide a safety net if your business is struggling or requires a different property.

In recent years, leases have generally become more favourable to tenants, being shorter and more flexible.

The one drawback of a short lease, or any lease for that matter, is the landlord may be able to force you out of the property at the end of the lease, even if you don't want to go. This could be a problem if your business is heavily dependent on its location, for example a successful restaurant.

Although owner occupiers arguably have more security than tenants, the Landlord and Tenant Act 1954 provides tenants with a significant amount of security of tenure, unless they've agreed to exclude the lease from the protection of the Act. This means that, after the fixed term of the lease has ended, the tenant has the right to remain in the property and apply for a new lease.

Landlords can only remove tenants for certain specified reasons, for example if they wish to occupy the property themselves or redevelop it. The landlord can also take back the property if the tenant has not complied with the terms of the lease or kept up with the rent payments.

Although there is protection for tenants, owning your own premises may give you more peace of mind and make you feel more in control of the destiny of your business.

You can always sell the property if you want to move location or cease trading. Alternatively, you could keep the property and rent it to another business.

The downside is it could take a long time to find a buyer and there may be early repayment charges on the mortgage. Also, you may not recover all the initial purchase costs such as SDLT.

Property is essentially a long-term investment so it may be better to rent if you don't think you'll be staying in the same location for very long.

### Capital Growth
As a property owner you will enjoy any increase in the property's value. This is arguably the key attraction of buying and why renting is often likened to throwing money away.

However, as we all know, property prices can go down as well as up. Commercial property is a specialist area and knowledge of the *residential* market in your area will not necessarily help you make a successful commercial property investment.

In many towns around the country you will find strong demand for rental flats and houses but commercial properties (especially high street shops) have lain empty for years.

If you expect the type of commercial property you use in your business to go up in value in the years ahead then you may be better off buying rather than renting.

### Residential versus Commercial Mortgages
Commercial property mortgages often come with less attractive terms than residential mortgages. The deposit may be higher, the interest rate payable may be higher and the mortgage term (the number of years you're given to repay the loan) may be shorter.

### Summary
Reasons for buying instead of renting business premises include:

- Benefiting from the property's capital growth
- Giving your business greater security as to its location

However, renting property has its own advantages including greater flexibility (if you have a short-term lease) and lower upfront costs.

## 10.3   WHO BUYS?

Having made the decision to buy your business premises, the next decision is *who* should buy it. The main choices are to buy the property through the company or to buy it personally, in your own name. While there are other alternatives, in this section we will confine ourselves to considering these main options.

### Why Buy Personally?
The main reason many company owners choose to buy their business premises personally is to protect this valuable asset (the property) from any future trading difficulties that could lead to a problem with the company. To put it bluntly, if the company goes bust, the property is protected.

This protection is not utterly foolproof. There are some circumstances where the owner of an insolvent company can be forced to sell their own personal assets to meet the company's debts, and banks will often ask for personal guarantees in any case. However, keeping the business premises out of the company will often still protect the property from the company's creditors.

Keeping the property separate may also be useful in facilitating a sale of the company, although this depends very much on the exact circumstances of the case. If you own office premises from which you run your company, it may be easier to sell the company, or its business, without the additional complication of a property that the purchasers may have no need for. Alternatively, however, if you are running a restaurant, hotel, or any other property-based business where the location itself is an intrinsic part of the trade, then it may be easier to sell the whole company, or its business, if the property is held within the company.

Finance is another key issue that needs to be considered. You may find it is easier, or cheaper, to get a mortgage on your business premises if you buy the property personally.

### Tax Considerations
There are a great many tax matters to consider when deciding whether to buy property through your company or personally. However, we can start by dispelling a couple of issues where the ownership of the property will not generally make any difference.

Business Rates are paid by the occupier, or user, of the property, rather than the owner so these will remain the same whatever ownership structure you use.

Assuming the property is entirely commercial property, with no residential element, the Stamp Duty Land Tax (SDLT) payable on its purchase will remain the same (see Section 10.2). However, it is important to be aware that, if the property is initially purchased personally and then subsequently transferred to the company, SDLT will be payable again, and will be based on the market value of the property at the date of transfer.

### Capital Taxes

Major tax differences do arise when we come to the main capital taxes, CGT and Inheritance Tax. Let's take CGT first.

If the company owns the property, it will not pay CGT on a sale of the property, but will pay CT on any gain arising. The CT rate applying could be either 19% or 25%, or an effective rate of 26.5% may apply to some or all of the gain (see Section 2.1 and Chapter 12).

Companies that held a property before December 2017 will benefit from indexation relief to reduce the amount of capital gain chargeable to CT. This is beneficial where it applies but is now irrelevant when planning for future purchases (see the Taxcafe guide *Using a Property Company to Save Tax* for further details of indexation relief).

In the absence of any potential CGT reliefs, an individual company owner selling their company's business premises personally, will generally pay CGT at 20%. This assumes the property has no residential use and has never had any such use during the individual's ownership.

The 20% CGT rate is reduced to 10% where any part of the gain falls within the individual's basic rate band and is also subject to their annual exemption (£3,000 from 2024/25 onwards).

### Example A

*Ben owns the small workshop that his company uses to trade from. In May 2024 he sells the workshop, realising a gain of £103,000. Deducting Ben's 2024/25 annual exemption of £3,000 from his capital gain leaves him with a taxable gain of £100,000.*

*Ben's taxable income for 2024/25 is £35,270, meaning he has £15,000 of his basic rate band remaining to cover part of his taxable gain (see Appendix B). Hence, Ben's CGT bill will be:*

| | |
|---|---|
| *£15,000 x 10%* | *£1,500* |
| *£85,000 x 20%* | *£17,000* |
| *Total* | *£18,500* |

*This represents an overall effective rate of 18%. The company would have paid at least £23,545 and possibly up to £27,295 on the same gain (assuming no indexation relief is available and depending on the overall level of the company's profits: see Section 2.1).*

In this case, we can readily see that personal ownership leads to a lower tax bill on the property's sale. Furthermore, Ben will not face the problem of having to extract sale proceeds from the company and thus potentially face further tax bills on dividends, salary, or other payments made to him.

At present, company owners will generally pay less tax on non-residential property gains than would have been paid if their company owned the property.

There will be a few exceptions, where the gain is small, the company is paying CT at 19%, and the company owner's annual exemption is not available. But these will be pretty rare. Even if we stack absolutely everything in the company's favour, the maximum possible saving would be just £500. Not only is this maximum potential saving too small to concern us, it is highly unlikely any saving at all will arise in the vast majority of cases.

More likely, we will be looking at a gain similar to the one in the example. If the company has other, regular taxable profits between £50,000 and £147,000, the £103,000 gain described above would suffer CT at an effective rate of 26.5%, or £27,295.

At other profit levels, the CT cost would be less, such as £25,750 if the company is making regular annual profits of £250,000 or more; or £23,545 if the company is breaking even. That last figure is the best the company can do, tax-wise, unless it is making losses.

As for Ben, even in the worst case scenario, where he is a higher rate taxpayer with income of at least £50,270, and has used his annual exemption elsewhere, the CGT arising would be just £20,600: still £2,945 less than the company's lowest tax bill.

So, as far as capital gains on non-residential property are concerned, it seems pretty clear that owning the property personally is currently the better option.

But all that is based on what we know at the moment. I began my tax career in 1983 and I can tell you, over the years since then, there have been many periods when we would have reached a different conclusion.

What really matters though is not the past, but what the future holds. For example, if the new Labour Government (or any future government for that matter) decides to increase CGT rates, this could make owning property personally less attractive.

### Capital Gains Reliefs

Our analysis so far has not taken account of any potential reliefs on capital gains. There are three major reliefs potentially available on business premises:

- Business asset disposal relief (BADR)
- Holdover relief
- Rollover relief

Each of these reliefs may apply to property used in the company's trade. At present, they may also apply to furnished holiday lets on the same basis. The reliefs do not apply to other rental properties.

For the rest of this section, when I refer to trades, this currently also includes furnished holiday lets: but see Section 1.6 regarding future changes, and for further information.

How you own your business property will affect your ability to claim these reliefs. Before we start to compare company and personal ownership, however, let's look at what the reliefs mean.

### Business Asset Disposal Relief (BADR)

Capital gains qualifying for this relief are subject to a CGT rate of just 10%, regardless of whether the individual making the gain is a basic or higher rate taxpayer. Each individual can only qualify for BADR on a lifetime maximum of £1m of capital gains.

For a higher rate taxpayer making disposals of non-residential property, or other assets on which the CGT rate would normally be 20%, the 10% BADR rate also, confusingly, represents a saving of 10%. You'll see both these 10% rates cropping up in this section, so don't be confused: one is the rate of tax paid; the other is the amount of tax saved.

### Holdover Relief

Where property is gifted or sold at under value to another person (an individual, a trust, or a company), the capital gain arising is generally computed as if the property had been sold at market value. However, where the property qualifies for holdover relief, any gain arising in excess of the gain based on the actual proceeds (if any) can be 'held over'.

The held over gain is then deducted from the transferee's base cost for CGT (or CT) purposes so that it effectively becomes taxable when they dispose of the property themselves.

This relief is extremely useful in business succession planning and is examined in detail in the Taxcafe guide *How to Save Inheritance Tax*.

**Rollover Relief**
Where the proceeds derived from the sale of qualifying property are reinvested in new property, or certain other qualifying assets, for use in a trade, within the period beginning one year before, and ending three years after, the sale, the gain arising can be rolled over into the new purchase.

No tax is payable on the amount rolled over, but the base cost of the new purchase is reduced by the same amount. Hence, the tax on the ultimate sale of the replacement asset will be increased.

The whole of the qualifying sale proceeds must be reinvested in order to obtain full relief. Any amount not reinvested within the required timescale remains taxable.

The replacement asset may be used in the same trade, or in a different trade carried on by the same company. Under the proposed changes discussed in Section 1.6, the gain on a furnished holiday let sold before April 2025 can still be rolled over where the proceeds are reinvested in trading premises (but not a furnished holiday let) after the furnished holiday letting tax regime has been abolished, but within the usual timescale described above.

**Relief Summary**
The position for these three key reliefs on a disposal of business property can be summarised as follows:

| Relief | Company Ownership | Personal Ownership |
|---|---|---|
| Business Asset Disposal Relief | Not available on sale of a property | Available on associated disposals (see below) |
| Holdover Relief | Not available | Available |
| Rollover Relief | Available | Available |

It is important to note, when viewing this table, that BADR and holdover relief may be available on the ***shares*** in the company, even if not on the properties it holds.

As far as rollover relief is concerned, the new asset must be used in a trade carried on by the same company.

The new asset must also be purchased in the same way the old property was held. In other words, where the old property was held personally, the proceeds must be reinvested by the company owner personally or, where the property was held by the company, the company must reinvest the proceeds.

**Associated Disposals (for Business Asset Disposal Relief)**
Where the company qualifies as your 'personal company' (see below), you may be entitled to BADR on an associated disposal of property used in the company's trade, but which you own personally. In many cases, this will reduce your CGT rate to just 10%, leading to substantial further savings. However, there are many restrictions on BADR on associated disposals, which can mean the relief is hard to obtain in practice.

Firstly, the relief is only available where the owner is also disposing of shares in the company. The stake being disposed of must generally be either at least a 5% stake, or their entire remaining stake out of an earlier stake of at least 5%.

The property must have been used in the company's trade for at least two years immediately prior to the disposal of the company shares or, if earlier, cessation of the company's business. In the latter case, the disposal must take place within three years after cessation.

The property must also have been owned for at least three years at the date of disposal.

BADR is restricted where any payment (i.e. rent) has been received by the owner for use of the property after 5th April 2008. Where the property was acquired after that date and a full market rent was received throughout the period of use in the company's business, no BADR will be available. Where the property was acquired earlier, or rent was charged at a lower rate, there will be a partial restriction in the relief.

The BADR available on an associated disposal is also restricted to reflect any periods when all or part of the property was not being used in a qualifying business carried on by the company.

### Example B
*Susan owns an office building in Glasgow which she purchased on 6th April 1999 for £200,000. On 6th April 2024, she sells the building for £800,000, realising a gain of £600,000.*

*From 6th April 2004 to 6th April 2024, she rented 75% of the property to her own company, Trinity Trading Limited, which qualifies as her personal company for BADR purposes. She charged Trinity 60% of the market rent for its lease of the property until selling the company on the same day she sold the property. Her gain is eligible for BADR as follows:*

| | |
|---|---|
| *Gain related to qualifying use in personal company* | |
| *£600,000 x 20/25 (years) x 75%* | £360,000 |
| *Less: Restriction for rent charged* | |
| *£360,000 x 16/20 (years) x 60%* | £172,800 |
| *Gain qualifying for business asset disposal relief* | £187,200 |

*The restriction for rent charged applies for the 16 years from 2008 to 2024, as a proportion of the total period of qualifying use: 2004-2024.*

*Ignoring her annual exemption, Susan's CGT bill will be:*

| | |
|---|---|
| *£187,200 x 10%* | *£18,720* |
| *£412,800 x 20%* | *£82,560* |
| *Total* | *£101,280* |

Charging her company rent has led to a restriction in Susan's BADR, which has cost her an additional £17,280 in CGT (£172,800 x 10%). Obviously, this restriction can be avoided by not charging your company any rent, but is this strategy either possible or desirable? That's the question we will consider in Section 10.4.

For the moment, it is worth pointing out that each individual is restricted to maximum total lifetime claims of £1m in BADR. Hence, if Susan's share sale yielded a gain of at least £812,800, the restriction in BADR on her property would be of no consequence.

One could also take the view that the restriction is of no importance where her total qualifying gains for BADR purposes, now and in the future, are likely to exceed £1m: although some commentators feel BADR may be scrapped altogether at some point in the foreseeable future.

Under the proposals described in Section 1.6, an associated disposal of a furnished holiday let will only qualify where the relevant qualifying disposal of company shares (as described above) takes place before 6th April 2025. Subject to this, and the other conditions described above, BADR will remain available after 5th April 2025 on an associated disposal of a property used in the company's furnished holiday letting business.

## Property in the Company

The restrictions applying to associated disposals do not apply to a BADR claim on a disposal of shares in a qualifying personal company (see below). Where the company owns its business premises, the value of those shares is, of course, enhanced by the value of the property it owns. Potentially, a £600,000 gain like the one made by Susan in Example B above, might effectively be fully covered by BADR on a sale of her shares in the company. If so, this could effectively save her up to £41,280 in CGT (£412,800 x 10%).

But there are some problems with this strategy. Firstly, the company shares will only qualify for BADR provided the company is not carrying on substantial non-trading activities. HMRC generally regards 'substantial' as 20% or more of the company's overall activities. This could be a problem for Susan as, in Example B, her company utilised just 75% of the office building and may therefore have rented out the surplus space (25%) if it had owned the property.

While renting out surplus space on a temporary basis can arguably be regarded as merely incidental to the underlying trading activity, this activity appears to have continued for many years (since 2004) and therefore would have meant the company had an investment activity which, in turn, might have threatened Susan's eligibility for BADR on her shares.

All is not lost, however, since case law tells us the question of whether company shares qualify for BADR must be considered by taking all the relevant factors into account. Even if 25% of the company's assets were employed in an investment activity (property rental), it is unlikely this activity accounted for more than 20% of other key factors, such as management time, company turnover, gross profit, etc.

HMRC's 20% 'rule' is really only a guideline. In a recent case, it was held that non-qualifying investment activities would only be regarded as substantial where they were of material or real importance in the context of the company's activities as a whole.

Sadly, while this could be helpful, it still leaves a lot of room for doubt in a case like Susan's. To avoid any argument over the issue, it is wise to keep both non-qualifying income and non-qualifying assets below 20% of the totals for the company as a whole, in order to safely preserve the company's trading status wherever possible. According to HMRC's manuals, they would then accept the company was a qualifying trading company for the purposes of BADR.

Put another way, going over 20% doesn't necessarily mean your BADR claim will fail, but it does mean you are likely to face a challenge from HMRC.

In this context, it is worth remembering it is only the activities in the last two years prior to disposal of the company's shares, or cessation of its trading business (as the case may be) that affect the owner's BADR claim on the shares. Hence, in Susan's case, the previous use of the property (from 1999 to 2004) would not affect her BADR claim on company shares if the company held the property. This contrasts with the restrictions to BADR on an associated disposal as per the original Example B above.

In summary, when it comes to claiming BADR on company shares, it is vital to be aware of all the qualifying rules and excessive amounts of property rental or other investment activities can lead to the loss of the relief, BUT there is also room for a good deal of optimism on the question of incidental investment and non-trading activities: so take professional advice before you make any assumptions!

Note that, under the proposals discussed in Section 1.6, for disposals of shares after 5$^{th}$ April 2025, furnished holiday letting will cease to be treated as a qualifying activity for BADR purposes. However, subject to the usual conditions, the relief will remain available on a disposal of shares within three years after a company ceased its furnished holiday letting business before 1$^{st}$ April 2025 and did not carry on any other trade after the cessation.

### Personal Companies

While companies themselves do not qualify for BADR, company owners may benefit from this relief when they dispose of shares in a qualifying personal company or, as we have seen, assets used in such a company's trade.

The definition of a personal company for the purposes of BADR is broadly as follows:

i)   The individual holds at least 5% of the ordinary share capital
ii)  The holding under (i) provides at least 5% of the voting rights
iii) The company is a trading company (see above)
iv)  The individual is an officer or employee of the company (an 'officer' includes a director or company secretary)

v)   The individual must either:
      a) Have at least a 5% interest in both the distributable profits and net assets of the company by virtue of their holding under (i), or
      b) Be entitled to at least 5% of the sale proceeds arising on a disposal of the company's entire ordinary share capital

Each of these rules must be satisfied for at least two years immediately prior to the disposal in question or, where the company has ceased trading, for at least two years immediately prior to the cessation. In the latter case, the disposal must take place within three years after cessation.

Where a qualifying business has been transferred to a company in exchange for shares, the individual's period of ownership of the business prior to the transfer can be counted towards the two-year qualifying period for their shares in the company.

**The Short Version**
The personal company rules have grown pretty complex but, for a small private company with only a single class of ordinary shares, tests (i), (ii) and (v) are usually satisfied simply by holding at least 5% of the ordinary shares. Hence, assuming you are also a director of the company, the only test you will generally need to worry about is the one we have already examined in detail: namely test (iii), do you have a 'trading company' for the purposes of BADR.

**Inheritance Tax**
If your company is a qualifying unquoted trading company, the value of your shares will qualify for 100% business property relief for Inheritance Tax purposes as long as you have held them for at least two years (generally speaking). This means the value of any property held by your company will be completely sheltered from Inheritance Tax.

To be a qualifying company for business property relief purposes, the company only needs to be engaged 'wholly or mainly' in qualifying trading activities. 'Wholly or mainly' effectively means more than half, or over 50%. This is obviously a much easier target than the over 80% required for BADR purposes.

However, to preserve full business property relief on the company's shares, all its activities must be an integral part of the same qualifying business.

Hence, for example, the rental of the surplus space in Susan's office building must be organised and run as an integral part of the company's main trading business.

Where you own a property personally, but use it in your company's trade, the property will only qualify for 50% business property relief (again, the property will, generally speaking, need to have been held for at least two years). Furthermore, only the part of the property actually used in the company's business will qualify. In Susan's case, in our example, this would reduce her business property relief on the property to just £300,000 (£800,000 x 75% x 50%), leaving £500,000 of its value exposed to Inheritance Tax and giving her family a potential tax bill of up to £200,000 (£500,000 x 40%).

The restriction in business property relief needs to be weighed against some of the CGT and Income Tax advantages of holding your company's business premises personally. Some business owners' strategy is to hold the property personally for the majority of their life and then transfer it into the company when they grow older, as their life expectancy shortens.

### Example C

*Afia is a wealthy old woman. Among her many assets is her unquoted trading company, Greatlady Ltd. She also owns a factory worth £1.6m, which is used by the company. Greatlady Ltd is currently worth £1.2m. If Afia were to die with things as they stand, her personal representatives would be able to claim business property relief as follows:*

| | |
|---|---|
| *Greatlady Ltd: £1.2m @ 100%* | £1,200,000 |
| *Factory: £1.6m @ 50%* | £800,000 |
| *Total* | £2,000,000 |

*Sadly, Afia falls ill and doesn't have long to live. She therefore decides to undertake some Inheritance Tax planning. She transfers the factory into the company. She is able to avoid CGT on this transfer by using a 'holdover relief' election (see above). SDLT is, however, payable on the market value of the property. In this case, the SDLT amounts to £69,500 (see Section 10.2). To fund this SDLT, Afia uses £69,500 out of her private wealth to pay for additional shares in Greatlady Ltd, issued by way of a rights issue.*

*Greatlady Ltd will now be worth £2.8m and, when Afia sadly passes away a short time later, the whole of this value will be covered by business property relief.*

*The overall value of Afia's estate will be virtually unchanged except for the £69,500 paid in SDLT. However, this simple piece of planning will save her family £347,800 in Inheritance Tax.*

The Inheritance Tax saved is made up of the additional £800,000 (50%) in business property relief on the factory plus the £69,500 reduction in Afia's estate, at the prevailing Inheritance Tax rate of 40%: £869,500 x 40% = £347,800. Taking account of the SDLT payable on the property transfer, the overall net tax saving achieved by the family amounts to £278,300 (£347,800 – £69,500).

Note that issuing the new shares by way of a rights issue means these are treated as part of Afia's original shareholding for the purposes of business property relief. Hence, by structuring her new investment into her existing qualifying trading company as a rights issue, she was eligible for full business property relief immediately.

Unlike BADR, there is no further restriction in business property relief if your company pays you rent for using your property. For further details on business property relief, see the Taxcafe guide *How to Save Inheritance Tax.*

**Capital Allowances**
How the property is owned will also affect the capital allowances available. The first, major point to note is that, if you own the property personally, you will only be eligible for capital allowances if you charge the company rent. Your entitlement to capital allowances is also dependent on the level of rent you charge.

If you are entitled to any capital allowances on plant and machinery within the property (you usually will be: see Section 10.5), your claim will have to be restricted if you are not charging full market rent. Charge, say, 80% of market rent and you will only be able to claim 80% of the allowances to which you would otherwise be entitled.

Furthermore, the property will not be brought into qualifying use for the purposes of the structures and buildings allowance (Section 10.6) until you begin to charge full market rent. Hence, this entitlement will be lost for any period prior to charging full market rent for the first time.

If you make a loss renting the property to your company, you can set your capital allowances off against any other taxable income you have: BUT only if you are charging a full market rent.

Another important point to consider is the fact only companies can claim the additional allowances available on new, unused plant and machinery covered in Section 8.5.

Having said that, however, if you own the property personally (and charge rent), you will still be eligible for the annual investment allowance on up to £1m of qualifying expenditure in each tax year. That's usually enough for most small company owners. Furthermore, the company will have its own annual investment allowance available as well.

Another area where you need to be careful if you own the property personally is that the company will only be eligible for capital allowances on any expenditure it incurs on fixtures, fittings, and the structure of the property itself, if it has a qualifying legal title in the property (generally a formal lease granted at a premium).

Where you do grant a formal lease, this can affect the capital allowances you are entitled to personally. It can also lead to SDLT liabilities, as we saw earlier, and other potential tax consequences: see the Taxcafe guide *How to Save Property Tax* for details.

In practice, the simplest approach, where you own the property, is to merely grant the company a licence to occupy and then make sure that you, personally, incur any expenditure on new fixtures and fittings or property improvements. You will also need to charge a full market rent to get the full benefit of the available capital allowances.

The company can still claim capital allowances on moveable items within the property, as well as claiming CT relief for other expenditure, such as repairs and maintenance (but see Section 10.5 regarding major replacement work on integral features).

**In Conclusion**

Owning your company's business premises personally provides opportunities for significant CGT savings, although there are some pitfalls to watch out for when it comes to the ultimate sale of the company or cessation of its business.

There are also some capital allowances issues to be considered, but these can generally be overcome by structuring your arrangements carefully.

The major downside in many cases is a significantly increased exposure to Inheritance Tax on the property. However, this can often be avoided where appropriate action is taken before death.

Another benefit to holding your company's business premises personally is the ability to pay yourself rent: one of the most tax-efficient ways to get money out of your company. We will look at this in the next section.

## 10.4 SHOULD YOU PAY YOURSELF RENT?

If you decide to hold your company's business premises personally, you will, if you choose, be able to pay yourself rent. But, given that rent represents taxable income in your hands, why would you want to do this?

The first reason is the simple, practical, one. You may need the rental income in order to cover costs related to the property: principally, in most cases, mortgage interest.

This practical issue is also matched by the tax treatment. The only way to get tax relief for costs incurred on the property personally is to receive sufficient rental income to cover those costs. The company, in turn, will get CT relief for the rent it pays to you, thus effectively passing on the relief for those costs.

### *Example D, Part 1*
*Basira owns her company's trading premises personally. She bought the premises with a mortgage on which she pays interest of £40,000 per year. She incurs other costs related to the property of around £5,000 per year. Without charging her company rent, these costs of £45,000 per year cannot be relieved for tax purposes.*

*However, if Basira charges her company an annual rent of £45,000, she will be able to set her costs off against this income, leaving her in a break-even position with no Income Tax to pay on this income. Meanwhile, the company will be able to claim the rent for CT purposes, providing tax relief of up to £11,925 (at 26.5%).*

There are no restrictions in Income Tax relief for interest or finance costs related to *non-residential* property. Relief for interest or finance costs related to *residential* property that you rent to your own company is restricted to basic rate (20%) only. In this case, this is likely to include most furnished holiday lets.

You can charge your company any level of rent you wish, from zero to a full market rent.

Like Basira in Example D, Part 1, you could choose to simply cover your costs but, in other cases, it may be desirable to increase your rent to a higher level, anything up to full market rent. This carries some significant advantages.

Firstly, as we saw in Section 10.3, charging a full market rent ensures you will maintain full, unrestricted entitlement to any available capital allowances. But that's not the only advantage rent brings.

**Profit Extraction**
Paying yourself rent is one of the most tax efficient forms of profit extraction. In many cases, the rent payment will even have an overall negative tax cost. This beneficial outcome has become much more common following the increase in CT rates from 1st April 2023 (see Section 2.1).

*Example D, Part 2*
*Let's say, like many small companies, Basira's company has a marginal CT rate of 26.5%. Let's also say Basira has no other sources of income, apart from anything she takes out of her company, and a full market rent for the business premises would be £100,000 per year. Hence, if Basira charges a full market rent, she will have a taxable rental profit of £55,000.*

*The first £12,570 of Basira's rental profit will be tax free, as it is covered by her personal allowance. However, it also attracts CT relief, thus giving rise to an overall positive tax benefit of 26.5%, or £3,331.*

*The next £37,700 of rental profit will be subject to basic rate Income Tax at 20%, but will continue to attract CT relief at 26.5%, thus giving rise to an overall tax saving of 6.5% on this part of the rent, yielding a net benefit of £2,451 (£37,700 x 6.5%).*

*The final £4,730 of rental profit pushes Basira into higher rate tax at 40%. However, as usual, this attracts CT relief at 26.5%, giving rise to an overall net tax cost of just 13.5%, which is much less than higher rate tax on dividend income at 33.75%.*

*In all, Basira can extract a total of £55,000 in profit with an Income Tax cost of £9,432 but a CT saving of £14,575: an overall positive tax saving of £5,143. This is far better than simply paying herself a dividend of £55,000, which would have produced an Income Tax cost of £4,851 and no CT saving at all.*

An annual saving of £5,143 instead of an annual cost of £4,851: that means Basira could be almost £10,000 better off each year.

While payments of rent are a very tax efficient form of profit extraction, they can be beaten, or sometimes perhaps simply equalled, by following some of the strategies we looked at in Chapter 5 and Section 6.4.

Note that the property income allowance, which can sometimes exempt up to £1,000 of rental income, is not available on rent paid to you by your own company: see the Taxcafe guide *How to Save Property Tax* for further details.

**The Downside**

As we can see, paying yourself rent is a pretty tax efficient form of profit extraction and is better than dividends where it can be justified. However, as discussed in Section 10.3, payment of rent will lead to a restriction in your BADR on a qualifying disposal of the property.

Without BADR, the CGT payable by a higher rate taxpayer on disposal of a business property will generally double (the rate increases from 10% to 20%).

Naturally, there are some business owners for whom BADR on an associated disposal is not an issue. These include company owners:

- Who have, or will, use their £1m maximum lifetime allowance for BADR on other capital gains, including the shares in the company that rents your property
- Whose shares do not qualify for BADR (e.g. a property investment company owner)

In other cases, the owner needs to weigh up the tax savings created by the payment of rent against the additional CGT cost on the eventual sale of the property. However, in this context, it's worth remembering the maximum saving yielded by BADR is just £100,000.

If you're making the kind of savings we saw in Example D, it only takes ten years and you've saved almost as much as the lost CGT relief: and getting that relief in ten years' time is far from certain!

### 10.5 CAPITAL ALLOWANCES ON PROPERTY

Capital expenditure on property effectively falls into four categories for the purposes of capital allowances:

- Integral features
- Other fixtures and fittings qualifying as plant and machinery

- Construction expenditure qualifying for the structures and buildings allowance (see Section 10.6)
- Non-qualifying expenditure

This is effectively a hierarchy. The highest item on the list the expenditure qualifies as determines how it will be treated. First, we look at integral features; then we see if it might otherwise qualify as plant and machinery; what's left might qualify for the structures and buildings allowance; then the dregs after that don't qualify for anything at all.

In that last category, we will find land and most expenditure on residential property. However, some expenditure on furnished holiday lets (at present) and communal areas within a rented residential property, but outside any individual dwelling, may qualify as plant and machinery. This also extends to qualifying expenditure on plant and machinery affixed to the exterior of a property divided into multiple dwellings, or in the garden or grounds of such a property.

Commercial, or non-residential, property expenditure may fall under any of the above headings of course.

In short, for the purposes of this section, qualifying properties are:

- Commercial or non-residential property
- Furnished holiday lets (at present: but see Section 1.6)
- Residential properties divided into multiple dwellings (but not where the expenditure is within an individual dwelling)

Plant and machinery allowances on qualifying assets within these properties may be claimed by:

- Companies using commercial property in their own trade
- Companies renting out property as a landlord
- Owner/directors renting property to their own company (note, property is unlikely to qualify as a furnished holiday let in the director's hands in these circumstances, even if the company uses the property in its furnished holiday letting business)

Assets within qualifying properties that qualify as plant and machinery for capital allowances purposes include:

- Integral features (see below)
- Furniture, furnishings, white goods, baths, showers, sanitary ware
- Kitchen and cleaning equipment

- Televisions, radios, music systems, and similar equipment
- Gardening tools and equipment
- Manufacturing or processing equipment
- Sound insulation and gas or sewerage systems provided to meet the special requirements of a qualifying trading activity
- Storage or display equipment, counters and checkouts, cold stores, refrigeration and cooling equipment
- Computer, telecommunication and surveillance systems, including wiring and other links
- Fire and burglar alarms, sprinklers and fire-fighting equipment
- Strong rooms and safes
- Moveable partitioning where intended to be moved in the course of a qualifying trading activity
- Decorative assets provided for public enjoyment in hotels, restaurants and similar trades
- Advertising hoardings, signs and displays

Expenditure on the alteration of a building for the purpose of installing qualifying plant and machinery also qualifies for plant and machinery allowances itself.

Apart from integral features, all the above items are eligible for the same capital allowances as other plant and machinery, like vans or computers, which we saw in Chapter 8: including the annual investment allowance, full expensing, and, for expenditure incurred before 1$^{st}$ April 2023, the super-deduction. In addition to these allowances, the items listed in Section 8.6 qualify for 100% enhanced capital allowances.

Expenditure on the items listed above (apart from integral features) that is not covered by any other allowances will fall into the main pool (see Section 8.7) and attract writing down allowances at 18%.

Assets must be purchased new and unused to qualify for full expensing, the super-deduction, or enhanced capital allowances. Subject to this, qualifying assets within property are usually eligible for the same rate of capital allowances whether they are purchased separately, or as part of the purchase of the property.

Where a second-hand property is purchased, the purchaser and seller generally have to agree a value for the qualifying fixtures within the property and make a joint election (known as a Section 198 Election), which the purchaser has to submit to HMRC within two years of the date of purchase in support of their capital allowances claim.

The agreed value can be anything between £1 and the original cost to the seller of the qualifying items. Sellers generally prefer a low value as this prevents or minimises balancing charges, but this is a matter for negotiation.

When purchasing second-hand commercial property, it is also important to obtain a copy of any applicable allowance statement to support a structures and buildings allowance claim (see Section 10.6).

## Integral Features
The following items are classed as integral features:

- Electrical lighting and power systems
- Cold water systems
- Space or water heating systems, air conditioning, ventilation and air purification systems and floors or ceilings comprised in such systems
- Lifts, escalators and moving walkways
- External solar shading

Integral features are eligible for the annual investment allowance in the same way as other plant and machinery. New, unused integral features purchased by a company are eligible for the 50% first year allowance that we looked at in Section 8.5.

Any amounts not covered by the annual investment allowance, including the other unrelieved 50% of expenditure on which the first year allowance has been claimed, fall into the special rate pool (see Section 8.7) and attract writing down allowances at just 6%.

Expenditure on replacing part of an integral feature within a qualifying property is classed as capital expenditure if, within any twelve-month period, such expenditure amounts to more than half the cost of replacing the entire feature. Capital allowances remain available on the expenditure in the same way as other expenditure on integral features.

## Final Points
Expenditure on thermal insulation of an existing commercial property or furnished holiday let (at present: see Section 1.6) qualifies for the same capital allowances as integral features.

See Sections 8.10 and 8.11 for planning issues relevant to larger companies with total qualifying plant and machinery expenditure in excess of £1m.

For further information regarding plant and machinery allowances, see the Taxcafe guides *Using a Property Company to Save Tax* (for property, and assets within property, owned by a company), or *How to Save Property Tax* (for property, and assets within property, owned by a director).

Expenditure on qualifying assets within furnished holiday lets incurred by companies up to 31st March 2025 will continue to be eligible for the full range of capital allowances discussed in Chapter 8 and, as explained in Section 8.9, the abolition of the regime will not, in itself, give rise to any balancing charges.

## 10.6   THE STRUCTURES AND BUILDINGS ALLOWANCE

The structures and buildings allowance (SBA) applies to expenditure on the construction, renovation, improvement or conversion of qualifying non-residential property. It is available to:

- Companies using commercial property in their own trade
- Companies renting out non-residential property
- Owner/directors renting business property to their own company

The SBA is given as a straight-line allowance on qualifying cost at the rate of 3% (2% prior to 1st April 2020). The main provisos are:

- All contracts for construction works on the relevant project must have been entered into after 28th October 2018
- The structure or building is used in a business chargeable to UK CT or Income Tax; including a trade, profession, or 'ordinary' property business (i.e. not a furnished holiday let)
- The cost of land, including rights over land, does not qualify
- Property in residential use does not qualify (see further below)

Where any contract for the construction of a property was entered into before 29th October 2018, the SBA cannot be claimed on the property itself. However, this does not prevent later projects for renovation, conversion or improvement work on the property from qualifying.

SBA is limited to the 'net direct costs relating to physically constructing the asset'. Where relevant, this will include demolition costs, the costs of land alterations or preparations necessary for the construction and other direct costs of bringing the structure or building into existence.

240

However, in addition to excluding the cost of land, SBA does not cover the cost of:

- SDLT and other purchase costs
- Obtaining planning permission
- Other land alterations beyond what is necessary for the construction (e.g. landscaping, although landscaping that results in the creation of a separate structure does qualify)
- Land reclamation
- Land remediation (a separate relief is sometimes available)

The SBA cannot be claimed on expenditure that qualifies for plant and machinery allowances, including integral features and other qualifying fixtures (Section 10.5).

The SBA claim generally commences on the later of the date the expenditure is incurred, and the date the building or structure is first brought into qualifying use. However, in the case of renovations or improvements to property already in qualifying use, the claim may commence on any of the:

i) Last day works are carried out in relation to the project,
ii) First day of the next accounting period commencing after (i), or
iii) First day of the next accounting period after the day the expenditure is incurred

For example, in the case of a company with a $31^{st}$ December accounting date carrying out improvements to a property over the period from October 2024 to $31^{st}$ March 2025, the company may choose to claim the SBA:

- From $31^{st}$ March 2025 using option (i),
- From $1^{st}$ January 2026 using option (ii), or
- From $1^{st}$ January 2025 for expenditure incurred up to $31^{st}$ December 2024 and from $1^{st}$ January 2026 for the remainder, using option (iii)

There isn't much advantage to option (ii), apart from simplicity. Whether option (i) or (iii) is best will depend on the particular circumstances of each case.

Expenditure incurred prior to the commencement of the owner's business is treated as if it were incurred on the date of commencement.

There is no limit to how long prior to commencement the expenditure was incurred (subject to the rule that all contracts must have been entered into after 28th October 2018, as stated above).

The SBA is reduced on a time apportionment basis:

- In any accounting period of less than twelve months' duration,
- If the building or structure had not yet been brought into qualifying use at the beginning of the period, or
- Where the SBA claim commences part way through the period (as detailed above)

The SBA ceases when a full claim for all periods since the expenditure first qualified would total 100%. In most cases, this will take thirty-three and a third years, so the allowance is a 'long player' (if you don't understand that reference, dear reader, ask your parents!) The SBA also ceases if a qualifying building or structure is demolished.

Following the increase in the rate of SBA in 2020, the earliest possible claims are now due to expire in August 2052, although I strongly suspect we will see more changes before then!

When a building or structure is sold, entitlement to the SBA transfers to the new owner. The SBA available for the year of sale is apportioned between the seller and purchaser, with the seller retaining entitlement for the day of transfer. There are no balancing allowances or charges at the point of sale.

Where a qualifying property is purchased from a developer, SBA may be claimed on the purchase price, but with appropriate exclusions for the cost of the land, integral features, and other fixtures qualifying for plant and machinery allowances (see Section 10.5). The expenditure is deemed to be incurred on the date of purchase in these cases.

### *Example*
*Scorpion Ltd purchases a new industrial unit from a developer for £300,000: £60,000 of this cost relates to the land, and £40,000 represents integral features and other fixtures qualifying as plant and machinery, so the amount qualifying for SBA is £200,000. Scorpion Ltd has a 31st December year end and starts to use the building on 1st April 2024.*

*The company will be able to claim SBA of £4,508 in 2024 (£200,000 x 3% x 275/366), followed by £6,000 (3%) in each subsequent year.*

## Residential Use

The SBA is not available when a property is in residential use. This includes:

- A dwelling house (i.e. normal residential property including houses, flats, apartments, etc.)
- Residential accommodation for school pupils
- Student accommodation (property that was either purpose built or converted for student use and is available for occupation by students at least 165 days per year)
- Residential accommodation for the armed forces
- Homes providing residential accommodation (but see the exception below)
- Prisons or similar institutions

There is an exception for care homes providing residential accommodation together with personal care for the elderly, disabled, people with mental disorders, or people suffering from alcohol or drugs dependency.

A 'dwelling house' is a building, or part of a building, that has all the facilities required for normal day to day living. Typically, therefore, hotel rooms do not usually constitute dwellings and a hotel would usually qualify for SBA. A guest house would, however, usually be a dwelling house and would not usually qualify.

Any structure on land in residential use, such as the garden or grounds of a house, is itself deemed to be in residential use. Additional facilities provided with serviced apartments (such as a gym or swimming pool) are also deemed to be in residential use and excluded from the SBA.

If the first use of a property following the qualifying expenditure is residential (as defined above), the SBA will never be available on that expenditure. Later expenditure on the same property may qualify, however: if it is subsequently converted into non-residential use.

Where a building or structure has both qualifying and non-qualifying use, the qualifying costs must be apportioned and the SBA may be claimed on an appropriate proportion. However, no relief is available on workplaces within a dwelling house; or where the proportion in qualifying use is insignificant (generally taken to mean 10% or less).

### The Allowance Statement
SBA claims require an allowance statement identifying the relevant building or structure, together with:

*   The date of the earliest contract relating to the relevant project,
*   The amount of qualifying expenditure, and
*   The date the property was first brought into qualifying use

The owner who incurs the qualifying expenditure makes the allowance statement. Subsequent owners must obtain a copy.

### Interaction with Capital Gains
The amount of SBA claimed by a seller must be added to their sale proceeds for the purposes of calculating the chargeable gain arising on a disposal of the property.

### 10.7   WORKING FROM HOME

Small company owners running their business from home are entitled to claim tax relief for the costs incurred. This can be achieved in a number of ways.

Like other employees, they could enter into a homeworking arrangement or claim the measly allowance of £26 per month. These options are covered in detail in Section 7.19 but are only really suitable if the company has business premises.

Where the company has no other premises, it can logically be argued on basic principles that the costs of working from home are incurred wholly, exclusively, and necessarily for the purposes of the director's employment. This means the director can be reimbursed a suitable and reasonable proportion of their household costs. The amount reimbursed will not give rise to a benefit in kind and will qualify for CT relief.

#### *Example*
*Simon runs his company from home. His house has five rooms excluding the kitchen, bathroom and hallways. He uses one room as his study from where he works around sixty hours per week on average (not unusual for a small company owner). The study is also used privately around twelve hours per week. The variable household costs on the property (see below) total £3,000 per year.*

*Simon can therefore claim £500 (£3,000 x 1/5 x 60/72) in respect of his household running costs.*

That's £500 Simon has managed to extract from his company tax free, while also producing a CT saving of at least £95 at the same time (£500 x 19%).

It's not much though, is it? And the reason is that a claim based on basic principles is restricted to variable costs only, like heating and lighting. This is because only the variable costs can be said to be wholly, exclusively, and **necessarily** incurred for the purposes of the director's employment.

Note, exclusive business use of part of your home can result in losing part of your CGT exemption on its sale. However, it is only *exclusive* business use that causes a problem; anything up to 99% is fine. For more details, see the Taxcafe guide *How to Save Property Tax*.

### Increasing the Claim
The 'number of rooms' method used above is not the only method that can be used. Any reasonable method for apportioning household costs is acceptable, such as floor area, for example.

In some cases, it may be possible to argue that some of the fixed costs are also necessarily incurred, such as where an extension has been built specifically to provide additional working space, but there we do start to run into the danger of losing out on the property's CGT exemption.

But there's a better way to get effective relief for more of your household costs.

### Non-Exclusive Licence to Occupy
The owner/director can grant their company a non-exclusive licence to occupy the working area within their home. It needs to be non-exclusive to ensure you don't run into CGT problems and also to ensure you can actually use the relevant room privately when you want to.

Provided the payments the company makes to you under the licence represent a reasonable rate for the working facilities you are providing, based on space, hours of usage, etc, there will be no benefit in kind and the company will get CT relief for the payments.

### *Example Continued*
*Simon grants his company a non-exclusive licence to occupy his study. He charges the company £500 per month (£6,000 annually). This now represents rental income, but he is able to set off the same proportion of variable costs as before **and** a proportion of his fixed costs.*

*Let's say Simon's fixed costs amount to £9,000 per year, so his total annual household costs are £12,000. He can therefore claim a deduction of £2,000 against his rental income (£12,000 x 1/5 x 60/72).*

The company is now getting CT relief of at least £1,140 (£6,000 x 19%) and Simon is effectively receiving £2,000 tax free. His rental profit of £4,000 is taxable, but we've seen what a tax efficient way rent is to extract profits from your company haven't we? (Section 10.4)

**Household Costs**
Costs that may be claimed include:

**Variable**
- Heating and lighting (electricity, gas, etc.)
- Metered water
- Cleaning

**Fixed**
- Mortgage interest or rent
- Council Tax
- Water rates
- Buildings insurance
- Repairs to the general fabric of the building (e.g. boiler or roof repairs)

Broadband probably falls into the fixed category in most cases these days.

Costs specific to the company's business may also be claimed, such as the cost of a business telephone line.

# Chapter 11

# Other Expenses

## 11.1  OFFICE SUPPLIES AND EQUIPMENT

If your company has dedicated premises there are lots of additional expenses that can be put through the company.

Many of these items will also be purchased regularly by company owners personally for their own private homes. These items cannot, of course, be claimed for tax purposes but when purchased specifically for your business premises it's a different matter.

Most items can be purchased online or at bricks and mortar shops. When comparing prices online it's important to make sure you're comparing apples with apples. For example, you should check whether the business you're buying from is VAT registered or not. Many small businesses that sell online on platforms like Amazon and eBay are not VAT registered.

For example, if a non-registered business quotes you £100 and a VAT registered business quotes you £110, you may be better off buying from the VAT registered business because you will be able to recover VAT of £18.33 (assuming the item is a standard-rated product and you meet all the necessary criteria to recover the VAT: see Chapter 3).

When buying from bricks and mortar shops, some are better than others at issuing detailed receipts. For example, LIDL provides a VAT breakdown on its till receipts, Morrisons and Tesco do not (although each item on the receipt will display a marker that tells you whether the item is standard rated or zero rated). At most shops you can request a proper VAT receipt at the checkout and this often involves simply punching a different button on the cash register.

If you're in a shop such as a supermarket and buying items for both your business and home, remember to separate out the business items and pay for them separately using your company card.

If buying items for your business involves a *dedicated* drive to the shops, this will count as a business journey on which tax relief can be claimed. For example, if you drive to the local supermarket for the sole purpose of buying some toilet rolls for your business, you can claim up to 45p per mile from your company (see Section 9.4).

Some of the items that you purchase for your business premises will count as capital expenditure (typically office equipment and other assets); others will count as revenue expenditure.

For tax purposes it doesn't usually make much difference because most capital expenditure qualifies for 100% tax relief in the year of purchase thanks to the annual investment allowance or full expensing. Purchases of new items before 1$^{st}$ April 2023 will often qualify for the super-deduction (Section 8.5) and give you more than 100% relief, so it's worth separating these out. This is still worth mentioning because some company owners will not yet have completed their accounts for periods that include some spending prior to 1$^{st}$ April 2023.

It's also important to keep a record of what you have purchased so your accountant can allocate each item of expenditure correctly.

Examples of spending on bigger ticket items that are found on many company premises and qualify for tax relief include:

- Desks and chairs
- Computers
- Printers
- Telephones
- Carpets, curtains and blinds
- Lights (e.g. uplighters)
- Filing cabinets
- Bookshelves
- Waiting room sofas and TVs
- Tools

If purchased new before 1$^{st}$ April 2023, the above items will generally qualify for the super-deduction, thus giving you extra tax relief. The same is true of smaller items qualifying as capital expenditure, so it's worth the effort of separating them out when you put your accounts together. See Section 8.1 for guidance on what constitutes capital expenditure generally, as well as the points below regarding software.

Apart from software, we've marked other items included below that might constitute capital expenditure with a 'C'.

There are lots of smaller ticket items that are almost too many to mention:

- Software
- External hard drives and memory sticks C
- Paper and envelopes
- Ink cartridges
- Extension leads C
- Stamps
- Pens
- Scissors, staplers C
- Toilet paper and toilet cleaning products
- Light bulbs
- Hand soap
- Waiting room newspapers and magazines
- Keys for the building C
- Padlocks C

As far as software is concerned, according to HMRC guidance: *"Most off-the-shelf computer software is now acquired under licence. If the licence is paid for by regular periodical payments then these should be treated as revenue expenditure and normally spread over the useful life of the software. If a lump sum payment is made for the software licence, and it is evident that the useful life of the software is greater than two years, consideration should be given to treating the payment as capital expenditure."*

If your premises have a kitchen area tax relief can be claimed for items such as:

- Glasses and mugs
- Kettles C
- Coffee machines C
- Tea, coffee, milk, sugar, biscuits
- Microwaves C
- Toasters and toasted sandwich makers C
- Cutlery
- Fridges (for storing milk and packed lunches) C
- Vacuum cleaners C
- Other cleaning equipment and supplies

If your premises have grass, plants or shrubs that have to be kept presentable, it should be possible to claim tax relief for items such as:

- Lawnmowers C
- Strimmers C
- Hedge cutting equipment C
- Garden shears and other garden tools
- Garden gloves, eye protection etc
- Weedkiller

In these days of 'elf and safety' the company will also be able to claim tax relief for items such as:

- Fire extinguishers and fire blankets C
- Carbon monoxide and smoke detectors C
- First-aid kits
- Eye-wash equipment

Most businesses that have their own premises also spend money on a whole range of *services*. Typical items on which tax relief can be claimed would include:

- Electricity and gas
- Water
- Broadband and telephone charges
- Business Rates
- Insurance
- Postage franking equipment hire
- Couriers
- Refuse collection
- Gardening services
- Window cleaning
- General cleaning

## 11.2   ADVERTISING, MARKETING AND SPONSORSHIP

Advertising and marketing are core business activities for generating new customers. As you would imagine, most advertising and marketing expenditure is incurred wholly and exclusively for the purposes of the business and can be claimed for tax purposes.

This would include:

- Online ads on websites like Amazon, Google and Facebook
- Search engine optimisation fees
- Newspaper, TV and radio ads (including design and development)
- Bulk mailings and email marketing
- Fliers and brochures
- Directory listings and premium subscriptions to websites like LinkedIn
- Free product samples
- Exhibition costs (hiring stands, etc.)

Spending on advertising hoardings, signs and displays is more likely to fall under capital expenditure, but will still qualify for immediate tax relief thanks to the annual investment allowance or full expensing. If they were purchased new before 1$^{st}$ April 2023, they may qualify for the super-deduction (see Section 8.5).

### Sponsorship or Donation?
The following cash payments made by companies automatically qualify for CT relief:

- Payments to a registered charity
- Payments to a community amateur sports club (CASC)
- Contributions to grassroots sports through a recognised sport governing body
- Direct contributions of up to £2,500 per year to grassroots sports

From 1$^{st}$ April 2024, the automatic reliefs for payments to charities and CASCs apply to payments to qualifying UK-registered entities only. Previously, these also applied to entities registered in the European Economic Area (provided HMRC accepted them as having qualifying status before 15$^{th}$ March 2023).

Grassroots sports are usually sporting facilities or activities that are open to the public generally.

There are also special schemes for qualifying payments to support cultural activities, including:

- Theatre tax relief
- Orchestra tax relief
- Museums and galleries exhibitions tax relief (until 31$^{st}$ March 2026)

However, these items tend only to apply where there is no direct benefit to the company. Hence, they are more like donations. Furthermore, they all come with strict rules and limitations.

Having said that, most of these items will certainly enhance the company's standing in the community and may therefore be beneficial to the company's business. We've all seen those giant cheques payable to charities with the smiling company director handing them over. It does no harm!

In other cases, for genuine sponsorship costs that directly benefit the company, we have to look to basic principles.

**Sponsorship**
With sponsorship your company can enhance its reputation by becoming associated with, say, a sports team or sporting or cultural event. Sponsorship also includes product placement.

You may, for example, think it's worthwhile for your company to sponsor the local football team, with the company's name displayed in match programmes and on team shirts.

Sponsorship spending will be fully tax deductible as long as it is incurred wholly and exclusively for the purposes of the company's business.

Where problems arise is when there is a *non-business purpose*. This will often be the case when the company owner has a personal interest in the activity being sponsored or the payments benefit family members.

For example, if your company sponsors the local football team that you support, and the sole reason for the sponsorship is to help the team financially, the expenditure is not for business purposes and will be disallowed.

In one case the sponsorship of a local rugby team was disallowed because the payments were made in part to help the club obtain better players without going into debt.

If the sponsorship doesn't have commercial characteristics this will indicate that it is not for business purposes. This doesn't mean the sponsorship has to be a commercial success. What matters is the *purpose* of the spending, not the outcome. It may be a complete waste of money but as long as the sole purpose is to benefit the business, the spending will be allowed.

However, where the sponsorship fails to generate results (more sales for example), failure to take steps to improve matters may indicate the arrangement is not commercial.

Further evidence that may show a lack of commerciality includes when there is no review of how the sponsorship has benefited the business or if such a review only considers the success of the sponsored party, not the benefits enjoyed by the business.

Having proof that the sponsorship has benefited the business would, of course, be helpful in justifying a claim.

Examples of sponsorship that may be viewed as not for commercial reasons could include:

- Sponsoring a relative or close friend
- Paying what the sponsored party wants without putting the business first
- Having disregard for the commercial benefits, for example, a small local business operating solely in Edinburgh sponsoring an event in Cardiff

You can expect HMRC to be most sceptical of the sponsorship's commercial underpinnings when the parties are connected.

A personal interest in the activity or a family connection will not always prevent the expense being tax deductible. In one case, a company was able to obtain CT relief for the cost of sponsoring the racing driving career of the director's daughter. The company owned hotels near Silverstone and the sole reason for the sponsorship was to promote the business, the benefit to the daughter was incidental.

### Hospitality
Often those who sponsor events are entitled to a certain number of free tickets, private boxes, or other benefits as part of the sponsorship package. Where the sponsorship includes an element of hospitality, this portion will not be allowed for CT purposes.

Some types of sponsorship spending fall under the normal definition of entertainment and the cost will therefore be disallowed in full.

### Benefits in Kind
In some cases, the sponsorship spending may result in a taxable benefit on the directors if HMRC regards the sponsorship spending as benefiting them personally.

## 11.3 WEBSITES AND OTHER INTERNET COSTS

These days you can make a living online even if you do not have your own website. Selling on Amazon and eBay are obvious examples. If you do want a website for your business though, is the cost of developing it tax deductible?

The short answer is yes. There is some debate as to whether such spending is revenue or capital in nature but, in tax terms, there is usually little practical difference.

Revenue expenses can always be deducted in full immediately when calculating the taxable profits of the business. Capital expenditure used to be written off over many years but, these days, thanks to the annual investment allowance and full expensing, most capital expenditure (apart from cars and buildings) is fully tax deductible in year one.

Hence, despite the uncertainty surrounding this revenue versus capital issue, most companies should still be able to claim an immediate tax deduction for their website development costs.

Even if the expenditure is not covered by the annual investment allowance, it will almost always involve the acquisition of a new, unused asset, and will qualify for full expensing (Section 8.5). In short, immediate 100% tax relief is almost guaranteed.

**Capital versus Revenue**
Generally speaking, it is hard to see how the capital versus revenue issue could matter in relation to website development costs. For expenditure incurred before 1ˢᵗ April 2023, however, we are in a strange, 'upside down' world since, thanks to the super-deduction, it will pay most companies to treat as much of the expenditure they incurred as capital as they can justify.

According to HMRC's *Capital v Revenue Expenditure Toolkit*, if a business spends money developing a website that creates an enduring asset, the spending should be treated as capital expenditure (for further details, see the previous edition of this guide).

It is a joyous thing when HMRC's own guidelines can be used to help generate additional tax relief, so it's well worth considering whether spending incurred before 1ˢᵗ April 2023 might justifiably be treated as capital expenditure qualifying for the super-deduction.

Nonetheless, where you have a simple website used solely to advertise or promote your business, it would generally be appropriate to simply claim the development costs as revenue expenditure.

According to HMRC, spending on initial research and planning, before the website is developed, should also normally be treated as revenue expenditure.

**Maintaining and Updating a Website**
Once your website is up and running, the cost of maintaining and updating it (e.g. changing prices), including web hosting costs, should be classed as revenue spending and will be fully tax deductible.

**E-commerce Platforms**
Back in the early days of the internet, if you wanted a sophisticated e-commerce website that sold products online you would typically have to go to a web developer and the cost could run to thousands of pounds.

These days for a modest monthly subscription of £20-£30, small businesses can set up a fully functioning online store using one of the e-commerce platforms such as Shopify. These platforms will give you online tools to help you create your website (complete with shopping cart, etc), host your website, and process orders. The monthly subscription cost will be fully deductible as a revenue expense.

**Advertising**
If you want to advertise your business online using Google Adwords, Facebook or some other website then, like most advertising costs, the cost is usually fully tax deductible.

**Transaction Costs & Commissions**
When you sell online, you will inevitably incur a variety of charges: credit card transaction fees, commissions to resellers, product listing fees, etc. All of these costs are deductible when calculating the taxable profits of your business.

However, sometimes these costs are a bit opaque: there is no invoice as such to pay; the costs are simply deducted from your balance (although an invoice should be available to download).

It is important not to forget these costs and give the details to your accountant when your accounts are being prepared, so that your taxable profits are not overstated.

## 11.4   COMPANY PENSION CONTRIBUTIONS

With the increase in CT, many companies are enjoying more tax relief on pension contributions they make for their directors and employees.

Previously, companies enjoyed at most 19% tax relief, but this has risen to 26.5% for companies with profits between £50,000 and £250,000, and 25% for companies with profits in excess of £250,000. For example, a company with profits of £100,000 would previously have saved £1,900 in CT by making a pension contribution of £10,000. Now it will save £2,650.

Because dividends are paid out of profits that have already been subjected to CT, some company owners may find it more appealing to make pension contributions instead of paying themselves additional dividend income.

Provided the pension contribution, together with any other remuneration (salary, benefits, etc) received by the director or employee is justified by the work they do for the company, it will be a tax-deductible expense. When it comes to pension contributions for owner/directors, we gave you our view on this issue in Section 2.2: if the profits are being made, there is little reason to doubt the contribution is justified.

There are several reasons why pension contributions are an attractive alternative to dividends:

- Like salaries, company pension contributions enjoy CT relief. As stated above, they're a tax-deductible business expense.
- When you eventually withdraw money from your pension, up to 25% can be taken tax free.
- Unlike salaries, there is no National Insurance on income withdrawn from a pension.
- Pension income is taxed at the regular Income Tax rates, typically 20% or 40%. By contrast, the combined tax rate (CT and Income Tax) on dividend income is approximately 32% for basic-rate taxpayers and 50% for higher-rate taxpayers who own companies with profits in excess of £250,000. Slightly higher rates will be suffered by many owners of smaller companies with profits between £50,000 and £250,000.
- When you start withdrawing money from your pension, you could find yourself in a lower tax bracket than you are now (many retirees are basic-rate taxpayers).

Putting all this together, it's possible you could ultimately pay Income Tax on your pension withdrawals at an effective average rate of just 15%. By contrast, you may face a combined tax rate that is possibly two, three, or even more times higher if the same money is paid out as dividend income.

There is, of course, a major drawback with pensions: your money is locked away until you are 55 (rising to 57 in 2028). Nevertheless, when you do reach the minimum retirement age, you can make unlimited withdrawals.

Another drawback with pensions is you are potentially exposed to any future increase in Income Tax rates. Essentially, your savings are at the mercy of future governments. Having said that, we believe pension contributions are still worth making in many cases.

### *Example – Higher-rate Taxpayer*

*Lesleyanne owns a company that makes profits of approximately £100,000 and is a higher-rate taxpayer (i.e. her taxable income is more than £50,270). Let's say she is trying to choose between taking an additional £1,000 of the company's profit as a dividend and getting the company to invest £1,000 in her self-invested personal pension (SIPP).*

*With a dividend the company will face a marginal CT rate of 26.5%, which means it will pay £265 tax, leaving £735 to distribute. Lesleyanne will then pay Income Tax at 33.75%: £248. The total combined tax rate on the dividend will be roughly 51%.*

*A company pension contribution will enjoy CT relief, so the whole £1,000 will go straight into Lesleyanne's SIPP. Ignoring investment growth (it doesn't affect the outcome), when she eventually withdraws the money from her pension, the first £250 will be tax free and the remaining £750 will be subject to Income Tax.*

*If Lesleyanne is a basic-rate taxpayer when she retires in the future, she will pay 20% tax (£150), leaving her with £850 overall. Thus, her effective overall tax rate will be 15%. If Lesleyanne is a higher-rate taxpayer when she retires (for example, if she ends up with a significant amount of rental income from buy-to-let properties) she will effectively pay 40% tax on her taxable pension income (£300), leaving her with £700 overall. Thus, the effective tax rate on her pension withdrawals will be 30%.*

*If Lesleyanne does not have much income from other sources when she starts withdrawing income from her pension (possibly from age 55), it's possible some of her pension withdrawals will be tax free, being covered by her Income Tax personal allowance.*

*We will ignore this possibility for the remainder of this section, so as not to overstate the potential benefits of pensions. When Lesleyanne eventually reaches state pension age her state pension will probably use up most or all of her Income Tax personal allowance, which means she will pay tax on all income withdrawn from her private pension.*

*In summary, Lesleyanne's choice is between paying tax at roughly 51% on her additional dividend income and paying tax at 15% or possibly 30% on her pension withdrawals.*

What this example shows is that, for company owners who have not already built up significant pension savings, a company pension contribution is an extremely attractive alternative to additional dividend income.

Of course, one must never lose sight of the fact that your pension savings are placed in a locked box until you are at least 55. So, a company pension contribution is only an attractive alternative to a dividend if you have already withdrawn enough money from your company to cover your living costs.

In the above example, we assumed the company has a marginal tax rate of 26.5%. If its profits are no greater than £50,000, the combined tax rate on Lesleyanne's additional dividend income will be roughly 46%; if its profits are greater than £250,000, the combined tax rate will be just over 50%: compared with 15% or possibly 30% on her pension withdrawals.

Are company pension contributions attractive if you're a basic-rate taxpayer (taxable income less than £50,270)? Let's find out:

### Example – Basic-rate Taxpayer
*Poppy is a company owner and a basic-rate taxpayer. She too is trying to choose between taking £1,000 of the company's profit as a dividend and a £1,000 company pension contribution.*

*Let's assume the company's profits do not exceed £50,000, which means it will pay CT at 19%. With a dividend the company will first pay CT of £190, leaving £810 to distribute. Poppy will then pay Income Tax at 8.75%: £71. The total combined tax rate on the dividend is roughly 26%.*

*If the company has profits in the £50,000 to £250,000 bracket, it will face a marginal CT rate of 26.5%, which means it will pay £265 tax and the total combined tax rate on the dividend will be roughly 33%.*

*With a company pension contribution instead, the whole £1,000 will go straight into Poppy's SIPP. As with Lesleyanne, the effective tax rate on her pension withdrawals will be either 15% if she is a basic-rate taxpayer when she retires or 30% if she is a higher-rate taxpayer.*

*In summary, Poppy's choice is between paying tax at between 26% and 33% on her additional dividend income and paying tax at 15% or possibly 30% on her pension withdrawals.*

What this example shows is that, if you are currently a basic-rate taxpayer, a company pension contribution is a reasonably attractive alternative to additional dividend income.

However, pension contributions will not be very attractive if you end up wealthier in retirement and become a higher-rate taxpayer. This could happen if, for example, you inherit or accumulate a significant amount of assets and the income takes you over the higher-rate threshold before you start withdrawing money from your pension.

Finally, please note that in this section we have not provided a comprehensive overview of the pension tax reliefs and rules. For further information see the Taxcafe guide *Pension Magic*.

# Chapter 12

# Saving Corporation Tax

## 12.1 THE NEW CORPORATION TAX REGIME

In this chapter, we will examine the new CT regime applying to company accounting periods starting after 31$^{st}$ March 2023.

In the March 2021 Budget, the then Chancellor Rishi Sunak announced the main rate of CT would be increased from 19% to a new rate of 25% with effect from 1$^{st}$ April 2023. This is one of the most significant tax increases in recent times, adding almost a third to many companies' tax bills.

The new 25% rate does not apply to all companies. Companies making annual profits of £50,000 or less benefit from the small profits rate of 19%. In other words, companies with annual profits of no more than £50,000 have not suffered any increase in CT.

Companies with annual profits between the 'lower limit' of £50,000 and the 'upper limit' of £250,000 also pay a reduced rate of CT, somewhere between 19% and 25%. This is achieved by applying a system of marginal relief.

Marginal relief is given at a rate of 3/200ths on the amount by which profits are less than the upper limit of £250,000.

### Example
*Nevis Ltd makes a profit of £180,000 for the year ending 31$^{st}$ March 2025. Its profit is therefore £70,000 less than the upper limit. The company's CT bill is calculated as follows:*

| | |
|---|---|
| *£180,000 x 25%* | *£45,000* |
| *Less Marginal Relief* | |
| *£70,000 x 3/200* | *(£1,050)* |
| *Corporation Tax due* | *£43,950* |

*In this case, the company's overall effective CT rate is 24.417%.*

The effective rate given after marginal relief can also be regarded as the average rate, i.e. the average rate of CT paid on all the company's profits.

## Short and Long Accounting Periods

The lower and upper limits of £50,000 and £250,000 respectively are reduced where the company draws up accounts for a period of less than twelve months. This is done on a pro rata basis, based on the number of days in the accounting period.

Hence, for example, where a company has a nine-month accounting period ending on 31$^{st}$ December 2024, the upper limit will be £188,356 (£250,000 x 275/365) and the lower limit will be £37,671 (£50,000 x 275/365).

Where a company draws up accounts for a period of more than twelve months, this is treated as two accounting periods for CT purposes: the first twelve months and the remainder.

## Earlier Periods

Accounting periods that spanned 1$^{st}$ April 2023 are also affected by the new regime, but only on the part of the company's profit arising after 31$^{st}$ March 2023. This is generally calculated on a simple time apportionment basis.

For example, where a company made a profit of £100,000 for a twelve-month accounting period ended 31$^{st}$ December 2023, £75,342 (£100,000 x 275/365) of this profit is deemed to arise after 31$^{st}$ March 2023. The company is then treated as if it had made this profit in a nine-month accounting period, as discussed above. The remaining £24,658 of profit deemed to arise before 1$^{st}$ April 2023 is simply taxed at the old CT rate of 19%.

The upshot of all this is that companies with profits of more than £50,000 for accounting periods that straddled 1$^{st}$ April 2023 suffer a variety of different marginal CT rates, which we have set out in Appendix A (the rates given apply to the whole twelve-month accounting period).

For the rest of this chapter, we will focus purely on accounting periods commencing after 31$^{st}$ March 2023, and thus falling wholly within the new regime.

## 12.2   MARGINAL CORPORATION TAX RATES

In Section 12.1, we looked at the total CT payable and saw an example of the resultant average CT rate.

Average tax rates and total tax bills are important for budgeting and cashflow purposes. In tax planning, however, we are far more concerned with *marginal* tax rates.

As explained in Section 2.1, a marginal tax rate is the rate of tax suffered on each additional £1 of income or profit or, to look at it another way, the rate of tax saving available on each additional £1 of allowable expenditure.

Governments almost never mention marginal tax rates and politicians seldom seem to understand them, which is a great shame because it is marginal tax rates that so often drive taxpayer behaviour. For example, an individual with a salary of £65,000 and four children qualifying for child benefit will generally have a marginal tax rate of 62% in 2024/25 (combining Income Tax at 40%, National Insurance at 2%, and the Child Benefit Charge). If their boss asks them to work overtime at the weekend to help the company's productivity, what incentive do they have, knowing they will keep just 38p out of every additional pound they earn in return for giving up a weekend with their family?

So, as we can see, marginal tax rates have a very real impact on the economy. And the bad news is many small companies will be suffering the highest marginal CT rate under the new regime.

As explained in Section 12.1, once a company's profits exceed the £50,000 lower limit, they are subject to CT at the main rate of 25% but also benefit from marginal relief at 3/200ths on the amount by which the company's profits are less than the upper limit.

This means every additional £1 of profit between the lower limit and the upper limit effectively suffers two tax charges: 25p in CT and 1.5p in lost marginal relief. Hence, the marginal CT rate on profits falling between the lower and upper limits is 26.5%.

So, while the Government will only ever mention the main rate of 25% and the small profits rate of 19%, there are actually three marginal CT rates as follows:

| **Annual Profits** | **Marginal CT Rate** |
| --- | --- |
| Up to £50,000 | 19% |
| £50,000 to £250,000 | 26.5% |
| Over £250,000 | 25% |

These bands apply to a company with no associated companies, for a twelve-month accounting period commencing after 31$^{st}$ March 2023.

## 12.3 ASSOCIATED COMPANIES

Where the company has associated companies, the higher CT rates (26.5% and 25%) kick in earlier, at lower profit levels. This is done by dividing the lower and upper limits by a factor of one plus the number of associated companies. For example, if the company has four associated companies, the limits are divided by five.

The impact on the upper and lower limits is illustrated by the table below (assuming a twelve-month accounting period).

| Number of Associates | Lower Limit | Upper Limit |
|---|---|---|
| 0 | £50,000 | £250,000 |
| 1 | £25,000 | £125,000 |
| 2 | £16,667 | £83,333 |
| 3 | £12,500 | £62,500 |
| 4 | £10,000 | £50,000 |

For example, if you own two companies that are associated, each company will pay 19% CT on the first £25,000 of profit and 26.5% on the next £100,000. Once either company has more than £125,000 profit, it will pay 25% tax on all its profits.

Where two companies are associated, it can potentially cost *each* company up to £1,875 in extra CT *every year*. That's a total additional tax burden of up to £37,500 over a ten-year period. Add to this the fact associated companies are also connected companies for the purposes of the employment allowance (Section 6.2), and we can see being associated can be very costly indeed!

On the other hand, an associated company may sometimes lead to an overall tax saving, or it may make no difference at all.

We will look at the costs and benefits of associated companies in more detail in Section 12.4 but, since it is such an important issue, we will first take a thorough look at *when* a company is associated for CT purposes (which will also mean it is connected for the purposes of the employment allowance: see Section 6.2).

### When are Companies Associated/Connected?
The basic rule is that two companies are associated with each other if one company is under the control of the other, or both companies are under the control of the same person or persons.

In the simplest case, where a company has a single class of shares and a person owns more than 50% of those shares, then that person controls the company. So, if you own more than 50% of the shares in two or more companies, those companies are associated. End of story.

In other cases, control is assumed to exist where a person, or group of persons, possesses, or is entitled to acquire, rights that entitle them to more than 50% of the company's share capital, voting rights, distributable income (assuming all available income were distributed), or assets on a winding up.

Deemed control may also arise where a person is a loan creditor (i.e. the company owes them money) and their rights as a loan creditor, plus any other rights they hold, entitle them to more than 50% of the company's assets on a winding up. This does not apply where the loan creditor is a bank or other financial institution, but could apply where an individual (or another company that is *not* a financial institution) is owed money by the company.

Control could also arise where, as a matter of fact, a person has ultimate control over the company.

### Some Examples

**A:** *Pennine Ltd owns all the shares in Cheviot Ltd and 75% of the shares in Kinder Ltd. Pennine Ltd therefore controls both Cheviot Ltd and Kinder Ltd and the three companies are all associated.*

**B:** *Dave owns all the shares in Helvellyn Ltd and 51% of the shares in Striding Ltd. Dave therefore controls both companies and they are associated.*

**C:** *Andrea, Brenda, and Claire each own one third of the shares in Scafell Ltd. Andrea, Brenda, and Diane each own one third of the shares in Snowdon Ltd. Andrea and Brenda together are able to control both Scafell Ltd and Snowdon Ltd and the companies are therefore associated.*

Example C demonstrates a key point: where any combination of two or more persons taken together, are able to exercise control over more than one company, those companies are associated.

**D:** *Kristine and Lauren each own 50% of the shares in Macdui Ltd and 50% of the shares in Braeriach Ltd, although Kristine runs Macdui Ltd on a day-to-day basis and Lauren runs Braeriach Ltd.*

*Nonetheless, despite the day to day management of the companies, Kristine and Lauren together are able to control both Macdui Ltd and Braeriach Ltd by virtue of their shareholdings and the companies are therefore associated.*

***E:*** *Emily, Fiona, and Gabby each own one third of the shares in Malvern Ltd. Emily, Helen, and Maggie each own one third of the shares in Pentland Ltd. The companies are **not** associated: there is no combination of two or more persons that is able to control both companies.*

***F:*** *John owns 50% of the shares in both Wainwright Ltd and Fells Ltd. The other 50% of Wainwright Ltd is owned by Paul. The other 50% of Fells Ltd is owned by George. On the face of it, the companies do **not** appear to be associated as there is no combination of two or more persons that is able to control both companies.*

The position in Examples E and F is based on the assumption there is no other relationship between the shareholders other than their common shareholdings. We will revisit these examples later to see how they would be affected by such a relationship.

The position in Example F would also be different if both companies' constitutions had some form of deadlock clause whereby John had the casting vote in the event of a dispute between the shareholders. This would mean John was able to exercise control over both companies and they would have to be treated as associated companies for CT purposes. It would not matter whether, in practice, John ever used his casting vote, the fact he was entitled to do so would be sufficient to make the companies associated.

Companies with 50/50 shareholdings often pose a difficulty in applying the associated companies rules as, even without the existence of a casting vote, or 'golden share' (sometimes used to produce the same result), there will frequently be a question hanging over the issue of who, in practice, ultimately controls the company. To avoid the risk of two companies being associated, it may make sense to ensure different persons hold more than 50% of the shares in each company. Naturally, this has commercial implications that need to be considered.

***G:*** *Indira owns all the shares in Moruisg Ltd, plus 40% of the shares in Loyal Ltd. Her husband, Romesh, owns the remaining 60% of the shares in Loyal Ltd. In practice, however, Indira exerts ultimate control over Loyal Ltd, as her husband acts in accordance with her instructions. Indira therefore controls both Moruisg Ltd and Loyal Ltd and the companies are associated.*

*H: Lester owns all the shares in Vorlich Ltd. His wife, Jane, owns all the shares in Stuc Ltd. Jane has also loaned £400,000 to Vorlich Ltd and, taking the loan into account, she would be entitled to 80% of the assets of Vorlich Ltd in the event of a winding up. Jane is therefore deemed to have control of Vorlich Ltd, meaning Vorlich Ltd and Stuc Ltd are associated companies.*

Note that the marital status of the shareholders in Examples G and H is irrelevant, the companies would be associated even if the shareholders were unmarried, or even if they had no other connection at all. The same could be said of Example D (although I did not mention marital status there).

But marital status, or other close relationships, can make a difference in other cases, and we will look at that later.

### When Does an Associated Company Need to be Counted?
An associated company does not need to be counted for the purposes of the upper and lower limits if it does not carry on any trade or business at any time during the relevant accounting period. This means we can discount dormant companies and companies that merely hold assets passively, with no attempt to carry on any trade or business.

Companies that may be discounted include a company that only holds cash on deposit, and has no other activities, or a company that only holds a property that is not being rented, developed, or used for any other business purpose. For example, it is quite common for people to own an overseas holiday home through a company. If the company does not rent out the property, or carry on any other activities, it may be ignored for the purposes of the associated companies rules. The same would be true of a company that held a UK holiday home and did not carry on any other activities, although this would have other tax consequences.

A company that owns a property occupied by another company for the purposes of its business will, however, usually have to be counted, and it seems likely this remains the case even if no rent is charged (as a lease or licence to occupy will generally exist).

Where a company's only activity is to hold investments such as stocks and shares, it will be debatable whether it is deemed to be carrying on a business. If the investments are passive, with little or no investment activity carried out, the company may be regarded as inactive, so that it need not be counted for the purposes of the associated companies rules.

266

Where, however, the company is actively trading its investments, a business will exist and the company will need to be included.

Passive holding companies also do not need to be counted. These are companies that exist solely to hold shares in subsidiary companies, and have no other assets or activities of their own. The holding company must own more than 50% of the shares in all its subsidiaries, and must redistribute all dividends it receives to its shareholders.

It is possible that Pennine Ltd in Example A above might qualify as a passive holding company, although this depends on the facts of the case. This would not prevent Cheviot Ltd and Kinder Ltd from being associated with each other, but it would mean each of them only had to count one associated company for CT purposes.

Subject to the above points, all associated companies must be counted for the purpose of reducing the upper and lower limits, including overseas companies and companies subject to different rates of CT (see Section 12.6).

As explained in Section 6.2, associated companies are also connected companies for the purposes of the employment allowance. Clearly, this only matters if two or more associated companies have UK-based employees (including directors being paid a salary).

**Spouses, Families, and Other Associates**
In some cases, the associated/connected company net is cast even wider. Where there is substantial commercial interdependence between two companies (see below), shares and other rights held by a shareholder's associates must be counted in deciding if the companies are under the control of the same person or persons. Associates for this purpose include spouses, close relatives (as per heading (ii) in Appendix C), business partners, and certain trusts and estates.

Nonetheless, there are many people who are not your associate for these purposes including, most importantly, an unmarried partner. Do not forget, however, that anyone becomes your associate if they are also your business partner.

Assuming they are not also a business partner, an unmarried partner is not your associate even if you have children together. However, it is important to remember your children are an associate of both of you.

Shares held by an 'associate of an associate' (e.g. your unmarried partner who is the mother of your child) do not need to be counted for the purposes of the associated companies rules. However, your associate (e.g. your daughter) may need to count shares held by all *their* associates (e.g. both you and her mother).

## Substantial Commercial Interdependence

As explained above, where there is substantial commercial interdependence between two companies, shares held by spouses, close relatives, and certain other associates must be included when looking at the question of whether the same person, or group of persons, controls the companies.

Three types of link may determine whether there is substantial commercial interdependence between two companies. Where any of these links exist, the companies have substantial commercial interdependence. The types of link we need to consider are:

### Financial Interdependence

Two companies are financially interdependent if one gives financial support to the other (for example, if one company makes a loan to the other). Companies are also financially interdependent if they both have a financial interest in the affairs of the same business.

### Economic Interdependence

Two companies are economically interdependent if they share the same economic objectives, the activities of one benefit the other, or they have common customers.

### Organisational Interdependence

Two companies are organisationally interdependent if they have common management, employees, premises, or equipment.

Where two people living together each run their own separate company from home, this alone does not amount to substantial commercial interdependence. Provided there are no other links between the companies, they will not be associated.

### *Examples Revisited... and Some More*

*E Revisited: Emily, Fiona, and Gabby each own one third of the shares in Malvern Ltd. Emily, Helen, and Maggie each own one third of the shares in Pentland Ltd. Fiona and Helen are sisters. The companies will be associated if there is substantial commercial interdependence between them since, if this is the case, Fiona and Helen are effectively treated as the same person and, together with Emily, they control both companies.*

**F Revisited:** *John owns 50% of the shares in both Wainwright Ltd and Fells Ltd. The other 50% of Wainwright Ltd is owned by John's elder son, Paul. The other 50% of Fells Ltd is owned by John's younger son, George. Although the companies provide slightly different services, they have a common customer base, meaning there is substantial commercial interdependence between them. The companies are therefore associated for CT purposes.*

**I:** *Natasha owns all the shares in her software company, Klibreck Ltd; her husband, Ivan, owns all the shares in his garden landscaping company, Slioch Ltd. They each have their own business premises and there are no other links between the companies. The companies are **not** associated for CT purposes.*

**J:** *Oriel owns 51% of the shares in Cairngorm Ltd, a company specialising in interior design, and 49% of the shares in Lochnagar Ltd, a company set up to run virtual fitness training classes. Oriel's wife, Priti, owns the other 49% of Cairngorm Ltd and 51% of Lochnagar Ltd. Oriel runs Cairngorm Ltd and Priti runs Lochnagar Ltd. Both of them run their company from their shared home, but there are no other links between the companies. The companies are **not** associated for CT purposes.*

**K:** *Suzy owns all the shares in her successful company, Saddleback Ltd. Her husband, Trevor, has just started his own company, Skiddaw Ltd, in which he owns all the shares. Suzy has loaned £250,000 to Skiddaw Ltd, but there are no other links between the companies. Suzy's loan does not entitle her to more than half the assets of Skiddaw Ltd in the event of a winding up (or under any other circumstances). In this scenario, there is no substantial commercial interdependence and the companies are **not** associated for CT purposes.*

*However, the companies **would** be associated if:*
a) *Taking account of her loan, Suzy would be entitled to more than half the assets of Skiddaw Ltd in the event of a winding up. She would then be deemed to control both companies.*
b) *Saddleback Ltd had made the loan and, as a result, it would be entitled to more than half the assets of Skiddaw Ltd in the event of a winding up. Saddleback Ltd would then be deemed to control Skiddaw Ltd.*
c) *Saddleback Ltd had made the loan (but (b) does not apply).*
d) *In order to make her loan, Suzy had borrowed money from Saddleback Ltd.*
e) *In order to make her loan, Suzy had borrowed from a bank and had secured her bank loan against Saddleback Ltd's assets.*

*Note: (a) and (b) would apply in any case; (c), (d), and (e) apply because Suzy and Trevor are associates.*

*Under any of (b) to (e), Saddleback Ltd would be providing financial support to Skiddaw Ltd, meaning there was financial interdependence between the companies. However, if Suzy obtained the funds for her loan by taking a dividend out of Saddleback Ltd, this would not create substantial commercial interdependence between the companies and, in the absence of any other links, they would not be associated (unless (a) applied).*

*If any of (a) to (e) applied, the companies would cease to be associated at the end of the accounting period in which Skiddaw Ltd repaid the loan (assuming, in the case of (a) and (b), that the entitlement to the assets of Skiddaw Ltd also ceased on repayment of the loan).*

**L:** *Quentin owns all the shares in his interior design company, Dorain Ltd; his wife, Rhona, owns all the shares in Criese Ltd, a company set up to run her antiques business. Quentin often sources antiques through Criese Ltd to use in his interior design projects and Rhona allows him a small discount on her usual prices. The activities of Criese Ltd benefit Dorain Ltd and the companies also have some common customers. There is therefore economic interdependence between the companies and they are associated for CT purposes. This would remain the case even if Criese Ltd charged Dorain Ltd and its customers the full market price for the antiques.*

**M:** *Tina owns Cobbler Ltd, a company that imports shoes from Italy for distribution in the UK. Her mother, Una, owns Uisinis Ltd, which operates a chain of shoe shops. Uisinis Ltd occasionally buys some shoes from Cobbler Ltd, but this is always for the same price, and on the same terms, as other customers. Furthermore, the shoes sourced from Cobbler Ltd only account for a small proportion of Uisinis Ltd's sales. There is an economic relationship between the companies, but it is insufficient to amount to economic interdependence. In the absence of any other links, the companies are **not** associated for CT purposes.*

**N:** *Victoria runs an outdoor clothing shop through her company, Diffwys Ltd. Her father, Victor, owns the adjacent hardware store, which he runs through his company, Rhinog Ltd. Both companies share the same 'back office' area at the rear of the stores and use the same clerical staff for their administration. As the companies share common premises and employees, there is organisational interdependence between them and they are associated for CT purposes.*

**O:** *Walter runs a building company, Schiehallion Ltd. He owns 90% of the shares, his wife, Xena, owns 10%. Xena's father, Grigor, also runs a building company, Glencoe Ltd, and owns all the company's shares.*

*There is economic interdependence between the companies as Schiehallion Ltd often carries out work for Glencoe Ltd as a subcontractor. In fact, it was through Walter's business relationship with Grigor that he met Xena.*

*At first glance, it would appear the companies are not associated as Walter controls Schiehallion Ltd; Grigor controls Glencoe Ltd; and the two men are not associated with each other. (As explained above, shares held by associates of associates are not counted for this purpose.)*

*However, every shareholder's position must be considered, including Xena's. As there is substantial commercial interdependence between the companies, shares held by her associates are counted. Her husband, Walter, and her father, Grigor, are both her associates, so she is therefore deemed to control both companies and they are associated.*

As we can see from Example O, the existence of a minority shareholder effectively brings more associates into play, meaning the company may end up having additional associated companies. A minority shareholder like Xena is effectively a 'linking person' who ends up causing the companies to be associated.

However, a person cannot be treated as a linking person in this way if they do not actually own shares in either company. If Xena did not own any shares in *either* Schiehallion Ltd or Glencoe Ltd, the companies would not be associated.

### Married Couples (and Other Close Relatives)
Examples I, J, and K demonstrate it is possible for married couples to each run their own company without falling fowl of the associated companies rules, even if they run their companies from home.

It is even possible for each spouse to have a minority shareholding in the other spouse's company. The 51/49 shareholdings used in Example J work well in this context but, as we saw in Example D, 50/50 shareholdings would mean the companies were associated, regardless of the couple's marital status, and regardless of whether the companies have any other links.

Nonetheless, with careful planning, a married couple can each benefit from the 19% small profits rate on up to £50,000 of company profits, as well as the £5,000 employment allowance for National Insurance purposes (if their company qualifies: see Section 6.2). Similar principles apply to other family members.

However, in all cases where different companies are controlled by spouses, close relatives, or other associates (as defined above), it is important to avoid substantial commercial interdependence between the companies and, as we saw in the examples above, there are many ways of falling into this trap.

## Unmarried Couples

Unmarried couples are not associates for CT purposes and hence, where each of them controls their own company, those companies will not usually be associated, even if there is substantial commercial interdependence between them. This will include cases where each partner has a minority shareholding in the other partner's company but, as usual, 50/50 shareholdings will mean the companies are associated (as we saw in Example D).

There are other pitfalls to watch out for too. If one partner lends money to the other partner's company, they will be deemed to control that company if, as a result, they would be entitled to more than half its assets on a winding up. The partners' companies will then be associated.

If the couple are also business partners, they will be associates for CT purposes and, as far as everything we have discussed in this section is concerned, they would be in the same position as a married couple.

If the couple have children, there is a risk attached to giving those children any shares in either partner's company. The child would then become a linking person (similar to Xena in Example O) and, if there is substantial commercial interdependence between the companies, they will be associated.

Lastly, it is important the ultimate control of each company does indeed lie with a different partner. If the position in reality is that one partner actually controls both companies then they will be associated (see Example G).

Subject to these points, however, an unmarried couple will usually be able to each set up their own company and benefit from the 19% small profits rate on up to £50,000 of profits in each company: even when the companies have substantial commercial interdependence. Each company may also be able to benefit from the £5,000 employment allowance.

## Example P

*Sanjeev and Yvonne are an unmarried couple who have been living together for many years. Yvonne owns all the shares in Bowfell One Ltd, which operates a pub and through which all the wet sales (drinks) are made. Sanjeev owns all the shares in Bowfell Two Ltd, which operates a restaurant within the same building. The companies have common customers, employees, and premises: there can be no doubt there is substantial commercial interdependence. But they are not associated because Sanjeev and Yvonne, being unmarried, are not associates for CT purposes.*

*Hence, assuming none of the pitfalls described above apply, the combined operation could make profits of up to £100,000 taxed at the small profits rate of 19% (on the basis each company made profits of £50,000).*

Compared with using a single company to run the pub/restaurant, the couple could save up to £3,750 in CT and £5,000 in employer's National Insurance *every year*. Note, I have assumed in this case that both companies are registered for VAT. See Section 12.4 for a further discussion of this issue.

### Associated Companies Summary

If you control more than one company, those companies are associated, it's as simple as that.

In other cases, you have to count companies where you and other people together are able to control more than one company.

Sometimes, you also have to count companies controlled by your spouse, a close relative, or certain other people (or you and those people together), but only where your company and theirs have a significant financial, economic, or organisational relationship.

## 12.4   COSTS AND BENEFITS OF ASSOCIATED COMPANIES

The maximum combined additional costs for two companies of being associated with each other are £3,750 in CT and £5,000 in employer's National Insurance. When considering the impact of these costs, it is important to remember these are annual costs: not a mere one-off.

The maximum CT cost of £3,750 arises because each company has had its lower limit for small profits rate purposes halved, from £50,000 to £25,000. This in turn means an extra £25,000 is taxed at the marginal rate of 26.5%, instead of the small profits rate of 19%: an increase of 7.5% in the effective tax rate. The cost for two companies of being associated is thus £25,000 x 7.5% x 2 = £3,750.

This maximum cost arises when both companies have annual profits anywhere between £50,000 and £125,000, but there remains some cost whenever either company has profits anywhere between £25,001 and £249,999.

These additional CT costs will often arise where a company owner decides to set up a second company: we'll look at the costs and benefits of doing this later. They can also arise in other circumstances, such as where two companies owned by people classed as associates (see Section 12.3) have substantial commercial interdependence.

The question then is: do the economic benefits of that substantial commercial interdependence outweigh the additional tax cost. In this context, it is important to remember that, to meet an extra tax cost of £3,750 each year, the companies would need to make an additional £5,102 in combined annual profits between them. This is because the companies will be suffering a marginal CT rate of 26.5% (£5,102 less 26.5% equals £3,750).

If both companies have employees, we also have to factor in the additional cost to one company of not having an employment allowance available. This will generally be at least £479 (see Section 6.4) and could be up to £5,000, although there may sometimes be no cost at all, such as when a company has a single director and no other employees (see Section 6.2).

Nonetheless, in many cases, to recoup the additional tax costs caused by being associated could mean the two companies need to make additional combined pre-tax profits of up to £10,102!

Let's say, for example, the only reason two companies must be treated as associated is that they share the same business premises. Naturally, sharing their business premises gives rise to a saving. If that saving amounts to more than £10,102 per year, it remains worthwhile, despite the additional tax costs, but if the annual saving is substantially less than this, it could be worth at least one of the companies looking for different premises.

**Common Control**
Where two or more companies are controlled by the same person, or persons, they will always be associated, regardless of whether there is substantial commercial interdependence.

There are often good reasons for having more than one company (although I have seen cases where it was simply to satisfy the owner's ego) but it frequently comes at a price. At the very least, you should know what that price is, in order to satisfy yourself it is a cost worth bearing. In some cases, it will make sense to reduce the number of companies you have, or refrain from forming new ones.

Naturally, there are many sound, commercial reasons for keeping different businesses, or different parts of a business, in separate companies, and these must be considered. In particular, many people with both a trading business and a property letting business like to keep these in separate companies, or are forced to by mortgage lenders. Furthermore, putting a property letting business inside an existing trading company can be disadvantageous for both CGT and Inheritance Tax purposes; although there are also potential advantages if you plan it well (see the Taxcafe guides *Using a Property Company to Save Tax* and *How to Save Inheritance Tax* for more information).

Reducing the number of existing companies you have will involve some form of corporate reorganisation, which may sometimes be a difficult, or costly, exercise. These matters are beyond the scope of this guide, but must be borne in mind. What I will do now, however, is look at the cost, or benefit, of having more than one company in terms of annual CT costs alone (we will look at employer's National Insurance and VAT later).

**When Does It Matter?**
If you already have a company making annual profits between £25,000 and £125,000, forming a second company will do no harm, provided that second company makes annual profits of at least £25,000.

This is because your £50,000 small profits rate band will be divided between your two companies, giving them a lower limit of £25,000 each. As long as both companies fully utilise their reduced small profits rate band of £25,000, nothing is lost.

### *Example Q, Part 1*
*Caroline has an existing company, Lomond Ltd, that makes an annual profit of £125,000. She is about to start a new venture and is uncertain whether to put her new venture in a separate company. She expects the new venture to yield annual profits of £40,000. If she puts the new venture in her existing company, it will make a total profit of £165,000, giving it a CT bill of:*

| £50,000 x 19% | £9,500 |
| £115,000 x 26.5% | £30,475 |
| Total | £39,975 |

*Alternatively, if she puts the new venture in a separate company, the CT bill for her two companies will be as follows:*

**Lomond Ltd**

| £125,000 x 25% | £31,250 |

*(profits equal reduced upper limit of £125,000)*

**New Company**

| £25,000 x 19% | £4,750 |
| £15,000 x 26.5% | £3,975 |
| Total | £8,725 |

*The total tax paid by both companies is £39,975, the same as it would have been if Caroline had put her new venture in her existing company.*

The position will be different, however, if the second company does not make sufficient profit to fully utilise its small profits rate band of £25,000.

### Example Q, Part 2

*As it turns out, Caroline's new venture only makes a profit of £10,000 in its first year. If she is using a single company, this will give Lomond Ltd a total profit of £135,000 taxed as follows:*

| £50,000 x 19% | £9,500 |
| £85,000 x 26.5% | £22,525 |
| Total | £32,025 |

*If she had put the new venture in a separate company, the CT bill for her two companies would be as follows:*

**Lomond Ltd**

| £125,000 x 25% | £31,250 |

**New Company**

| £10,000 x 19% | £1,900 |

*The total tax paid by both companies is £33,150 or £1,125 more than it would have been if Caroline had put her new venture in her existing company.*

In effect, Caroline has wasted £15,000 of her small profits rate band, meaning an extra £15,000 has been taxed at 26.5% instead of 19%: the extra 7.5% tax on £15,000 amounts to £1,125.

If the new venture had broken even, the extra tax would have been £1,875, which is the cost of paying 7.5% more on half the lower limit of £50,000 (7.5% x £50,000 x ½ = £1,875).

The same cost (£1,875) would arise if the new venture made a loss and the two companies formed a group (see Section 12.7). However, if the companies were merely associated and not grouped, the loss could not be relieved and the extra cost would be even greater. (Having said that, the risk of losses is one of the main commercial reasons for forming separate companies: although the benefits of loss relief can often still be preserved with a group company)

The same principles effectively apply where you have an existing company making annual profits of less than £25,000 and plan to start a new venture. If the new venture yields profits of more than £25,000, putting it in a separate company will mean you have wasted part of your small profits rate band.

However, if neither your existing company, nor your new venture, ever makes profits of more than £25,000, having a second company will make no difference, as all profits in both companies will be taxed at the small profits rate.

Nonetheless, it is important to be aware that the CT rates apply to a company's total taxable income, profits and capital gains. While you may have two companies that you never expect to produce an annual profit of more than £25,000, if one of them has some sort of windfall, such as a capital gain on disposal of a property, for example, you may still suffer an additional cost.

**Benefits of Additional Companies**
Where you have an existing company already making annual profits of £250,000 or more, its profits will be taxed at 25% regardless of how many associated companies it has. Hence, there is effectively nothing to lose by forming a second company.

Furthermore, there could even be an annual saving of up to £1,500. This is because the new company may enjoy the small profits rate on up to £25,000. Having profits taxed at 19% instead of 25% is a rate saving of 6%, with a maximum potential benefit of £1,500 (£25,000 x 6%). To achieve the same saving with a single company would require annual cost savings of £2,000 (equivalent to £1,500 after tax).

Achieving the maximum potential saving of £1,500 is difficult, however. It requires the second company to make a profit of exactly £25,000. If the new company's profit is any less, part of the small profits rate band is wasted, reducing the overall saving by 6% of the shortfall; if the new company's profit is any more, some of it is taxed at 26.5%, reducing the overall saving by 1.5% of the excess. Once the new company's profit reaches £125,000, the saving is eliminated altogether.

So, whether the effort is worthwhile is perhaps debatable: although there will be cases where the new company's profit level is fairly predictable, at least within a reasonable range. For example, if the owner of an existing company with profits of £250,000 or more sets up a second company for a new venture and makes profits of, say, £35,000 in that new company, there is still an overall saving of £1,350. To achieve the same saving with the existing company would require annual cost savings of £1,800.

And it's worth remembering, where the existing company is already making profits of £250,000 or more (and will continue to do so), there is nothing to lose (as far as CT is concerned): provided, that is, the new company does not make any losses that cannot be relieved (easily avoided by forming a group: Section 12.7).

Technically, savings are possible whenever the existing company has profits of more than £125,000, but the potential savings are less (where profits are less than £225,000) and there is a downside risk that, if the new company makes less than £25,000 profit, there will be an overall increase in the CT cost.

Note, my analysis so far is based on the second company being used to house *additional* profits, with the existing company continuing to make profits of at least the same amount. Annual savings of up to £1,500 are still possible where part of the existing business is transferred into another company, but the existing company will generally need to continue making profits of at least £250,000. Such restructuring is also more difficult to carry out effectively: although there are always exceptions.

**Costs and Benefits of Multiple Companies**
As we have seen, the potential costs or benefits of forming a second company are dependent on the profit levels of both the original, existing company, and the new company. Costs arise where part of the small profits rate band is wasted; benefits may arise where profits can be separated out in a new company to be taxed at the small

profits rate of 19% instead of the main rate of 25%; or where an existing company has less profit taxed at the marginal rate of 26.5%.

Similar principles apply when we look at the costs or benefits of forming third, or subsequent, companies, although the thresholds to consider are different (see Section 12.3), and the maximum impact gradually diminishes the more companies we look at. From a tax planning perspective, the position grows steadily more complex, as we need to look at the profit levels in each of the companies.

In summary, forming additional companies can lead to extra CT costs, small CT savings, or no change at all, depending on the circumstances.

It is important to be aware of the potential extra costs, even if the commercial benefits of having additional companies outweigh them. The risk of extra CT costs is limited if all associated companies are also group companies.

The potential savings are generally too small to be of any practical value in their own right, but may provide an additional incentive when they fit alongside a good commercial rationale for using multiple companies.

**Multiple Companies and the Employment Allowance**
Earlier in this section, we discussed the potential annual cost of up to £5,000 caused by the fact that, where two or more companies are associated, only one of them can claim the employment allowance. Where you control two or more companies yourself, however, this will generally not be a problem.

Firstly, if your main company already fully utilises its employment allowance, there is effectively no cost in forming additional companies (you won't get any extra employment allowance, but you won't lose out either). In other cases, it is possible to employ everyone you need to run all your companies in a single company, then recharge the relevant costs to the other companies, thus preserving the full benefit of your employment allowance. While this is common practice, it does require specialist advice to get it right.

**VAT and Associated Companies**
In Section 3.2, we discussed how it is generally unwise to form an additional company simply to avoid having to register for VAT.

Furthermore, in a case like Example P in the last section, both companies would probably have to register for VAT if their *combined* turnover exceeded the VAT registration threshold. This can be avoided in such a case, but it requires some very careful management to keep the businesses completely separate for VAT purposes. Having said that, if you're aiming to benefit from the other tax savings we looked at in that example, both companies probably need to register for VAT anyway.

But there are cases where separating businesses into separate companies can be beneficial for VAT purposes, such as where:

- The companies run genuinely separate businesses and at least one of them has turnover below the VAT registration threshold
- One company operates the flat rate scheme and another company has VAT exempt activities (e.g. residential property letting)

On the other hand, it is sometimes helpful to form a VAT group, in order to simplify admin and avoid having to charge VAT on inter-company sales or management charges. This has to be applied for but is not dependent on having a group for CT purposes.

### 12.5   COMPANIES WITH DIVIDEND INCOME

Dividends received by companies are, in themselves, generally exempt from CT. However, dividends received from external investments may lead to an increase in the CT payable on the rest of the company's profits. This is because CT rates are based not on the company's taxable profits but on its 'augmented profits'.

Augmented profits are made up of the company's taxable profits **plus** dividends received, except dividends from subsidiary companies: broadly speaking, companies in which the recipient company owns more than 50% of the share capital.

If the company's augmented profits do not exceed the lower limit, the company is unaffected and continues to pay CT at the small profits rate of 19%, and only on its taxable profits.

If the company's augmented profits exceed the lower limit, the company is subject to CT at the main rate of 25%, but only on its taxable profits.

If the augmented profits are less than the upper limit, the company is then entitled to marginal relief. However, under this scenario, the marginal relief is calculated based on its augmented profits then also reduced by the proportion of taxable profits to augmented profits.

## 12.6 EXCEPTIONAL COMPANIES

The tax rates set out in previous sections apply to the vast majority of companies paying UK CT. However, there are a few exceptions to be aware of. While the companies listed below are, or may be, subject to different CT rates, they generally still have to be included as associated companies, where appropriate, subject to the points in Section 12.3.

### Close Investment Holding Companies

Close investment holding companies are not eligible for the small profits rate or marginal relief and must pay CT at the main rate of 25% on all profits arising after 31$^{st}$ March 2023.

A company is a 'close investment holding company' if it is a close company and does not exist wholly or mainly for a qualifying purpose. 'Wholly or mainly' is taken to mean more than half the company's activities.

Most family and small owner-managed companies are close companies. Broadly speaking, a company is a close company if it is under the control of five people or less. Control is generally deemed to exist where more than 50% of the company's shares are held. For this purpose, shares held by an individual's connected persons (Appendix C) must be treated as if held by the individual themselves. A company where all the shareholders are directors is also a close company.

Fortunately, qualifying purposes include carrying on a trade or renting property to unconnected persons. Hence, the vast majority of trading companies, or companies carrying on a property letting business, will **not** be close investment holding companies and will be eligible for the small profits rate or marginal relief, where appropriate.

Renting property to group companies (Section 12.7) is also a qualifying purpose, but *not* renting property to other associated companies.

### Non-Resident Companies
Non-UK resident companies are not eligible for the small profits rate or marginal relief and must pay tax at the main rate of 25% on any profits or gains subject to UK CT. Among others, this affects non-UK resident companies renting out, or developing, UK property.

### Other Companies Paying Tax at Different Rates
Different tax rates may apply to members of multinational groups; companies operating in the oil and gas sector; and large companies in the banking sector. Different rates may also apply to companies trading in Northern Ireland at some point in the future, although the date of introduction for this special regime remains uncertain.

### 12.7 GROUP COMPANIES

In Section 12.4, we looked at the impact of associated companies. Companies can be associated in a number of ways, including when they form a group.

However, group companies carry the distinct advantage that any losses arising in a group company can be set off against the profits in another group company. This is known as 'group relief'.

Broadly speaking, two companies are grouped for group relief purposes when one company owns at least 75% of the shares in the other company, or when a third company owns at least 75% of the shares in both of them.

### Example
*Laura owns 51% of the shares in Arkle Ltd and all the shares in Eildon Ltd. Arkle Ltd also has three subsidiary companies: it owns 100% of the shares in Beacon Ltd; 75% of the shares in Clent Ltd; and 60% of the shares in Dunmoor Ltd.*

*While all five companies are associated, only Arkle Ltd, Beacon Ltd, and Clent Ltd are group companies. Hence a loss arising in Clent Ltd could be set off against the profits in Beacon Ltd. However, losses arising in either Dunmoor Ltd or Eildon Ltd could not be set off against profits in any of the other companies, even though they are associated.*

### Optimising the Value of Group Relief
Where companies are grouped, losses arising in one company can be relieved against profits in any other group company. Any amount of loss can be relieved against any other group company's profits.

This flexibility is useful when we consider the different marginal tax rates applying.

### Example Continued

*For the year ending 31$^{st}$ March 2025, the results for the companies in the Arkle Group are as follows:*

| | |
|---|---|
| *Arkle Ltd:* | *£75,000 profit* |
| *Beacon Ltd:* | *£25,000 profit* |
| *Clent Ltd:* | *£20,000 loss* |

*Each company has four associated companies, meaning its lower limit is £10,000 and its upper limit is £50,000. The first £10,000 of profit in each company is taxed at 19%; the next £40,000 suffers an effective marginal rate of 26.5%; anything over £50,000 is taxed at 25%.*

*Hence, the best way to relieve Clent Ltd's loss is to first set £15,000 against Beacon Ltd's profit, thus bringing its chargeable profits down to £10,000; then set the remaining £5,000 of the loss against Arkle Ltd's profit. This saves CT as follows:*

| | |
|---|---|
| *Beacon Ltd £15,000 x 26.5%* | *£3,975* |
| *Arkle Ltd £5,000 x 25%* | *£1,250* |
| *Total (both companies)* | *£5,225* |

As the example demonstrates, the best strategy is to first set losses against any group profits being taxed at the 26.5% marginal rate, then any excess against profits being taxed at the main rate of 25%. Only once these options have been exhausted should losses be set against profits subject to the small profits rate.

This is a good example of why marginal tax rates are generally more important in tax planning than average, or overall tax rates. Before the group relief claim, Beacon Ltd's average tax rate was 23.5%, whereas Arkle Ltd's was 25%. However, the best value for the first £15,000 of Clent Ltd's losses came from setting them against Beacon Ltd's profits, saving tax at the marginal rate of 26.5%.

Once Beacon Ltd's tax rate had been brought down to 19%, the best saving came from setting the remaining £5,000 against Arkle Ltd's profits, saving tax at 25%.

The best tax savings are all about looking at marginal rates, and we will see more of this type of planning in the next section.

## 12.8  MARGINAL RATE TAX PLANNING

Your company's marginal tax rate determines the amount of tax saved by: incurring deductible expenditure; reducing taxable income; or claiming tax reliefs and allowances.

Opportunities for marginal rate tax planning arise whenever there is a change in your company's marginal tax rate. Generally speaking, this occurs when profits rise above, or fall below, either the lower limit (usually £50,000) or the upper limit (usually £250,000).

### *Example*
*Gavel Ltd is anticipating profits of just £50,000 for the year ending 31st March 2025, meaning it will pay CT at 19%. For the year ending 31st March 2026, however, the company expects its profits to increase to £100,000, meaning its marginal CT rate will be 26.5%.*

*These projected profit figures are before exceptional repairs costing £30,000, which the company plans to carry out in the first half of 2025. If the expenditure is incurred by 31st March 2025, it will save tax at 19%, or £5,700; if it is incurred later, it will save tax at 26.5%, or £7,950.*

In this case, the company will save an additional £2,250, or 7.5% of the expenditure, by deferring it into the next accounting period.

### Marginal Rate Savings
Assuming twelve-month accounting periods and no associated companies, deferring taxable profits into a later accounting period will generally produce *additional* tax savings as follows:

*   Profits about to fall below £50,000: 7.5%
*   Profits expected to rise above £250,000: 1.5%
*   Profits about to drop from over £250,000 to less than £50,000: 6%

Conversely, *accelerating* taxable profits into an earlier accounting period will generally produce *additional* tax savings as follows:

*   Profits expected to rise above £50,000: 7.5%
*   Profits about to fall below £250,000: 1.5%
*   Profits about to shoot up from less than £50,000 to more than £250,000: 6%

This, of course, all assumes that altering the timing of taxable profits does not, in itself, alter the company's marginal tax rate: although, in most cases, there would still be some saving even if this did happen.

Profit movements between less than £50,000 and more than £250,000 from one accounting period to the next may seem odd, but they do happen, especially given that capital gains made by the company will be included in its taxable profits.

In this section, we will look at the three main ways to alter the timing of taxable profits:

- Accelerate or defer tax-deductible expenditure
- Accelerate or defer taxable income
- Accounting adjustments

One point worth mentioning at this stage is that accelerating taxable profits will mean suffering extra tax a year early. In the example above, by deferring its repairs expenditure, Gavel Ltd will have £5,700 more tax to pay on 1$^{st}$ January 2026 and will have to wait until 1$^{st}$ January 2027 to enjoy the £7,950 reduction in its CT that produces the additional saving of £2,250.

This can, however, effectively be viewed as making an investment of £5,700 that returns a profit of £2,250 after one year. That's an investment yield of almost 40%, so it's pretty worthwhile.

Where the additional tax saving is 6%, this equates to an investment yield of a little over 31.5%, so it's still very good. Where the additional tax saving is only 1.5%, however, the 'investment' is less attractive, producing a yield of just 6%.

**Deductible Expenditure**
Marginal rate tax planning is not about incurring additional expenditure: it is seldom wise to spend extra money just to save tax. It is about the timing of expenditure. Because changing that timing can change the value of the tax relief you get for the expenditure.

Naturally, there are many types of expenditure a company is unable to control the timing of, such as business rates or employee's wages. Furthermore, under the accruals basis of accounting that companies must always follow, expenditure is recognised as it is incurred rather than when it is paid. Hence, simply paying a bill early or late will not alter the timing of your company's tax relief, or the marginal tax rate that applies.

Furthermore, even when you can alter the timing of when expenditure is incurred, the commercial implications of deferring or accelerating that expenditure need to be weighed up: the decision should not be driven by tax rates alone.

Accelerating expenditure also has cashflow implications that will need to be considered, although sometimes you may only need to accelerate the expenditure a short time to achieve the additional tax saving.

Leaving aside these considerations for the moment, expenditure that can sometimes be accelerated or deferred includes:

- Repairs and maintenance (where there is some discretion over timing)
- Advertising and promotion
- Travel and subsistence (by altering the timing of business journeys)
- Employee bonuses (where these are discretionary or gratuitous, rather than contractual)
- Staff entertaining
- Staff recruitment (agents' commission will generally be a deductible expense)
- Pension contributions (i.e. voluntary contributions for the owner/director themselves, or perhaps for other key employees, but **not** contractual entitlements the company's employees have, or compulsory contributions under auto-enrolment)
- Equipment, software, vans, commercial vehicles, and other asset purchases qualifying for the annual investment allowance or full expensing (see Chapter 8)
- Legal and professional costs, such as business advice, or consultancy (provided these are not capital expenditure or regular, annual costs that would be recognised in the accounts in any case)

Purchases of trading stock can sometimes be accelerated or deferred, but this, in itself, will not alter the timing of tax relief for the expenditure (but see below regarding accounting adjustments for trading stock).

Directors' salaries or bonuses can usually be deferred or accelerated fairly easily, but the Income Tax consequences are far more important, so these should not generally play a part in marginal rate tax planning for the company.

### Taxable Income
It is not generally possible to reduce **taxable** income without reducing **actual** income: something that, again, is seldom wise. Hence, marginal rate planning is not generally about reducing overall long-term income, only about altering the timing of when that income is received, or taxed.

Here are some possible steps for accelerating income into an earlier accounting period where the company has a lower marginal tax rate:

- Complete orders and projects and bring billing up to date. Accounting rules often require part-completed work to be brought into account, but there is still a large element of profit dependent on completion and billing in many cases. For example, two half completed projects are, in accounting terms, likely to yield less profit than a single completed project of the same size.
- Connected businesses (e.g. wife has her own company, husband also has his own business): make extra sales to connected businesses in advance of the company's accounting date.

Deferring income is fairly easy (delay sales or project completions) but seldom wise from a commercial point of view.

### Accounting Adjustments

Most company owners leave accounting adjustments to their accountant (it's what you pay them for, after all). However, it's worth understanding the part these adjustments can play in marginal rate tax planning. Carefully considered accounting adjustments can slightly alter the timing of company profits. While accounts must be prepared on a reasonable, 'true and fair' basis, there is often some leeway in the exact amount of each adjustment.

Where the aim is to defer taxable profits, there is no real downside (for tax purposes) to making whatever accounting adjustments can be justified. This means maximising accruals, provisions, and other profit deductions, while minimising prepayments and other adjustments that increase taxable profits.

This is all worthwhile from a tax perspective, even if the company's marginal tax rate is expected to stay the same. However, the commercial consequences of reducing the company's reported profits need to be considered, especially if you are thinking of applying for a bank loan or selling the business in the near future.

Where the aim is to accelerate taxable profits, this involves minimising accruals, provisions, and other profit deductions, while maximising prepayments and other adjustments that increase profits.

However, as well as the cashflow considerations created by paying extra tax a year early that we looked at above, it's also important to bear in mind it is only worth increasing the profits taxed at a lower rate if the relevant accounting adjustments will subsequently reverse and thus reduce profits in later accounting periods taxed at higher marginal rates. In other words, we need to be looking at timing differences that will reverse in a later accounting period.

**Capital Gains**
Deferring or accelerating property and other asset disposals that yield capital gains could give rise to tax savings. However, there are practical issues to consider too. Furthermore, as large amounts are usually involved, the gain itself will often change the company's marginal tax rate, so each case must be considered on its own merits.

An important point to note, however, is that, for capital gains purposes, a sale is deemed to take place on the date of unconditional contract.

# Marginal Corporation Tax Rates 2018 to 2024

| Year Ending: | Small Profits Rate | Marginal Rate | Main Rate |
|---|---|---|---|
| 31-Mar-2018 to 31-Mar-2023 | n/a | n/a | 19.000% |
| 30-Apr-2023 | 19.000% | 19.616% | 19.493% |
| 31-May-2023 | 19.000% | 20.253% | 20.003% |
| 30-Jun-2023 | 19.000% | 20.870% | 20.496% |
| 31-Jul-2023 | 19.000% | 21.507% | 21.005% |
| 31-Aug-2023 | 19.000% | 22.144% | 21.515% |
| 30-Sep-2023 | 19.000% | 22.760% | 22.008% |
| 31-Oct-2023 | 19.000% | 23.397% | 22.518% |
| 30-Nov-2023 | 19.000% | 24.014% | 23.011% |
| 31-Dec-2023 | 19.000% | 24.651% | 23.521% |
| 31-Jan-2024 | 19.000% | 25.288% | 24.030% |
| 29-Feb-2024 | 19.000% | 25.865% | 24.492% |
| 31-Mar-2024 | 19.000% | 26.500% | 25.000% |

Due to a bizarre quirk caused by the fact 2024 is a leap year, for twelve-month accounting periods ending on any date between 1st April 2023 and 28th February 2024, the small profits rate will apply to profits up to £49,863; the marginal rate will apply to profits between £49,863 and £249,317; and the main rate will apply to profits over £249,317.

For twelve-month accounting periods ending on any date from 29th February 2024 onwards, the small profits rate will apply to profits up to £50,000; the marginal rate will apply to profits between £50,000 and £250,000; and the main rate will apply to profits over £250,000.

These limits are subject to the rules for associated companies (Section 12.3).

## UK Tax Rates and Allowances: 2022/23 to 2024/25

| | Rates | 2022/23 £ | 2023/24 £ | 2024/25 £ |
|---|---|---|---|---|
| **Income Tax (1)** | | | | |
| Personal allowance | | 12,570 | 12,570 | 12,570 |
| Basic rate band | 20% | 37,700 | 37,700 | 37,700 |
| Higher rate threshold | 40% | 50,270 | 50,270 | 50,270 |
| | | | | |
| Personal allowance withdrawal | | | | |
| Effective rate/From | 60% | 100,000 | 100,000 | 100,000 |
| To | | 125,140 | 125,140 | 125,140 |
| Additional rate | 45% | 150,000 | 125,140 | 125,140 |
| | | | | |
| Starting rate band (2) | 0% | 5,000 | 5,000 | 5,000 |
| Personal savings allowance (3) | | 1,000 | 1,000 | 1,000 |
| Marriage allowance (4) | | 1,260 | 1,260 | 1,260 |
| Dividend allowance | | 2,000 | 1,000 | 500 |
| | | | | |
| **National Insurance (5)** | | | | |
| Primary threshold | | 11,908 | 12,570 | 12,570 |
| Rate:   Directors (Class 1) | | 12.73% | 11.5% | 8% |
| Upper earnings limit (UEL) | | 50,270 | 50,270 | 50,270 |
| Additional rate above UEL | | 2.73% | 2% | 2% |
| Secondary threshold (emp'rs) | | 9,100 | 9,100 | 9,100 |
| Rate:   Employers | | 14.53% | 13.8% | 13.8% |
| Employment allowance | | 5,000 | 5,000 | 5,000 |
| | | | | |
| **Pension Contributions** | | | | |
| Annual allowance | | 40,000 | 60,000 | 60,000 |
| | | | | |
| **Capital Gains Tax** | | | | |
| Annual exemption | | 12,300 | 6,000 | 3,000 |
| | | | | |
| **Inheritance Tax** | | | | |
| Nil Rate Band | | 325,000 | 325,000 | 325,000 |
| Main residence nil rate band | | 175,000 | 175,000 | 175,000 |

**Notes**
1. Different rates and thresholds apply to Scottish taxpayers (except on savings income and dividends)
2. Applies to interest and savings income only
3. Halved for higher rate taxpayers; not available to additional rate taxpayers
4. Available where neither spouse/civil partner pays higher rate tax
5. Thresholds and rates are those applying to company directors

# Appendix C
# Connected Persons

The definition of connected persons differs slightly from one area of UK tax law to another. The definition applying for Capital Gains Tax, SDLT, and Corporation Tax purposes is set out below, and also forms a reasonable guide to the definition for other purposes.

An individual's connected persons include the following:

i) Their husband, wife, or civil partner
ii) The following relatives:
   o Mother, father, or remoter ancestor
   o Son, daughter, or remoter descendant
   o Brother or sister
iii) Relatives under (ii) above of the individual's spouse or civil partner
iv) Spouses or civil partners of the individual's relatives under (ii) above
v) Spouses or civil partners of an individual under (iii) above
vi) The individual's business partners and their:
   o Spouses or civil partners
   o Relatives (as defined under (ii) above)
vii) Trusts where the individual is:
   o The settlor (the person who set up the trust or transferred property, other assets, or funds into it), or
   o A person connected (as defined in this appendix) with the settlor
viii) Companies under the control of the individual, either alone, or together with persons under (i) to (vii) above
ix) Companies under the control of the individual acting together with one or more other persons